German Unification

German Historical Perspectives Series
General Editors:
Gerhard A. Ritter and Anthony J. Nicholls

Volume I
Population, Labour and Migration in 19th- and 20th-Century Germany
Edited by Klaus J. Bade

Volume II
Wealth and Taxation in Central Europe: The History and Sociology of Public Finance
Edited by Peter-Christian Witt

Volume III
Nation-Building in Central Europe
Edited by Hagen Schulze

Volume IV
Elections, Parties and Political Traditions: Social Foundations of German Parties and Party Systems
Edited by Karl Rohe

Volume V
Economic Crisis and Political Collapse: The Weimar Republic, 1924–1933
Edited by Jürgen Baron von Kruedener

Volume VI
Escape into War? The Foreign Policy of Imperial Germany
Edited by Gregor Schöllgen

German Historical Perspectives/VII

German Unification

The Unexpected Challenge

Edited by
DIETER GROSSER

BERG

Oxford/Providence

First published in 1992 by
Berg Publishers Limited
Editorial offices:
165 Taber Avenue, Providence, RI 02906, USA
150 Cowley Road, Oxford, OX4 1JJ, UK

Library of Congress Cataloging-in-Publication Data
German unification: the unexpected challenge / [contributors]. Dieter
Grosser . . . [et al.].
    p.   cm.
   ISBN 0–85496–752–4
   1. Germany—History—Unification, 1990.   I. Grosser, Dieter.
DD290.25.O474   1992
943.087′9—dc20   91–44182
                                                                      CIP

British Library Cataloguing in Publication Data
German unification: the unexpected challenge.
  – (German historical perspectives)
   I. Grosser, Dieter   II. Series
   943.087

ISBN 0 85496 752 4

Printed and bound by Edwards Brothers, Inc., Ann Arbor, Michigan.

Contents

Editorial Preface   vii

Preface   viii

Contributors   ix

The Dynamics of German Reunification
Dieter Grosser   1

Reunification as an Issue in German Politics 1949–1990
Dieter Mahncke   33

Collapse from Internal Weakness – The GDR from
October 1989 to March 1990
Hannelore Horn   55

The GDR on its Way to Democracy
Uwe Thaysen   72

West Germany's Political System under Stress:
Decision-making Processes in Bonn 1990
Wolfgang Bergsdorf   88

Economic Unification
Uwe Andersen   107

The European Community: How to Counterbalance
the Germans
Beate Neuss   136

Fear of Germany and Security for Europe
Michael Wolffsohn   150

Germany – A Future with Two Pasts
Peter Graf Kielmansegg   180

Chronology   196

Basic Literature   199

Index   200

Diagrams, Table and Figures

Diagram 1 The Initial Formation of the Political Forces at the East German Central Round Table at the Inaugurating Session on 7 December 1989   74

Diagram 2 Seats and Votes at the East German Central Round Table since the Second Session (18 December 1989)   76

Diagram 3 The Political Frontline at the East German Central Round Table from the Second Session on 18 December 1989   78

Diagram 4 Periods and Functions in the History of the East German Central Round Table   84

Table 1 Federal Republic of Germany and German Democratic Republic: Comparison of Selected Economic and Social Indicators in 1988   110

Figure 1 Gross Domestic Product per caput from 1950 to 1989   116

Figure 2 Labour Market in May 1991   124

Figure 3 General Government Finances   129

Editorial Preface

The purpose of this series of books is to present the results of research by German historians and social scientists to readers in English-speaking countries. Each of the volumes has a particular theme which will be handled from different points of view by specialists. The series is not limited to the problems of Germany but will also involve publications dealing with the history of other countries, with the general problems of political, economic, social and intellectual history as well as international relations and studies in comparative history.

We hope the series will help to help overcome the language barrier which experience has shown obstructs the rapid appreciation of German research in English-speaking countries.

The publication of the series is closely associated with the German Visiting Fellowship at St Antony's College, Oxford, which has existed since 1965, having been originally funded by the Stiftung Volkswagenwerk, later by the British Leverhulme Foundation, by the Ministry of Education and Science in the Federal Republic of Germany, and, starting in 1990, by the Stifverband für die Deutsche Wissenschaft with special funding from C. & A. Brenninkmeyer Deutschland. Each volume is based on a series of seminars held in Oxford, which has been conceived and directed by the Visiting Fellow and organised in collaboration with St Antony's College.

The editors wish to thank the Stiftverband für die Deutsche Wissenschaft for meeting the expenses of the original lecture series and for generous assistance with the publication. They hope that this enterprise will help to overcome national introspection and to further international academic discourse and cooperation.

Gerhard A. Ritter   Anthony J. Nicholls

Preface

The purpose of this book is to show the processes leading to the unification of Germany in 1990. The contributions are based on lectures given at St Antony's College, Oxford, between January and March 1991. The authors are West German political scientists who have been observing the developments in the German Democratic Republic and the relations between both German states for years.

The collapse of the communist regime in East Germany and the accession of the German Democratic Republic to the Federal Republic of Germany came with breathtaking speed. Many details of these processes are still little known; every month new sources are discovered, new memoirs of participants published. The findings presented here are therefore preliminary hypotheses.

I am grateful to St Antony's College, especially to Mr Tony Nicholls, and to the Stifterverband für Deutsche Wissenschaft, who made the lectures and the publication possible.

Dieter Grosser

Contributors

Uwe **Andersen**
Professor of Political Science, University of Bochum

Wolfgang **Bergsdorf**
Ministerialdirektor in the Bundespresse- und Informationsamt,
Bonn, Professor of Political Science

Dieter **Grosser**
Professor of Political Science, University of Munich

Hannelore **Horn**
Professor of Political Science, Free University of Berlin

Peter Graf **Kielmansegg**
Professor of Political Science, University of Mannheim

Dieter **Mahncke**
Ministerialdirigent in the Bundesministerium der Verteidigung,
Bonn, Professor of Political Science

Beate **Neuss**
Assistant Professor, University of Munich

Uwe **Thaysen**
Professor of Political Science, University of Lüneburg

Michael **Wolffsohn**
Professor of Political Science, University of the Armed Forces,
Munich

DIETER GROSSER

The Dynamics of German Reunification

1. The Unanticipated Challenge

The partition of Germany was the result of the East–West conflict. When Soviet power declined in the eighties, the end of that conflict became a possibility. However, almost nobody in Germany thought that the decline of Soviet power might lead to the collapse of the German Democratic Republic (GDR) so soon, opening, perhaps only for a few months, a window of opportunity to achieve German reunification. That dramatic development, beginning in August 1989 with thousands of East German refugees crowding into the West German Embassy in Budapest, and ending with reunification on 3 October 1990, came as an unexpected challenge.

The lack of foresight is surprising. It had already been evident in 1988 that the Soviet Union was neither willing nor able to prevent Poland and Hungary breaking with socialism. Why did nobody in West Germany begin to analyse the effect this would have on East Germany?

One explanation is that the majority of West German politicians and opinion-makers, to say nothing of the experts on the German Democratic Republic among political scientists, failed to see the full extent of the economic débâcle and political discontent in East Germany. As a result, the stability of the socialist regime in the German Democratic Republic was overestimated. At most, Western observers expected attempts to exchange the Honecker regime for a regime along the Gorbachev lines, trying to increase economic

1

efficiency not only by administrative changes, but by reducing political oppression. Developments in Poland and Hungary should have shown that even a limited reduction of oppression might lead to the rapid disintegration of such a socialist system. West Germans seemed to observe a kind of taboo when considering the consequences for Germany of the change in Eastern Europe. Even in the summer of 1989, German reunification was not a topic for discussion in serious political or academic circles. This reluctance even to analyse the problem of partition was the main reason for the lack of foresight. It can be explained by looking at the history of the Federal Republic of Germany. Most of the founders of the Federal Republic saw the West German state as a transitory stage on the road to the reunification of Germany. This interpretation was widely accepted by West German public opinion until the mid-sixties. Even in the fifties, however, the allegedly provisional character of the Federal Republic and the high priority given to reunification in the 'Basic Law' was hardly consistent with reality. By overwhelming political and economic necessity, the young Federal Republic was drawn into close co-operation and integration with the West.

This made reunification impossible as long as the Soviet Union insisted that a reunified Germany should be within the Soviet sphere of influence, or at least neutralised. Already in the fifties West Germany found itself facing a dilemma: a majority of its citizens wanted integration with the West, because the political and economic advantages of this were huge, and were felt by almost everybody. But a majority also wanted reunification. Adenauer's solution to this dilemma was to make the West stronger through integration, and wait for Soviet power to wane. But in the fifties and sixties, Soviet power increased. West Germany's Western allies refused to run any risks in order to push back Soviet domination from Eastern Central Europe. The building of the Berlin Wall on 13 August 1961 marked the end of any German illusions that Adenauer's idea might work. Adenauer's numerous critics who, after 1961, demanded a more realistic policy failed to design a strategy which made Bonn's commitment to reunification consistent with the attempt to reduce tensions with the Soviet Union, the German Democratic Republic, Poland and Czechoslovakia. Better relations with the 'East', however, seemed to be imperative.

After the Cuban missile crisis of 1962, the United States and the Soviet Union began to look for crisis management; *détente* became a possibility. Bonn risked being isolated if it did not contribute to finding some arrangement which reduced the confrontation in Central Europe, the most sensitive and dangerous problem being the exposed and insecure position of West Berlin. Published opinions in West Germany changed. More and more opinion-makers no longer saw the partition of Germany as the main danger to peace in Europe. On the contrary, the insistence on reunification now appeared as a risk to West Germany's security. In the interests of peace, the Germans had to accept reality: the division of Europe and of their country.

In the late sixties this view was still not shared by the majority of the German people. But it steadily gained support, for several reasons: West Germany had become an affluent society, which had much to lose and which wanted security at all costs. West Germans had got used to the partition of their country; they now lived very well without reunification, and as the Berlin Wall had cut off personal contacts very effectively, East Germany, for most West Germans, simply became less interesting than the countries they travelled to in millions every summer. Another factor which contributed to this change of attitude towards reunification was the leftist trend which became influential in West Germany, as in many other countries, in 1968. Segments of the Free Democrats and the Social Democrats were the first to draw the political consequences. In 1968, they began to look for an arrangement with the East based on the *de facto* acceptance of the status quo.

When Willy Brandt became chancellor of a Social Democratic – Liberal coalition late in 1969, his most important aim was to achieve an arrangement with the Soviet Union, Poland, Czechoslovakia and the German Democratic Republic which would lead to reconciliation between Germany and its neighbours in the East, reduce the conflict between West and East Germany, guarantee the security of West Berlin and pave the way to improve the plight of the East Germans. Brandt's famous 'Eastern treaties', together with the Berlin agreement of the Four Powers, essentially brought the acceptance of the prevailing situation in Europe. The existing frontiers, including the frontier between West and East Germany and the Oder–Neisse line, were declared inviolable. The Soviet Union accepted the principle that West Berlin had a special relationship with the Federal Republic, and guaranteed civilian traffic between West Berlin and West Germany. Bonn recognised the German Democratic Republic as an independent state; the claim that the government of the Federal Republic was the legitimate representative of all Germans was relinquished.

Bonn, however, refused to legitimise the division of Germany. Recognition of the German Democratic Republic fell short of all aspects of international law; Bonn insisted that the two German states exchange only 'permanent representatives', not ambassadors. The preamble of the German–German Treaty (*'Grundlagenvertrag'*) stated that differences between the concluding parties remained in 'fundamental questions, among them the national question'. In order to ensure ratification of the German–German Treaty in the Bundestag, the Brandt government, before signing, handed a 'Letter on German unity' to the government of the GDR, expressing the West German view that the treaty was consistent with the aim of achieving German unity 'in the free self-determination of the German people'.

Bitterly criticised by most of the Christian Democrats, Brandt's *Ostpolitik* nevertheless was approved by a majority of the voters in the Federal elections in November 1972. One could argue, as Brandt did, that his government only gave up what was long lost. Or one could argue, as his critics did, that not only had he accepted Soviet hegemony over Eastern Central Europe, he had legally recognised it. One could point out that the German–German Treaty did not sanction the partition of Germany, and that the Federal Republic did not give up the right to act as an advocate of German reunification. Or one could reply that all this was of symbolic value only, the decisive fact being that the German Democratic Republic, a totalitarian dictatorship with no democratic legitimacy at all, had been recognised as equal and independent by the Federal Republic.

Almost two decades later Brandt's *Ostpolitik* is still controversial. When reunification came, the Social Democrats claimed that Brandt's policy of reconciliation with the East, especially with the Soviet Union and Poland, was the beginning of the long road leading to German unity. This argument has its merits. Without the *de facto* recognition of the Oder–Neisse frontier in the Warsaw treaty of 1970, Poland might have hesitated longer before shaking off Soviet domination. Without giving in to the Soviet wish to have the status quo in Europe accepted by the Federal Republic, mistrust of a 'revanchist' West Germany might have continued in Moscow to such a degree that the Gorbachev–Kohl accord of 1990 would have been unthinkable.

There is also the argument that Bonn's recognition of the GDR opened the way for numerous agreements between Bonn and East Berlin which improved the conditions under which people not only in East Germany, but also in West Berlin and even in West Germany had to live. Of special importance to many Germans were agreements allowing families separated by the German–German frontier to meet. Family reunions were practically the only way for people who were not reliable party members on official business (*Reisekader*) to see West Germany with their own eyes. The regime feared that visitors, returning home, might spread discontent with conditions in East Germany, and kept the numbers of citizens allowed to visit West Germany as low as possible, frustrating most of Bonn's efforts. Only in 1987 did the number of visits begin to rise sharply.

Contrary to many hopes, the celebrated formula 'change through *rapprochement*' coined by Egon Bahr, Brandt's most important adviser, proved to be far too optimistic. The East German regime did not change its character. It remained a dictatorship, employing all the techniques that totalitarian systems had developed to keep people subjugated. The hopes of some West German socialists that 'change through *rapprochement*' might lead to change in West Germany too, by undermining the capitalist system, were equally disappointed. Despite the considerable efforts of some journalists and quite a number of educators to present a positive picture of the German Democratic Republic, emphasising its full employment, social security and equality, the great majority of West Germans did not find the East German system in the least attractive.

Taken all together, the main effects of Brandt's *Ostpolitik* were a considerable lessening of the tensions between East and West Germany, far more security for West Berlin, and a limited extension of family contacts. These were achievements that should not be underestimated. On the other hand, the very lessening of the tensions fostered the impression that a stable, almost normal situation had been attained. Brandt had not opened a new road out of the old dilemma of how to achieve both German reunification and integration into the West. He had refused to accept the dilemma itself. Reunification was transformed into a symbolic goal that was no longer valid for practical politics. In 1972 a small majority, which grew with the years, considered this policy unavoidable and sensible.

When, in 1982, the Christian Democratic – Liberal Coalition took over the government, it did not change practical politics very much, only emphasising the symbolic goal of German reunification more strongly. For most West Germans, the partition of Germany had

become a fact of life. Living in a state that was highly successful
politically and economically, being used to high interdependence
with the European Community and the United States, having been
taught by history and by everyday experience that the nation state
had no future anyway, West Germans did not think their own
national question important any longer. Thus, they were not prepared at all for the consequences of the collapse of East Germany's
regime.

2. The Causes of the Collapse of the German Democratic Republic

(a)   The Decline of Soviet Power and the Policy of Gorbachev

The erosion of Soviet dominance over its Central and
Eastern European client states began in 1980, when the Soviet
Union was unable to prevent the disintegration of the Polish socialist system. Military intervention in Poland to keep the Polish United
Workers' Party in undisputed power was not possible; the Soviet
Union was already engaged in a civil war in Afghanistan, and feared
the international consequences of using force in Poland. Moreover,
there seem to have been doubts in Moscow whether intervention in
Poland would achieve its aim at all. Jaruszelski's martial law gave a
temporary respite to the Polish communists, but was unable to
re-establish their authority and leading role. The Polish crisis
strengthened the position of those members of the Soviet leadership
who thought drastic economic and political reforms necessary in all
socialist countries. Discussions about a kind of *perestroika* began in
Moscow long before Gorbachev became General Secretary. In East
Berlin the Polish crisis had the opposite effect: it strengthened the
position of those who thought reforms would destabilise the socialist
system. From the beginning of his tenure as General Secretary,
Gorbachev admonished the socialist 'brother countries' to follow the
Soviet Union on the road to reform. Reform for him at first meant
economic efficiency and acceleration of economic growth. In 1986,
Gorbachev began to speak of 'radical reforms' not limited to the
economy, but necessary for the political system and all areas of
society as well.[1] In January 1987, in his address before the Central
Committee, he announced for the first time the 'democratisation' of

the political system.[2] After this, *perestroika* and *glasnost* had become symbolic terms used with optimism by the opposition in all socialist countries, but regarded with growing anxiety by the orthodox ruling groups in East Berlin, Prague or Sofia.

In an important statement on 2 November 1987 Gorbachev redefined 'socialist internationalism' as 'unconditional and full equality; the ruling party's responsibility for the state of affairs of the country; its patriotic service to the people; concern for the common cause of socialism; respect for one another; a serious attitude towards what has been achieved and tested by one's friends; voluntary and diverse co-operation; a strict observance of the principles of peaceful coexistence by all'.[3] The message to the 'socialist brother countries' was clear: *glasnost* and *perestroika* were to strengthen, not to weaken socialism. The leading role of the communist party had to be preserved. The Soviet Union expected the other socialist countries to learn from Soviet experience and follow its reformist line. The Soviet Union, on the other hand, was willing to grant more 'equality' to the other socialist countries, meaning not only that they would have a wider scope to develop reformist strategies of their own, but implying that the Brezhnev Doctrine was no longer applicable.

In 1987, Gorbachev's position must have been convincing to the reformist group within the Soviet Union's communist leadership: as the Soviet Union was no longer able to stabilise the socialist system in the 'brother countries' from without, it had to be stabilised from within, by increasing economic efficiency and by gaining more support from the people. Exactly as in the Soviet Union, force was to be reduced, and consent was to be increased. But the essentials of the socialist system, including the leading role of the party and the socialist ownership of the most important means of production, were not to be jeopardised.

In the summer of 1989, however, Gorbachev's position of 1987 was already discredited as illusory. In the Soviet Union itself *glasnost* had given rise to countless informal groups, some of them outside the boundaries of any kind of socialism, and all of them challenging the dominant role of the Communist Party. The elections to the Congress of People's Deputies in March 1989, although heavily weighted to ensure a strong majority of CPSU members, had shown the strength of the opposition. The economic crisis had become more dangerous than ever, not at least because the reforms, though insufficient to increase output, had destroyed the co-ordination imposed by central planning. In Poland, the comeback of Solidarity had not been prevented even by martial law: the communists had been compelled to admit it to a 'Round Table' for joint crisis management, and the elections in June 1989 had been a triumph for Solidarity. At the summit meeting of the Warsaw Pact countries in Bucharest on 7–8 July 1989 Gorbachev was faced by harsh criticism from the East German, Czechoslovakian, Romanian and Bulgarian leaders. They demanded Soviet intervention against the 'revisionists' in Poland and Hungary, and blamed Gorbachev for concessions to the West. There is some suspicion that Gorbachev now began to engineer the overthrow of Honecker, Husak, Ceaucescu and Zhivkov, intending to replace them with persons pledged to his own policy.[4]

With the sources available today it is not possible to say whether Gorbachev really thought a reformist Socialist Unity Party (SED – the ruling communist party of the GDR) would have a chance to remain the strongest political force in East Germany, winning enough support from the people to save socialism and, with socialism, the existence of the German Democratic Republic as a separate German state. He probably saw no alternative to the overthrow of Honecker and his orthodox colleagues in Prague, Bucharest and Sofia: if they remained in power, they would not only be a threat to him, trying to form a coalition with his orthodox opponents within the Soviet Union, but they would go on ruining their countries until a revolution destroyed not only them but socialism as well.

Gorbachev's contribution to the downfall of Honecker is undisputed. First, his own policy of *perestroika* and *glasnost* had raised hopes in East Germany. When Honecker refused to follow Gorbachev, disappointment in East Germany was intense. Second, when he visited East Berlin on 7 October 1989, celebrating the fortieth anniversary of the founding of the GDR, he admonished Honecker to follow the Soviet example and try to win consent by political means, encouraging Honecker's critics within the SED leadership to exchange him for a General Secretary willing to accept Gorbachev's line. This came about on 18 October. Even more decisive was the Soviet refusal to use the Red Army to support East German forces if demonstrations got out of hand. Commenting on the turbulent events in Central and Eastern Europe after the fall of Honecker in Germany, of Zhivkov in Bulgaria and of Husak in Czechoslovakia, Gorbachev said that they were the result of *perestroika*, and meant a renewal, not the collapse of socialism.[5]

(b)   Hungary's Opening of its Frontier with Austria

The decline of Soviet power gave Hungary a chance for closer relations with the West. In the summer of 1989 Hungary was governed by the communist 'Hungarian Socialist Workers' Party', which had a strong reformist wing led by Imre Poszgay; the Prime Minister was Niklas Nemeth. This government partly initiated and partly accepted developments that led to pluralism and democracy, even before the formal change of the constitution. On 2 May 1989 Hungary began to dismantle its frontier fences at the Austrian border, which had effectively prevented illegal crossings up to that time. In the following months, more and more citizens of the GDR tried to leave their country via Hungary. Early in August, the situation became critical. Using the holiday season, East Germans began to seek refuge in the West German embassy in Budapest, demanding free travel to the Federal Republic.

Legally, the Hungarian government would have been compelled to extradite the refugees to the German Democratic Republic. Not even orthodox communists among the ministers, such as Horwath, the Minister of the Interior, wanted to do that; using force against the refugees would have been unpopular. A majority in the cabinet decided to open the frontier. But before allowing the refugees to leave for Austria, Nemeth and Horn were to fly to Bonn to meet Chancellor Kohl. This meeting took place on 25 August. Kohl, when told that the Hungarians would open the frontier for the East Germans, asked: 'What do you want to have in return?' Nemeth answered: 'Nothing. This is a decision for humanitarian reasons only. Our current negotiations about financial aid should be continued later. Nobody should think that we are selling the refugees for money.' Kohl was visibly shaken. With tears in his eyes he said: 'The German people will for ever be grateful to the Hungarian people.'[6]

At midnight on 11 September Hungary opened its frontier with Austria. The government of the GDR protested vehemently. The Soviet News Agency TASS criticised the Federal Republic of Germany for violating the sovereignty of the GDR, and even pointed out that the GDR was 'an inseparable member of the Warsaw Pact'.[7] This threat, as well as Ligachev's similar statements in East Berlin on the same day, indicates that at least some of the orthodox Moscow leaders were horrified at Hungary's opening of the frontier, seeing clearly that this could mean the end of the Honecker regime.

By the end of September more than 23,000 East Germans had left
their country via Hungary. On 30 September, after negotiations
between Bonn and East Berlin, more than 6,000 refugees, most of
whom had gone to Prague, some to Warsaw, asking for the protection of the West German embassies, were allowed to leave by special
trains to West Germany. Many of the refugees were skilled workers,
indispensable to East Germany's economy. Should the GDR prove
unable to stop the exodus, it might lead not only to the fall of the
Honecker regime, but to the collapse of the GDR itself.

(c)   Discontent and Opposition in the GDR

Exodus from the GDR was nothing new. From 1949 to
1961 almost three million people left East Germany illegally. On
13 August 1961 the Berlin Wall cut off the stream of refugees. At
great risk to themselves many tried to get out even after that. From
1962 to 1988 more than 170,000 succeeded in escaping, and 360,000
obtained permission to emigrate to West Germany. This was relatively easy only for people who were past working age. Countless
applications were refused. Many lost their jobs after handing in their
applications, and were kept waiting for years until they could leave.
Almost 30,000 of those permitted to emigrate were political prisoners, for whom the Bonn government had paid a ransom. The
undiminished desire of hundreds of thousands to leave the GDR was
the strongest indication of discontent with conditions in East Germany. For many, the GDR was a prison. As soon as there was a
chance to escape without risking imprisonment or life, the mass
exodus was bound to begin again.

Of course, those determined to leave the GDR at great risk were a
minority. The majority had found some way to live within the
system. There were highly privileged groups, from the carefully
selected members of the *Nomenklatura* – people qualified for the top
positions in party, administration or economy – to politically opportunistic artists and academics in universities and research institutions. There were large groups of people without any privileges, but
relatively content with the conditions of everyday life: their jobs
were secure, as long as they paid lip-service to the regime; housing
was not luxurious, but was cheap; basic consumer goods were
available on a restricted basis; and even cars, though extremely
expensive, were within the reach of many households. Complaints
about consumer goods shortages and extremely high prices for qual-

ity products were widespread. Politically, there was a tendency to apathy. Quite a few people suffered from the all-pervasive regimentation and control, the absence of civil liberties, the inability to criticise and change an inefficient and corrupt system. But for decades this minority did not dare to demand in public freedom of speech, freedom of organisation, reform of the system. Why did a few dissenters begin to do so in the eighties; and why did protest spread in summer 1989?

The answer is still speculative; a well-documented history of the last years of the GDR will be possible only much later. The following outline summarises the sources available today.

Economically, the road to catastrophe began in the seventies. Just like the other socialist economies, the GDR was unable to switch from extensive to intensive growth. With few incentives for product and process innovation, there was no way to increase labour and capital productivity at rates comparable to those achieved in capitalist economies. Without higher labour productivity one could not increase real wages. Without product and process innovation, competitiveness in international trade had to decline.

The leadership reacted to these problems in a way that might promise short-term political advantages, but was ruinous for the economy in the long run. In order to keep the masses content, wages were raised slowly, and basic commodities continued to be supplied at very low prices which were only made possible by high subsidies. In order to earn enough hard currency, exports to the West had to be increased; but they also had to be more and more subsidised. To compensate for the subsidies going into consumption, housing and exports, investment in capital stock was reduced, and investment in the infrastructure was neglected altogether. At the same time, high spending on defence and internal security continued, and billions were lost in a futile attempt to develop a microelectronic industry that could compete with Western products. As a result, the real income of consumers rose slightly in the eighties, but capital stock and infrastructure deteriorated rapidly. Even official statistics showed that growth rates fell after 1985. At the same time, hidden inflation caused by budget deficits became more and more dangerous.

The average East German consumer was used to shortages, especially of quality products. In the mid-eighties, shortages were as bad as ever. But with rising wages, they were felt more acutely. There is no statistical evidence that the standard of living began to decline. Objectively, people were better off economically than a decade before, not least because housing conditions had improved.

That the economy was heading for a severe crisis was known to the experts, above all to the managers and administrators. But they did not dare to criticise the policy of the Politbureau openly. Within the SED *Nomenklatura* there were some who wanted to follow the Gorbachev line. In 1987 Hans Modrow, then party chief of the district of Dresden, tried to find support for ousting Honecker.[8] But before October 1989 these 'reformers' within the ruling party had no chance. This was not only the result of the strict discipline exercised by the Honecker leadership. For the *Nomenklatura, perestroika* and *glasnost* were not a very attractive alternative. They had ex-perimented with economic reform in the years 1963–1970. In the opinion of most who were in charge of the economy in the eighties, the mixture of 'economic incentives' and central planning had not been a success, because it had led to the neglect of the planned sector, resulting in shortages of the most important investment and export goods. *Glasnost* seemed to be even more dangerous. With their close contacts with Soviet colleagues, the East German party bosses and managers already knew in 1987 that the CPSU was losing control of public opinion and was unable to keep criticism below the danger point. Would *glasnost* not lead to destabilisation in the ex-posed GDR? Honecker's stern refusal to change course and follow Gorbachev certainly had a solid following among people of influence in the SED. A 'revolution from above', as attempted by Gorbachev, was out of the question in East Germany. Change, if at all, had to come from below.

Even in January 1989 pressure from below had not become strong enough to cause the SED leadership serious worries. There were small opposition groups, most of them using the limited sanctuary of the church as a base, all of them carefully observed by the Stasi (state security). These groups had spread in the heyday of the peace movement, which the SED itself had helped to organise and encour-aged as long as it was directed against NATO's double-track deci-sion and Reagan's Strategic Defense Initiative. The Stasi, however, had not been able to control the peace movement in East Germany tightly enough. Quite a number of young people met in discussion circles sponsored by the church and began to criticise the armament policy of the Warsaw Pact countries as well. In 1983 environment, pollution and human rights were taken up as important issues by these groups. Thus nuclei of civic action groups had come into existence, their participants and protectors among the clergy well known to the Stasi, the number of their active members estimated at about 500 in summer 1989.[9] In the view of the Politbureau it was inconceivable that these groups would cause serious trouble. However, several factors contributed to create a potentially dangerous situation for the SED even before the exodus began.

Among the mass of citizens, discontent grew when, beginning in 1986, more and more people even of under 60 were allowed to visit relatives in West Germany. By 1989 millions of East Germans had seen the enormous difference in the standard of living with their own eyes, not just as it was presented by Western TV. This could not fail to create demands which the system was quite unable to satisfy.

Among those people who were both politically interested and critical of the system, above all among intellectuals outside the SED, Gorbachev's policy became a factor of great, perhaps of decisive, importance. In March 1989 there were elections to the Congress of People's Deputies in the Soviet Union. For the first time, Soviet citizens had a choice among several candidates in many constituencies. In the GDR, there were local elections in May. During the election campaign, the SED was confronted with criticism more open and intense than ever before. There were not only complaints about insufficient supplies of consumer goods, increasing pollution and inadequate medical services; according to Stasi reports, intellectuals and students frequently demanded that there should be several candidates for each elective post, as in the Soviet elections in March.

The elections on 7 May 1989 were rigged in the traditional way; officially, 98.85 per cent of the voters had supported the list of the National Front. Members of civil rights groups who had dared to monitor the election procedures denounced the election results as a forgery. There were public protests, even by the Protestant Church, and heated discussions and demonstrations. All these demands and activities were without precedent. People dared to protest against procedures they had known and endured for more than forty years. However, the hopes that the SED might concede at least part of the reforms that were being tried out in the Soviet Union, in Poland, and in Hungary, were shattered in June when the Politbureau gave full support to the rulers in Peking, who had used military force to crush popular opposition. When word spread that there might be a chance to get out of the GDR via Hungary, thousands were willing to go.

(d)   A Revolution with Faults

The SED regime faced a crisis even before the Hungarians opened their frontier to Austria on 11 September. During August, the number of East German refugees in Budapest and in the embassy in Prague increased. On 19 August the Hungarians allowed more than 600 East Germans to cross the border during a 'picnic' organised by the Pan-Europe Union, signalling that they were unwilling to force the refugees to return to East Germany. This caused even more East Germans to try to escape via Budapest. At home, there were demonstrations for unrestricted travel. Closely watched by the Stasi, the leaders of civil rights groups began to prepare for the founding of a social democratic party, of the 'New Forum', and of the other 'new groups' which were to challenge the leading position of the SED later. Within the churches, discussion circles multiplied. The Stasi seemed quite confident that it could control these developments. But the very fact that more and more citizens now dared to participate in activities which might land them in prison for years showed that the regime was no longer feared enough to be stable. It is possible that the top leaders did not realise this. More probable was that they were paralysed, not only because Honecker was in hospital undergoing a cancer operation, but because they had run out of options.

Gorbachev's strategy of winning support by reforms, if it would ever have had a chance, would by this time have come too late. The 'Chinese solution' would work only if the Soviets backed it. This could be expected only if Gorbachev was overthrown. Honecker had gambled on this, but had he been right? Honecker would have to resign because of ill health anyway. For members of the Politbureau, it was a time to prepare for the succession struggle, but not to take sides too early.

After 11 September the mass exodus began, with more than 20,000 emigrating via Hungary by the end of the month, and thousands trying to get out via the embassies in Prague and Warsaw. West German TV, which most East Germans could watch, showed the refugees arriving in the West, crying with happiness, blaming the SED for the years lost in oppression, showing their new green West German passports to the TV cameras, and thus demonstrating that they were citizens of the Federal Republic of Germany.

This exodus, televised into the living-rooms of those staying behind, was the beginning of the end of the regime. It had a double effect: the opposition was encouraged, and the *Nomenklatura* began to panic and split apart. Following the example of 'New Forum', more civil rights movements organised themselves GDR-wide. These movements got much attention on West German TV, but their influence on the course of events was less than it was believed, even by the Stasi, to be. A new, spontaneous form of protest developed. Leipzig set an example. After peace prayers every Monday there would be a demonstration against the regime. Organisation was not necessary, as everybody knew the time and place. In other cities this example was followed. Stasi and police reacted violently, brutally beating and arresting demonstrators. But the number of people participating in demonstrations increased steadily.

Incredible mistakes on the part of the party and the government contributed to the escalation. Giving in to West German and Czechoslovakian pressure to solve the problem of the 7,600 East German refugees in Prague, the GDR authorities provided special trains to transport them to Bavaria, not directly, but across the territory of the GDR. Once the trains were within the GDR, more people tried to board them, since they wanted to get out, too. When on 6 October the fortieth anniversary celebrations began, police brutality against protesting demonstrators reached a peak; the regime had to show an unbroken façade. But on 7 October Gorbachev, in a conference with Honecker and members of the Politbureau, urged the SED leaders to follow his course. His words 'history punishes those who come too late' became famous. Within the East Berlin leadership, a majority now was in favour of an attempt to stabilise the regime by at least some political concessions.

The first indications of this change of strategy came two days later in Leipzig. Honecker seems to have given the order to dissolve the demonstration expected on Monday 9 October by the use of arms. Special combat groups were kept in readiness. But local party chiefs, pressed by Kurt Masur, the famous conductor, and other well-known Leipzig citizens, appealed for non-violence on both sides. Politbureau member Egon Krenz claims that he himself, being in charge of internal security, gave the order not to use force to the police and the combat groups. At any rate, the demonstration, the largest so far in Leipzig, with 70,000 participating, was not dispersed. October 9 marked a turning-point.

People were no longer afraid that the police would use force against them. Mass demonstrations against the regime and for free elections and unrestricted travel were held in almost every large city, with little organisation, but with millions participating. They were non-violent, but showed overwhelmingly that the people were determined to achieve freedom at once.

The majority in the Politbureau tried to stem the flood with manifestations of its willingness to follow Gorbachev's example. On 18 October Honecker had to resign as General Secretary. His successor, Egon Krenz, was weak, opportunistic, and without solid support even within the bewildered SED. The demonstrations continued, as well as the exodus. Krenz tried to win some support by throwing the 'old guard' out of party leadership and government, blaming the Honecker group for everything that had gone wrong in the GDR. He even promised free elections. It was to no avail. In the view of the majority of the East Germans, the SED was completely discredited. People were no longer willing to accept an SED-dominated system, even if it promised reforms. They wanted total change. From 9 October on the German Democratic Republic was no longer in a crisis: it was in a revolution.

On 9 November the Berlin Wall was breached. Most probably the SED leaders had not intended this to happen. The Council of Ministers had only declared that in future GDR citizens could get permission for travel abroad without delay. But this declaration came as a surprise, at a press conference called to report the far less interesting plenary session of the Central Committee. Phrased in complicated bureaucratic jargon, the meaning of the declaration was not very clear, and it was interpreted by many watching on TV to mean that the frontier was open. At night, when thousands went to the checkpoints to see what was happening, the frontier guards, having no instructions about how and where permits were to be issued, let people cross over into the West. On the morning of 10 November hundreds of thousands of East Germans were in West Berlin. The SED was quite powerless to turn back the tide. Not only the Berlin Wall, but the frontier between East and West Germany collapsed within days. The total chaos in the SED leadership is best shown by the fact that the army command were preparing to send troops into East Berlin to restore order at the same time that the frontier guards were already acting as traffic police and helping the huge crowds to pass the checkpoints.

The opening of the frontier was not only the death-blow for the SED regime; it was the beginning of the end for the German Democratic Republic. The demonstrations continued, but the mood of the crowds changed. As before, people demanded free elections, the overthrow of the SED regime, the punishment of criminal and corrupt members of the old leadership. But in Leipzig on 20 November for the first time demonstrators not only shouted 'We are the People', but also modified this to 'We are one People'. 'Deutschland, einig Vaterland' ('Germany, united Fatherland') was also chanted, first by small groups, and then by the majority – this was a line of the GDR national anthem which, because of the presence of that line, was no longer officially allowed to be sung, but had to be 'hummed'.

This change of mood was soon evident all over the GDR. One explanation for it was the emotions millions had felt when the frontiers fell and people could come together. The East Germans realised how much they had missed while being imprisoned. The West Germans realised that they had been on the winners' side since 1949, though they shared not only the same language but the same history with the losers. There were, of course, also more mundane motives; not only the wish to get a share of West Germany's wealth, but a widespread and well-founded scepticism about whether the GDR as a separate and independent state would be able to break the power of the SED or be strong enough to escape from its economic misery.

In the weeks following the opening of the frontiers, the SED desperately tried to save its own existence. The party was re-organised, and renamed itself 'SED–PDS' ('Party of Democratic Socialism'). Krenz lost his offices, first in the party, then in the government. Early in December, the SED–PDS presented itself with a changed leadership. But most of the second-rank members, the people who had been in charge of the local party apparatus, of the administration, the economy, the media, the police and the army, still had their old jobs, and still decided what was to be done. In spite of the revolution from below, the old *Nomenklatura* was still by far the most influential group in the country. The citizens knew this very well. This was the main reason for the continuing demonstrations.

Until November, the government had been relatively unimportant, the power being concentrated in the Politbureau of the Party. This now changed. The central political figure now was Hans Modrow, Prime Minister since 13 November. In his government, the SED was still the dominant party. Of the 28 members of the Council of Ministers, 19 belonged to the SED, and 9 to the CDU or another of the former '*bloc* parties' which had been the vassals of the SED for so long, and had cautiously moved towards independence only since summer 1989. Modrow had been SED secretary for Dresden, enjoyed the reputation of being honest, seemed to be a reformer on the Gorbachev line, had a good image even in the West German media, and was backed by the Soviets. He knew of course that he was Prime Minister of a government which would last only until free elections, which had to come soon. But nobody could refute his argument that preparations for free elections would take time, at least a few months: the new parties that were still in the first stages of organisation would not have a fair chance in a campaign that came too soon. Modrow was determined to make good use of the time he had until the elections. His proclaimed aim was to lay the foundation for a socialist democracy in the GDR. Until January 1990 he seemed to believe that this might work, stabilising not only socialism but the very existence of the GDR as a separate German state. In this aim he failed. But his attempt to stabilise socialism was quite consistent with the attempt to keep his comrades in power as long as possible. Many members of the old *Nomenklatura* were able to use this opportunity to acquire real estate, firms or jobs that promised them income and influence even after free elections.

In the last days of November the Protestant and Catholic Churches of the GDR began to fear that the SED might try to slow down the reform process, provoking violent reactions, or that the demonstrations might get out of hand anyway, as tensions increased between groups desiring unification and groups wanting a reformed socialism in a separate GDR. Many members of the clergy now saw their role as mediators who had to make sure that the transformation of the system continued without violence. Non-violence, in their view, required some kind of arrangement between the SED and its former *bloc* partners in the government on the one side and the opposition groups and parties who still operated illegally on the other. The churches therefore invited the antagonists to a 'Round Table Discussion' on 7 December. This famous Round Table had an equal number of members from each side, with representatives of the churches acting as moderators. The declaration in which the Round Table members defined their intentions began as follows: 'The participants of the Round Table meet out of deep concern for our country steeped in crisis, for its independence and its enduring development.'[10] The Round Table did not want to be part of the government, but demanded to be informed and consulted before important decisions. It regarded its role as being a control mechanism, necessary until free elections had created a democratic parliament.

The Round Table had no legitimacy. It was an expression of public opinion only, and certainly not the most important expression. Far more important were the demonstrators, many of whom were already demanding reunification at a time when most representatives of the new groups and parties at the Round Table seemed to agree with the SED–PDS that there should be democratic socialism in an independent GDR. But the public, including the advocates of reunification, accepted the Round Table because it seemed to give the new groups and parties at least some influence, and might be an instrument to limit conflict. The SED–PDS regarded it as a mixed blessing. On the one hand, the insistence of the new groups and parties on controlling and influencing policy was regarded as dangerous by all those who wanted to retain or regain the dominant position of the SED–PDS. On the other hand, the well-publicised Round Table activities had a stabilising effect which was very much in the interests of the SED–PDS. The government, by discussing policy with at least part of the opposition, appeared to accept control and the necessity of compromise. As a result, the SED–PDS tried to keep the representatives of the new groups and parties at the Round Table as little informed and as powerless as possible, without risking open confrontation.

This strategy of the SED–PDS worked until 8 January 1990. The Modrow government had not only been slow to dissolve the Stasi, it even planned to reconstitute a new security service, employing at least part of the Stasi membership. The new groups and parties, above all 'New Forum', adamantly refused to accept this. Modrow did not want to give in, and insisted upon his new security organisation even in his statement before the People's Chamber on 11 January, arguing that the neo-Nazis had become a danger and had to be watched. Demonstrations and protest strikes forced Modrow to give in on 12 January. He had lost credibility. On 15 January a demonstration in front of the Stasi headquarters at Normannenstraße in East Berlin got out of hand and the demonstrators stormed the Stasi building. The revolution, for the first time, had used violence. Modrow was now faced with increasing criticism. His coalition partners in government, the former '*bloc*' parties, were considering leaving the government, realising that further cooperation with the SED–PDS might draw them into the abyss.

Modrow now changed his tactics. Bowing to an ultimatum from

the Round Table, he did what he had refused to do so far: he appeared before the Round Table to defend his policy, recognising the Round Table as an organ of extraconstitutional control (15 January). A week later, he invited the new groups and parties represented at the Round Table to join an all-party government, arguing that this was the only way to prevent the collapse of the GDR, as thousands were leaving for West Germany every day, social tensions were increasing, and the economy was crumbling.

After some hesitation, the new groups and parties did exactly what Modrow wanted. They sent their representatives to take part in a government of 'national responsibility' led by Modrow (28 January). They did not insist upon getting any ministries, however, being quite satisfied with participation at the Round Table and in the Council of Ministers. They also agreed to hold elections on 18 March, and not, as earlier planned, on 6 May. On the one hand, this early date seemed to be necessary, as neither the Volkskammer nor the Round Table represented the people; but on the other hand, the early date also meant that a rich and well-organised party like the SED–PDS or a party heavily supported by a West German partner, such as the CDU and the SPD, would have a far better chance to wage an effective campaign than the new groups, which lacked organisation, money and candidates. Modrow could be satisfied indeed. He had managed to integrate the Round Table into his government without weakening the position of the SED–PDS, which stayed in control of all important ministries, dominated the media, and could not hope for better conditions in which to wage the election campaign.

The seven weeks of Modrow's 'Government of national responsibility' saw the Prime Minister and the Round Table playing a political game which in all important aspects was out of touch with reality. On 30 January Modrow flew to Moscow, expecting support for his policy to stabilise the GDR. Gorbachev disappointed him, telling journalists even before the beginning of the conference with Modrow that the Soviet Union would not stand in the way of the self-determination of the German people.[11] After this, Modrow knew that reunification might come soon. His goal now became the prevention of a take-over of the GDR by the Federal Republic. In order to attain this, he had to improve the GDR's bargaining position. To this end he had the full support of most of the former opposition groups now sharing his government. The common denominator making co-operation between these groups and the SED–

PDS possible was the desire to save 'socialist achievements' such as social security and social benefits, and to try a 'third way' between the former 'bureaucratic' socialism and Western capitalism. This co-operation could be seen most clearly in the draft of a new constitution for the GDR, intended to be the legal basis for a democratic and socialist state entering into a lengthy bargaining process with the Federal Republic before consenting to reunification.

Of the former '*bloc* parties', Christian Democrats and Liberals no longer tried to prolong the life of the GDR. They now advocated rapid reunification, and largely accepted the guidance of their West German partner parties in the election campaign that began in February. The Social Democrats, who were free of the taint of having participated in the SED-controlled *bloc* system, had been most reluctant to join the Modrow government, were stronger advocates of rapid reunification than their West German partners, and hoped to become the strongest party in the March elections.

In the streets of the GDR, the demonstrations continued, now turning into election campaign rallies. Among the people participating in these manifestations of direct democracy, most demanded reunification as soon as possible, wanted to live as the West Germans did, and refused to be guinea-pigs for another experiment with socialism. The Round Table lost the little authority it had gained while it was perceived as fighting the Stasi. During the 'government of national responsibility' it was the central co-ordination committee in which most important decisions of the government were prepared. The government, however, was operating more and more outside the sphere of political reality. What really mattered in February 1990 was the interaction of East German citizens with West German politicians who campaigned in the GDR, the East Germans demanding, the West Germans offering, currency and economic union and rapid reunification.

The elections to the Volkskammer on 18 March 1990 showed that it was not the ideas of the Round Table, but the demands of the demonstrators that represented the mood of the voters. The success of the CDU could only be explained as a vote for the West German chancellor, who had been the one who most clearly offered reunification: the CDU won 40.8 per cent of the votes itself, and together with the Deutsche Soziale Union ('German Social Union') and the Demokratischer Aufbruch ('Democratic Awakening'), with whom it had formed an Allianz für Deutschland, even managed to log up 48 per cent. The defeat of the SPD (21.9 per cent) was the result of the impression that the West German SPD was divided on the all-important issue of reunification. The civil rights groups were annihilated. The most important of them had formed the Bündnis 90 ('Alliance 90'), which won only 2.9 per cent of the votes. The former SED, now the 'Party of Democratic Socialism', with 16.4 per cent, proved to be stronger than many had hoped, with its following concentrated mainly among the civil servants and intellectuals who had profited from the old regime. The overall result of the elections was definitely a mandate for a CDU-led government to prepare reunification.

The process that has transformed East Germany since September 1989 and March 1990, when the first democratic elections marked the end of the SED regime, is often called a 'peaceful revolution'. If a revolution is defined as the overthrow of a ruling group and the transformation of the political system by a protest movement backed by the people, what had happened might be called a revolution indeed. As a revolution, however, it had flaws, which were to cause trouble later.

One flaw was the lack of a revolutionary élite which led the attack against the old regime, won the support of the people, and was willing and able to occupy the top positions when reconstruction began. The civil rights groups so prominent in the first months had few active members wanting to become professional politicians. More importantly, these groups had the support of the people only when they protested against the SED, not when they declared that the future GDR should be a socialist democracy. The civil rights groups became less and less necessary even for organising the demonstrations, since people knew they could meet other people wanting to protest at fixed dates and places. West German TV was sure to report the events, needing little invitation from any such organisation. Co-operation with the SED–PDS in February and March 1990 was the final move which broke the already waning authority of the groups. In the view of many citizens, the members of 'New Forum' or 'Democracy Now' had contributed to the beginning of the uprising; but they certainly had not led it or brought it to a successful conclusion.

Neither could the East German Christian Democrats, the Liberals or the Social Democrats serve as a revolutionary élite. They had not led the attack against the SED regime – on the contrary, with the exception of the SPD, they had been part of the old system, and had hardly managed to distance themselves in time. De Maizière, when elected chairman of the CDU early in November 1989, had declared there were common interests with the SED, since socialism should be kept alive in the GDR.[12] All these parties depended heavily on West German support, not only in terms of money and expertise, but in ideas as well.

The problems caused by the absence of a revolutionary élite were aggravated by the lack of a broad basis from which to recruit able and reliable people for mid-level positions in administration and in the enterprises. Most of those who had professional qualifications and had made a career before 1989 had been members of the SED. Many able, courageous opponents of the regime had left the country. Even if there had been greater efforts to break the 'old-boy network' of SED members in the administration and the economy, there would not have been enough qualified people to replace them.

Another flaw of the revolution followed from its non-violence. Non-violence was thought necessary in order to demonstrate moral superiority and to avoid giving the regime an excuse to use even more brutal force. This idea might not have been realistic. Had the Soviets supported a 'Chinese solution', the East Berlin Politbureau would hardly have hesitated to crush the uprising with every means available. A related argument carried more weight: violence might escalate into civil war, tipping the scales in Moscow in favour of Gorbachev's orthodox opponents. If, however, the principle of non-violence was strictly observed, there was hardly any way to break the power and the self-assurance of the old *Nomenklatura* in time. The process of law against members of the *Nomenklatura* could not work at all in the GDR during the revolution, not only because there were hardly any prosecutors and judges who had not been members of the SED, but because thousands of high-ranking party functionaries, administrators and police officers who had committed crimes even by the standards of GDR law were given sufficient time (by the Modrow government) to destroy the evidence, with only some members of the civil rights groups protesting. As a result, the revolution succeeded in destroying the dictatorship of the SED leaders, but did not succeed in driving most of their active supporters out of positions of influence.

A further flaw of the revolution was the lack of realistic expectations regarding the future of East German society once the SED regime was overthrown. The ideas of reformist socialism combined with elements of direct democracy so popular in most civil rights groups were not attractive to the majority of the people. The majority wanted the civil liberties and the standard of living the West Germans enjoyed. Therefore they opted for representative democracy and a market economy. They had, however, no practical experience with these systems, having lived under political and economic dictatorship for almost half a century. Misconceptions fostered illusions, which are now widespread and may overburden the political system with expectations that cannot be met. Of course, people will learn. They will be able to play the game of democratic party politics soon. It will take them longer to learn the difficult rules of a market economy and realise that the celebrated 'social' component of the West German economic system allows high social benefits only if efficiency and economic growth have priority over the redistribution of wealth. For a time, without aid from the West, neither democracy nor the market economy may work well. This dependence on West German aid may lead to a lasting feeling of inferiority, and seriously impair the development of a political and economic culture adequate to a modern, creative society.

If one considers these flaws, it might be more appropriate to speak, not of a revolution, but of a process of rapid decolonisation triggered by the breakdown of the Soviet empire. When the Soviet Union was no longer able or willing to control its client state, the SED regime, in the final analysis only maintained by Soviet arms, had to crumble. The people pushed to hasten its downfall, but had neither the strength to destroy the old power structures completely nor the time and the resources to reconstruct their society by their own efforts alone.

3. Restricted Choice

If the speed of the collapse of the GDR was surprising, the rapidity with which reunification was accomplished in 1990 was staggering. Governments in Bonn, Moscow, Washington, Paris or London gave the impression that they were busy trying to catch up with events, realising that they had no option but to follow the tidal wave.

The government of the Federal Republic of Germany had welcomed and encouraged Hungary's opening of its frontier to East German refugees; but until November 1989 it had done little to influence the developments within the GDR. When, after 9 November, the exodus grew to more than ten thousand people every week, politicians realised that this could not continue indefinitely. There was no way to stop the exodus from the GDR by refusing work permits. According to the constitution, the East Germans were West German citizens. It would have been possible to cut the special benefits, which had been justified as long as people were fleeing from a dictatorship. Now, in a situation of open frontiers, and with reform of the East German system beginning, they could hardly be defended any longer. The government, however, doubted that cutting off the benefits would be sufficient to stop the exodus as long as the East Germans could not hope for rapid improvement of economic conditions in the GDR.

On 28 November Chancellor Kohl announced a ten-point programme. He offered 'comprehensive aid' for the GDR as soon as the political and economic transformation had been definitely decided, proposed 'confederative structures' to prepare the way for a German federation, and declared that the final aim was a 'peaceful Europe in which the German people can achieve its unity in free self-determination'. This programme was approved by a strong majority of the Bundestag, including most Social Democrats. In East Berlin Egon Krenz, still General Secretary of the SED, commented: 'If a confederation means that one assumes the existence of two separate, independent German states one can discuss everything.' Kohl at that time thought a period of two to three years would be required to attain the final goal of reunification. It would be necessary to win the consent not only of a democratically elected GDR government, but also of the 'Four Powers', which legally still held responsibility for 'Germany as a whole'.

Bonn's biggest worry late in 1989 was that the Soviet Union might consent to reunification only on terms unacceptable to West Germany, and that its Western allies, above all France and Great Britain, might try to postpone reunification as long as possible. British reservations were evident when Foreign Minister Hurd, visiting Berlin after the breaching of the Wall, declared that German unification was not on the agenda; Mitterand paid an official visit to the GDR on 20 December which could only be interpreted as an attempt to stabilise the GDR. The USA might not share the fear of a unified Germany's dominance in Europe, but it certainly expected a Soviet attempt to concede reunification at the price of weakening NATO and the EC. If West Germany had to choose between reunification and integration with the West, the majority of its citizens would have chosen integration with the West. In this situation, Kohl's ten-point programme, with its rather vague 'confederative structures', was representative of public opinion: the goal should be reunification, but the government should proceed with caution and in agreement with West Germany's allies and partners. As so often in the process leading to reunification, the actions of East German citizens rendered all political calculations obsolete within a few weeks. When some demonstrators in Leipzig first demanded reunification (20 November) there could still be doubts whether they spoke for the majority. When Kohl visited Dresden on 19 December he was welcomed by huge crowds, expecting him to achieve reunification as soon as possible. At the same time, there were indications that the East German economy was on the verge of total collapse, and that central planning was no longer working. The government was unable and perhaps unwilling to prepare the change-over to a market economy. It was no surprise that the exodus continued undiminished.

Kohl was now determined to shorten the process leading to reunification. The decisive move to accelerate developments was the proposal to introduce the West German currency, the Deutsche Mark, (DM) in East Germany. It was the most daring initiative of the Bonn government in the chain of decisions it took on reunification – highly controversial at first, but, in the opinion of most observers a few months later, necessary because there was no alternative.

Most economists debating the best way to transform the GDR's planned economy into a market economy wanted the transformation to come first. The monetary union was to follow when the change to a market economy had been accomplished and labour productivity in the GDR had been boosted from 30 per cent of West Germany's level to at least 75 per cent of it. During transformation, the producers in East Germany should be protected by flexible exchange-rates. This might mean a rate of 1 DM West to 5 Marks East at the beginning. With rising productivity and an increase in the competitiveness of East German products the exchange-rate for the East German Mark would improve. As a model for an economic union between two separate countries able to control migration from the weaker to the stronger economy this was sound textbook economics. As a model for both German states after the opening of the frontiers it was completely unrealistic. It would have worked only if the Federal Republic in the transition period could close its frontiers to East Germans looking for jobs in West Germany. Any such measure would have been unconstitutional; and, even if the constitution had been amended, it would have been impossible to enforce it. How could one prevent East Berliners working illegally in West Berlin, if, at an exchange rate of 1:5, they made more money working 8 hours in West Berlin than in two weeks in the Eastern part of the city?

Apart from being impractical, the model favoured by most economists had another very serious flaw: it made reunification impossible as long as the East German economy had not doubled labour productivity. Last but not least, it was not realistic even if judged on its economic merits alone. The idea that the GDR would be able to transform its economy and attain self-supported growth without massive aid in money and expertise from West Germany was preposterous. Massive aid, on the other hand, could be expected only after reunification.

The first West German politicians to propose the introduction of the DM in East Germany were not members of the government, but prominent economic experts of the opposition: Social Democrats Ingrid Matthäus-Maier and Wolfgang Roth, who were not speaking for their party. A few days later, Bonn noted with intense interest that Gorbachev had refused to give Modrow any guarantees for the continuing existence of the GDR (30 January 1990).

On 7 February the Kohl government offered monetary and economic union to the GDR. At first, most German economists, sharing the view of the President of the Bundesbank, Pöhl, were aghast. They feared that, without the protection of a low exchange-rate, most of East Germany's industry would be wiped out, and that the DM would be weakened by demand-pull inflation. After some wavering, most opinion-makers took the side of the government. People realised that, if one wanted to achieve reunification at all, monetary and economic union was the fastest and safest way to get it. It was the most effective means to convince the citizens of the GDR that conditions would improve soon, stopping the exodus. As soon as the monetary and economic union was implemented, the GDR's monetary, fiscal and economic policy would be controlled by Bonn, making full and formal reunification the inevitable next step. Some of the 'Four Powers' might very likely attempt to drive a hard bargain before consenting to reunification; but they could hardly prevent the monetary and economic union. Once this was established, however, pure political necessity would pressure them into accepting full legal reunification. For supporters of the Christian Democrats and Liberals, Kohl's proposal had an additional advantage: it gave the governing coalition in Bonn a splendid edge in the election campaign now being waged in the GDR.

On 10 February Kohl and Genscher flew to Moscow. They were reasonably sure that Gorbachev had changed his position, no longer attempting to stabilise the GDR, but accepting reunification at least in principle. Otherwise, the initiative for the monetary and economic union would have been far too risky. When they returned to Bonn, they had every reason to be in high spirits. Gorbachev had declared that he would respect the wish of the German people to live in one state. It seems that Gorbachev and Shevardnadze, despite harsh criticism from their orthodox opponents in party and army for not using military force to close East Germany's frontiers after 9 November, had decided to concede reunification, merely bargaining for terms as advantageous as possible.

The importance of the discussion in Moscow on 10 February for accelerating the process leading to reunification can hardly be overestimated. Even if they had intended to do so, Great Britain and France were now no longer in a position to slow down developments. Already on 13 February the foreign ministers of the USA, the UK, France, the Soviet Union, the GDR and the Federal Republic of Germany met in Ottawa, where a CSCE conference was held. They agreed on discussions on the 'external aspects' of reunification, with the Four Powers and both German states participating (the '4 plus 2' talks).

In the following months, there were two tracks of negotiations: there were the German–German negotiations, first on the state treaty on the 'Monetary, Economic and Social Union', and later on the Unification Treaty which was to be the basis of East Germany's accession to the Federal Republic of Germany. And parallel to the German–German negotiations, there were the 'Two plus Four' talks and a series of bilateral meetings between Bonn and the governments of the Four Powers to prepare a treaty regulating the external aspects of reunification.

German–German negotiations were facilitated by the CDU victory in the Volkskammer elections on 18 March. The new government led by de Maizière (CDU) was pledged to reunification, and wanted to have the monetary union as soon as possible – but of course on terms highly advantageous to the average citizen of East Germany. For political reasons, the Bonn government showed a tendency to give in to East Berlin's demand for a conversion rate of 1:1 for a large percentage of the cash and savings accounts holdings of East German citizens. The Bundesbank's fears that the money supply would be increased far above the production potential, causing inflation, were ignored.

Politically, this strategy was successful. Local elections in the GDR on 6 May showed an unbroken trend towards the parties which governed in Bonn. Economically, the fears of inflation proved to be unfounded. When monetary union came, on 1 July 1990, East German consumers did not indulge in a huge spending spree, and thus failed to cause the expected demand-pull inflation. Anticipating unemployment, many saved part of their new DM holdings. What they did spend, however, was largely spent on Western products. As predicted, many East German enterprises were soon facing ruin. In the summer of 1990, however, optimism that Western firms would be willing to invest in East Germany was still running high. This optimism was unfounded. The de Maizière government had done little to prepare the economy for monetary and economic union, and Bonn had neglected to insist on regulations to facilitate investment in East Germany. In retrospect the main obstacles to Western investments were the incompetence and resistance of many East German civil servants, the unsolved property situation, and the lack of reliable data on which to assess the value of East German enterprises – obstacles which should have been removed in time.

Preparing the political and legal basis for reunification was less difficult. In the new Volkskammer, the majority had accepted the position of the Bonn government. There was to be no new constitution for unified Germany, worked out and submitted to a plebiscite, but the short method provided for in Article 23 of the Basic Law: the GDR, represented by the Volkskammer, had to apply for accession to the area in which the Basic Law of the Federal Republic of Germany was valid. This procedure not only saved time; it reflected the determination of most West Germans that reunification should not change the essential characteristics of the political and economic system of the Federal Republic. The GDR, however, did not consent to reunification unconditionally. As in the State Treaty on Monetary, Economic and Social Union, the Unification Treaty, in its voluminous annexe, listed hundreds of regulations to cushion the impact of reunification on East German society – from family subsidies to rent controls to the hotly disputed abortion clause, permitting abortion during the first three months of pregnancy for a transition period.

On 23 August 1990 the GDR declared its accession to the Basic

Law. The Unification Treaty was concluded a few days later. The Bundestag and the Bundesrat gave their consent on 23 September. On 3 October Brandenburg, Mecklenburg–Vorpommern, Sachsen, Sachsen-Anhalt, and Thüringen – the five newly-founded federal states that were the successors of the former GDR – joined the Federal Republic.

The external aspects of reunification were dealt with in the 'Two plus Four talks' and in bilateral conferences of the Bonn government with the Four Powers. Of the problems to be solved, the definite and final recognition of the Oder–Neisse frontier between Germany and Poland proved to be the easiest. Kohl had been convinced for years that the recognition of this frontier would be part of the price of German unity. The opposition of a small number of representatives of refugee organisations did not matter, as a great majority in the Bundestag supported Kohl's position.

Far more difficult to solve was the most important problem in the 'Two-plus-Four-talks': Germany's membership in military alliances.

As late as 22 June Shevardnadze presented a draft of a treaty limiting the armed forces of a unified Germany to 250,000 soldiers. During a transition period of five years West Germany should stay in NATO and East Germany should remain a member of the Warsaw Pact organisation. The prerogatives of the Four Powers concerning Germany as a whole and Berlin in particular should continue until the end of the transition period. This proposal was not only unacceptable, it was impossible to put into practice. How could one part of united Germany be a member of NATO, the other part a member of the Warsaw Pact? The breakthrough came on 16 July, when Kohl met Gorbachev in the Caucasian resort of Kislovodsk. Gorbachev again showed his willingness and ability to abandon positions that had become untenable, provided he got something tangible in return. He consented to NATO membership for a unified Germany. Kohl promised economic assistance. The sum of transfer payments and credits for the Soviet Union agreed upon in 1990–1 exceeded 50 billion DM.

The negotiations were concluded in Moscow on 12 September 1990. The main clauses of the Moscow agreement, signed by the Four Powers and both German states, were as follows. Unified Germany would be a member of NATO. As long as Soviet troops remained in East Germany (until 1994), no NATO forces would be stationed on the territory of the former GDR. The Bundeswehr would be limited to 370,000 soldiers, including those units of the former East German 'People's Army' that were incorporated into the Bundeswehr. Bundeswehr units stationed on the territory of the former GDR would not be integrated into NATO. The unified Germany would neither produce nor use atomic, biological, or chemical weapons, and would remain a member of the non-proliferation treaty. The prerogatives of the Four Powers with regard to Germany as a whole and to Berlin would come to an end.

It is not possible yet to analyse in detail the complicated negotiations which made this result possible. The main work was not done during the 'Two-plus-Four talks', but in bilateral conferences, Genscher and Shevardnadze meeting ten times between February and July. The position of the Soviet Union was crucial. Without Soviet consent, a satisfactory solution of the security problem could not be attained. Fundamentally, Gorbachev and Shevardnadze were looking for co-operation with a unified Germany, realising that co-operation would be far more advantageous to the Soviet Union than the inevitable conflicts that would result from Soviet insistence on conditions which would be of doubtful benefit to Soviet security anyhow. This policy was not only far-sighted, it was courageous, because it was sure to encounter bitter opposition within the Soviet Union itself. A few weeks after the Moscow agreement of 12 September Gorbachev, in his domestic politics, moved nearer to the orthodox groups in party and army. It is an open question whether it would have been possible to achieve the same results if the 'Two-plus-Four talks' had continued into the winter of 1990–1.

Of Germany's Western allies, the United States supported Bonn's policy in all essentials. France, after Mitterand's ill-advised visit to East Germany in December 1990, accepted the inevitability of rapid reunification. The United Kingdom did not oppose it, but added complications to already difficult negotiations. Typical was British insistence on NATO manoeuvres on the territory of the former GDR, which endangered the conclusion of the Moscow agreement at the last moment.

With the end of the prerogatives of the Four Powers who had been the victors in 1945, and with reunification, the post-war epoch had ended for Germany. For the peoples of Eastern Central Europe, it had ended as soon as they were able to shake off Soviet domination. The full extent of the devastation Soviet-type socialism and Soviet domination had caused is seen only now, as the former socialist societies face the enormously difficult problems of transformation to

modern economies and to democracy. Before blaming the Soviet
Union for all the difficulties that have to be overcome when recon-
structing East Germany, Germans should bear in mind, however,
that without German aggression half a century ago neither the
partition of Germany nor Soviet domination over large parts of
Europe would have been possible.

Notes

1. M. Gorbachev, 'Perestroika near Neotlozna' in *Pravda*, 2.8.1986.
2. 'Materialy plenuma Centralnogo Komiteta KPSS', 27–28.1.1987, *Polis-
   dat*, Moscow, 1987, p. 7.
3. M. Gorbachev, *October and Perestroika, The Revolution Continues*, Moscow,
   Novosty Press, 1987, p. 28.
4. For a convincing analysis see Ernst Cux, 'Aufstieg und Fall des sowjetischen Kolonialreiches', *Neue Zürcher Zeitung*. Dec. 9–10, 1990.
5. *Isvestia*, Nov. 30, 1989.
6. Nemeth in an interview with F. Kurz, in Dieter Grosser, Stephan
   Bierling, and Friedrich Kurz, *7 Mythen der Wiedervereinigung*, Munich,
   1991.
7. *Deutschland Archiv*, Chronik der Ereignisse in der DDR. 1990, p. 4.
8. *Der Spiegel* 45, 1989 (6.11.1989), p. 23.
9. Martin Mantzke, 'Was bleibt von der DDR?', in *Europa Archiv* 24/1990,
   p. 738.
10. Uwe Thaysen, *Der runde Tisch, Óder: Wo blieb das Volk?* Opladen 1990,
    p. 50.
11. *Deutschland Archiv*, Chronik der Ereignisse in der DDR, 1990, p. 60.
    Karin Holzer, Interview with Hans Modrow, in Karin Holzer, 'Die
    Übergangsregierung Modrow', MA thesis, University of Munich, 1991.
12. *Die Wirtschaftswoche*, 13/1990, p. 18.

DIETER MAHNCKE

Reunification as an Issue in German Politics 1949–1990

Introduction

Three introductory remarks seem in order. Firstly, a word needs to be said about the expression 'reunification', because some observers and participants in Germany took pains in 1989 and 1990 to avoid it, preferring rather to talk about the 'unification of Germany'. Here, however, the term 'reunification' will be used, because this was the term predominantly used in Germany throughout the period since the end of the war. The issue in German politics was 'reunification', not unification.

Initially, the term encompassed the reunification of Germany as it existed within the boundaries of 1937. Obviously, this is no longer the case. As the agreement between the Four Powers and the two German states of 12 September 1990 stipulated, the Germany to be united constituted the then Federal Republic of Germany, the German Democratic Republic and Berlin.[1] The boundary issue is solved and settled,[2] despite some remaining discontent about this among some Germans.

However, those critical of the term 'reunification' may have been concerned about more than just the boundary issue. Apparently, *re*-unification to them implied a return to what they considered to be the 'old Germany': unfettered by alliances, irrational, militaristic and hegemonic. That, too, is an obsolete idea. Such a Germany no longer exists. Today's Germany is closely tied to its European and

33

North American partners in the European Community and in the Atlantic Alliance. A keynote of German foreign policy is co-operation, and one might well argue that present-day Germany is probably less nationalistic than either Britain or France, and more modern in its policies of integration and co-operation.

Another explanation for the reluctance by some to use the term 'reunification' – though this may be difficult to prove – is that those who had in the course of the seventies and eighties given up the aim of reunification found this differentiation rather useful: They could claim that they had only given up *re*unification in the sense of restoration; unification, however, they had always favoured.

Secondly, we might ask what can we learn from a review of reunification as an issue in German politics. From a 'political science point of view' the topic is interesting because it raises the questions of the role of consistency in policy and the role of principles and conviction versus apparent realities. In other words, it raises the difficult political assessment of when a policy is overtaken by events and becomes obsolete. Can one tell – before history makes its decision – whether a policy is steadfast and true to principle, or simply *stur* and *dickköpfig*, simply obstinate and out of touch with a changing environment? What indicators would there be for such an assessment? Are there any certain indicators at all, or does it really come down to the 'right feeling', perhaps even to luck?

Of course, these questions cannot all be answered here. What is being suggested is just that, if there is something to be learned from the topic, this is where one might look.

Finally, it must be pointed out that it is impossible within the limited space available here to do justice to many of the events during more than forty years in any degree of detail. The aim will hence primarily be to describe some general lines of development and to offer a few theses that may help to order some of the detail and give some basis for a further discussion.

Main Thesis

Reunification policy and practice can be divided into a number of phases:

- the Adenauer period;
- the beginnings of *détente* in the sixties;

- the new *Ostpolitik*;
- the seventies;
- and finally the eighties and reunification.

The overriding thesis to be presented here is that, while the question of reunification was always a controversial issue in German politics since the end of the war and indeed has remained so up to the present, it was at first – up to about the middle and late sixties – not an issue of principle (everybody, including the Communists in West and East Germany favoured it), but primarily an issue of practice and implementation. That is, the political differences concerned mainly the question not of *whether* but of *how* it was to be achieved. This changed in the course of the seventies and eighties, and the issue became less a question of practice (all parties now adhered to the concepts of *détente* and of dealing with the East Germans on an equal level) and increasingly a question of a principle that was no longer adhered to by all. In the course of 1990 we witnessed a turn-about again, as almost everybody once again proclaimed adherence to the principle, but differences grew about the means of putting it into practice: the pace, the cost and the methods.

The Adenauer Period

It is worth dwelling on Adenauer's ideas about reunification, because they provided the foundation for later policies and perhaps even – some today claim – the basis for ultimate success. They can be sketched quite simply.

It is untrue that Adenauer, the westward-oriented, Catholic Rhinelander, was not really interested in the reunification of Germany. He favoured reunification, but not at any price. Unification in his view was acceptable only in freedom and in a Western framework.[3] He was convinced that a united Germany – just like West Germany itself – should be removed from a central position between East and West, and tied firmly to the West, as a permanently Western country.

Adenauer recognised, however, that under existing circumstances reunification could not be achieved against the will of the Soviet Union. Since war was obviously out of the question one would have to wait for changes in the Soviet Union. These he believed would come about in three ways: China would abandon the Alliance with the Soviet Union, thus weakening it externally. Secondly, Soviet power would be undermined internally by the growing resistance of the people to the Soviet dictatorship (particularly in Eastern Europe) and, most importantly, by economic collapse. Adenauer was convinced – as he wrote in his memoirs – that when that day arrived the question of German reunification would be back on the agenda.[4]

He understood that such a day would possibly take a long time to arrive. Patience and perseverance – 'ein langer Atem' – would be required, and he repeatedly admonished not only the Germans to be patient, but his Western partners to persevere.[5] In the mean time the West needed to maintain its strength and its resistance to Soviet ambitions. Soviet aims in Europe would have to be consistently frustrated, so that Communist leadership would not be able to compensate for domestic difficulties with external successes. This was to be supplemented by a politically stable and economically thriving Western Europe, to which – Adenauer claimed – the East would then be magnetically attracted.

Both the 'policy of strength' and the 'magnetism theory' were subsequently scoffed at. But the real difference between Adenauer's approach and that of Kurt Schumacher and the Social Democratic Party lay elsewhere. While Adenauer wanted to pursue reunification within a Western framework, Schumacher felt that a German national approach would be much more promising. Almost all other differences, on substance and on timing, derived from this basic contrast.

Thus Adenauer wanted to finalise the moves toward Western integration – the European Defence Community, and then NATO, and the steps toward European economic integration – before starting out on a more active *Ostpolitik*. This can be seen in two major conflicts during the early years of the Federal Republic: the Soviet Note of March 1952 and the entry into NATO in 1954–5.

In the Note of 10 March 1952 (followed by several further notes up to 23 September 1952 and again in 1954 after the signing of the Paris treaties) the Soviet Union offered to accept German reunification in return for neutrality. Adenauer pressed the Western Allies to reject these advances. He was unwilling to start negotiations with the Soviet Union before his policy of integration of the Federal Republic into the West was firmly on course. More important, however, was his conviction that the offer was not a serious one in the first place: he felt that it was primarily intended to obstruct the

Federal Republic's course of co-operation and integration with the West.[6] But beyond that, even if it were a serious offer, Adenauer strongly felt that the result would be undesirable. Neutralisation of Germany would destroy the Western process of integration, the United States would withdraw, and old nationalistic rivalries would revive in Europe. Soon the whole of Europe would fall under the influence of the Soviet Union.[7] For what he thus considered to be neither serious nor desirable he was not willing to risk the confidence which the West was beginning to show towards the Federal Republic and which he considered so essential for the future of Germany.

The second and more important issue to arise was the completion of the treaties leading to West Germany's admission to the Atlantic Alliance in 1954–5. While Adenauer described this as the necessary foundation of his policy of reunification in freedom, the Social Democrats felt that the integration of West Germany into the Alliance (and Western Europe) was in fact incompatible with reunification. Of course, seen from a Soviet point of view – how could they accept a united Germany as part of a Western military alliance? – this seemed absolutely plausible.[8] According to Adenauer's line of argument, however, such a situation would come up only under completely changed circumstances which would then make it both more difficult to resist (because of Soviet internal and international weakness) and more acceptable (because the Soviet leadership would understand that Germany did not pose a threat).

For the Social Democrats, however, their approach of not looking at what seemed essential from a German point of view (freedom and security for a united Germany), but at what seemed acceptable ('negotiable') from a Soviet point of view confronted them with a dilemma from which they suffered right up to reunification in 1990. Almost up to the end they had claimed that reunification would never come about if Germany remained in NATO.[9]

Of course, Adenauer did not join the Alliance without Western concessions: West Germany gained both sovereignty and a formal commitment of the Western Allies (in Article 7 of the *Deutschlandvertrag*) to support the aim of German reunification. This commitment, which in subsequent years more and more observers tended to see as no more than lip-service, proved to be important in 1990, when the Western Powers, specifically Britain and France, ultimately came round to supporting reunification despite considerable political reservations.[10]

Once integration into the Atlantic Alliance had been achieved and integration in Western Europe was making progress, Adenauer opened up and embarked upon what was in fact a remarkably flexible *Ostpolitik*. He established (in 1955) diplomatic relations with the Soviet Union. This was necessary, he argued, despite the fact that the Soviet Union had diplomatic relations with the German Democratic Republic, because the USSR was one of the Four Powers responsible for Germany. Direct relations were thus imperative.

This would not be valid for other states, however. Should another state that had diplomatic relations with West Germany recognise the GDR this would be considered an 'unfriendly act' by the Federal Republic, and the West German government would decide on measures to be taken in response. This was the birth of the Hallstein Doctrine (actually formulated by Wilhelm Grewe), which itself became a controversial issue in the second half of the sixties. Although the Doctrine itself was open on what precise measures might be undertaken, it turned out that as a rule diplomatic relations were severed, the Hallstein Doctrine thus becoming practically synonymous with a break-off of diplomatic relations in those cases in which a state that had diplomatic relations with West Germany took up such relations with the GDR.[11]

After having taken up diplomatic relations with the Soviet Union Adenauer undertook two further moves which were kept secret at the time. In 1958 he offered the Soviet Union what was called an 'Austrian solution' for the GDR, i.e. Germany would accept the division of the country if the GDR was granted freedom. When the Soviet Union rejected this and tensions rose as a result of the Berlin crisis he offered the Soviet Union a truce (*Burgfrieden*) in 1962. Regardless of continuing differences the German question should be laid on ice for ten years. In this period German–Soviet relations could be developed and then a new effort at resolution of the German question could be made.[12] Both moves were rejected by the Soviet Union.

For many years Social Democrats as well as many writers accused the Christian Democrats of having 'missed an opportunity' for German reunification by not 'at least testing' the Soviet offer of 1952[13] (although in Adenauer's view even a positive result of such a test would have been undesirable). One wonders whether in private Soviet discussions in 1989 and 1990 there might sometimes have been a reference to a 'missed opportunity' from the Soviet point of view in the shape of the refusal of Adenauer's offer of 1958!

Throughout this period, however, Adenauer insisted on maintaining the basic principles of his *Deutschlandpolitik*, specifically that only the Federal Republic represented Germany and could hence speak for all Germans (*Alleinvertretungsanspruch*), and that any recognition of a second German state was out of the question. This and the rejection of negotiations on the Soviet Note in 1952 (his moves of 1958 and 1962 were kept secret) gave him the reputation of being inflexible, rigid, and perhaps not even seriously aiming for reunification. (Remarkably enough, information on Adenauer's moves was first published by the Brandt government in 1972, although probably not to show how flexible Adenauer had actually been, but rather to indicate that the Social Democrats were not, in fact, erring from the true path or – if they were – that they had had a notable precursor from the Christian Democratic side.)[14]

To sum up: During the first third of the period of German division since the end of the Second World War there were no differences on the aim of German reunification, and even differences on the territorial extent of a reunited Germany were at most embryonic.

Differences were deep with regard to the means of achieving the aim. Whereas Adenauer wanted to (and did) pursue his reunification policy from a firm Western base, the opposition Social Democrats felt that such ties precluded reunification. The opposition approach was thus a more national approach, and it was mainly on these grounds that they opposed NATO and membership in the European Economic Community.

In addition, the Social Democrats felt that the Adenauer governments were too rigid, that they were unwilling to take a risk in order to move toward reunification. (One of the most successful CDU campaign slogans in this period was indeed 'Keine Experimente' – 'No experiments'.) As time progressed and the East seemed to become more stable, the feeling steadily grew that a new and more flexible approach to reunification was required.

The Beginnings of *Détente*

Whether Adenauer's policy had been too rigid or not, after the building of the Berlin Wall in 1961 and the ensuing limited stabilisation of the GDR there was growing uneasiness and uncertainty. Were we really on the right track? Was our policy of maintaining our moral and legal positions (or legalistic positions as the critics said), of practically ignoring the GDR, not in fact hampering progress towards the aim of allowing the two parts of Germany to grow together? Were the people not actually growing apart, were they not losing contact with each other? And wasn't the overall development in Europe overtaking previous policies? Was it not imperative to recognise these 'new realities' in Europe and to adjust and adapt to them?

Certainly many Social Democrats thought so. 'We must achieve change by approaching each other' was the intended purport of Egon Bahr's slogan 'Wandel durch Annäherung'. But the Social Democrats were not alone. There was a general feeling within the German population that something needed to be done.[15] In June 1961 the Bundestag in a joint resolution had called upon the government to 'grasp every opportunity to normalise relations between the Federal Republic and the Eastern European states without sacrifice of vital German interests', while making the 'necessary legal reservations' and maintaining the aim of a free and united Germany.[16] As a result of German initiatives trade missions were established in Poland (1963) as well as in Romania, Hungary and Bulgaria (1964). The aim, however, was to encourage a greater independence of these countries from the Soviet Union – a policy which questioned rather than accepted the status quo. The Soviet Union reacted to this with a stronger effort to maintain a common foreign policy line toward the West German moves amongst its East European allies.

Nevertheless, the Soviet Union did respond to the German 'Peace Note' of March 1966 – in which negotiations on a non-aggression agreement were offered without, however, sacrificing the aim of reunification or prejudicing the boundary issue – and hence the Grand Coalition of CDU and SPD, which took power in autumn 1966 under the leadership of Chancellor Kurt Georg Kiesinger, felt encouraged to continue the initiatives. Indeed, within a few weeks after taking office the new West German government, with Willy Brandt as Foreign Minister, took up diplomatic relations with Romania.[17] The Hallstein Doctrine was amended by what came to be known as the 'birth defect theory', i.e. that since Romania had had the 'birth defect' of having had no choice with regard to the recognition of the GDR this case could again be accepted as an exception to the Hallstein Doctrine. In 1967 a trade mission was established in Prague, and in January 1967 diplomatic relations were taken up with Yugoslavia.[18] The 'birth defect theory' was quietly dropped. But despite the offer to extend negotiations even to include the GDR, little more could be achieved. In the summer of 1968 – as tensions rose in Czechoslovakia – the Soviet Union broke off the discussions that had proceeded on the basis of the Peace Note of 1966.[19] Rather, the Soviet Union and the GDR responded to the West German initiatives by a major effort to bring the East Europeans into line, making their relations with West Germany in fact dependent on the Federal Republic's relationship with the GDR.[20]

In addition, the Grand Coalition faced a major crisis with regard to the Hallstein Doctrine when, in rapid succession, the GDR was recognised by Iraq, Cambodia, Syria, Sudan and South Yemen. Since the Federal Republic had not maintained diplomatic relations with most of the Arab states since 1967, when these states had broken off relations after West Germany's establishment of diplomatic relations with Israel, the critical case turned out to be Cambodia.[21] Foreign Minister Brandt's position was that as long as the GDR was not prepared to improve its bilateral relations with the Federal Republic in the interest of the people, recognition of the GDR was to be considered as an unfriendly act. However, if West Germany always reacted by breaking off relations it might soon find itself isolated. Once the 'dam' thus far inhibiting general recognition of the GDR broke the GDR would in effect be granted sole representation (*Alleinvertretung!*) in all those states by which it was recognised. The Christian Democrats, on the other hand, feared that the dam would break *unless* a firm response was chosen. The question was finally resolved in a decision to 'freeze' relations with Cambodia, whereupon Cambodia decided to break off relations.[22]

Of course, all parts of the political spectrum felt frustration. But while the Christian Democrats believed that they had gone far in offering to negotiate with the GDR on the highest level – although not recognising it as a state, to sign non-aggression agreements with all members of the Warsaw Pact including 'the other part of Germany', and to establish diplomatic relations with all of them except the GDR, the SPD and the FDP felt that too little had been offered. The CDU pointed out how negative the response had been, with tensions even rising and obstruction increasing on the access routes to Berlin.[23] The Federal Republic had offered to declare formally that it would not use force to pursue its aims: the Soviet Union had instead demanded that the aims themselves should be abandoned. This was unacceptable to the Christian Democrats. The SPD, however, felt that if the Eastern reactions were hardly positive this only proved that German moves were too half-hearted, and hence insufficient. More had to be offered – specifically with regard to the acceptance of the reality of the second German state and the permanent nature of the German–Polish boundary – before improvements could be expected.[24] Such improvements should no longer be hampered by 'legalisms' or 'political formulae'.

The Free Democrats, in opposition during the Grand Coalition and able to give their thoughts free reign, certainly believed so. Under the leadership of Walter Scheel, who had succeeded the more conservative but by no means inflexible Erich Mende,[25] they began to develop ideas that ranged close to those of the Social Democrats;[26] and with the election victory in the autumn of 1969 and the subsequent forming of a coalition between SPD and FDP the 'new *Ostpolitik*' was launched.

Neue Ostpolitik

When the SPD–FDP coalition took over power in the autumn of 1969 by a narrow majority the situation was therefore as follows: all political parties in the Federal Republic wanted to improve relations with the East, including and indeed specifically with the GDR. The CDU/CSU, however – obviously marked by the continuity of twenty years of responsibility in government, possibly also by the electoral successes of the right-wing NPD[27] – wanted to move ahead step by step, and was careful to maintain the legal positions of German reunification policy. The SPD and the FDP, on the other hand, were prepared to accept 'the realities', as they said, i.e. explicitly the existence of two separate and independent German states and the boundaries of those two states, and implicitly the political situation in Eastern Europe, including Soviet hegemony.

The details of the process and results of the *neue Ostpolitik* are well known. The landmarks of this *Ostpolitik* were the treaties with the Soviet Union (August 1970), Poland (December 1970) and Czechoslovakia (June 1973), as well as the 'Basic Treaty' with the GDR (December 1972) and the Quadripartite Agreement on Berlin (September 1971). In addition the judgement of the Constitutional Court on the Basic Treaty with the GDR of July 1973 should be mentioned.[28]

The 'new *Ostpolitik*' basically had two aspects to it: it brought great movement – *but*, after all was said and done in the hectic and highly emotional political struggles of the early seventies,[29] it also upheld the cornerstones of German reunification policy,[30] more clearly and more permanently than was perhaps foreseen at the time.

Firstly, Brandt's *Ostpolitik* formally recognised the existence of two German states and abandoned the Hallstein Doctrine, thus opening up the road to general international recognition of the GDR – *but* the Federal Republic itself did not recognise the GDR under international law and it maintained the declared aim of German reunification, both in a letter handed to the Soviet Union and in the Resolution of the Bundestag of 17 May 1972 in connection with the ratification of the treaties with the Soviet Union and Poland.[31]

Secondly, West Germany signed a major treaty with the GDR on the improvement and intensification of relations between the two states – *but* the Federal Republic did not recognise the GDR as a foreign country, argued that the relations between the two states were of a 'special nature' (*inter se* relations), and maintained its position with regard to a single German citizenship.

Finally, the Eastern boundary with Poland was accepted in substance – *but* it was declared that ultimate and final recognition could come only in a peace treaty signed by the government of a united Germany.

When these reservations proved their validity as the reunification process proceeded in 1990, a debate arose in Germany about the role of the Christian Democratic opposition in bringing about these reservations, the Social Democrats maintaining that the reservations were of their own making, while the Christian Democrats claimed that the reservations were not only the result of their pressure (in a Bundestag in which the SPD–FDP coalition had lost its majority owing to several defections), but that to a significant extent the very wording had come from them.

Statements by Social Democrats at the time (as opposed to today) tend to support the Christian Democratic point of view.[32] It seems rather likely that the SPD–FDP coalition would have been less strict on some of the reservations had it been able to maintain a secure majority in the Bundestag. Christian Democratic pressure was significant because of their strong position in the Bundestag. While the 'letter on German unity' handed to the Soviet Union on ratification was (well) formulated in the Foreign Office, the first draft of the Bundestag joint resolution came from Rainer Barzel, then leader of the opposition. But, at the same time, there were members of the governing coalition who were convinced of the inherent validity of the reservations, and the coalition as a whole recognised in the course of the debate that unless these reservations were made the treaty might not pass scrutiny by the Constitutional Court. And indeed, when the Bavarian state government tested the 'Basic Treaty' concluded with the GDR before the Court in May 1973 (incidentally, against the personal conviction of the leader of the parliamentary opposition, Karl Carstens, who had succeeded Barzel and who felt that these were purely political questions to be decided upon by the relevant political institutions) the Court did reject the claim that the treaty was unconstitutional, but in a very detailed judgement emphasised and reaffirmed the reservations, and hence in practice accepted the Bavarian move (*inter alia* with regard to the upholding of the aim of German reunification, a single German citizenship, and the inclusion of Berlin in all treaties signed by the Federal Republic).[33]

The Seventies

The ensuing period was again a period of change and adaptation, perhaps more adaptation by the Christian Democrats and more change on the part of the SPD.

From the Social Democratic point of view the seventies – basically the period from ratification of the *Ostverträge* in 1972 to the loss of power in 1982 – were not very rewarding. 'Filling the treaties with life' as the phrase went, turned out to be difficult.[34] Poland, the Soviet Union, and particularly the GDR made use of every weakness or lack of clarity which the treaties offered them: with regard to the inclusion of (West) Berlin in the international activities of the Federal Republic, with regard to all areas of co-operation except economic co-operation, and with regard to the extension of free travel and the free flow of information, to mention just a few of the areas of controversy.

Even the Conference on Security and Co-operation in Europe (CSCE), which was successfully concluded with the signing of the 'Final Act' in Helsinki in August 1975, and which was to become one of the major instruments for furthering human rights and freedom in Eastern Europe, did not bring dividends immediately. At this stage it was still uncertain whether it was going to be more of an instrument of the status quo or of change. By the time it had become mainly an instrument of change and borne fruit, the government in

Bonn was again being led by the Christian Democrats (who in 1975 had voted against the CSCE Final Act in the Bundestag).

With regard to the reunification issue there were perhaps two important changes. Among the Social Democrats, frustrated by the tedious progress in relations with the East, more and more felt that a stable and 'normal' situation would only come about if and when the status quo was really and finally accepted: German division and all. SPD–FDP *Ostpolitik* had been predicated on change and adaptation, on the acceptance of 'the realities'; and if there were difficulties or lack of progress there were many who were ready to believe that change, adaptation and the 'acceptance of realities' had just not gone far enough. Ironically we can thus witness a situation where the Social Democrats gradually move away from the Christian Democrats and many of the Free Democrats on the principle of reunification, while simultaneously the Christian Democrats are rapidly moving closer to the SPD on its practical policies. Indeed, when the CDU/CSU took over power in 1982 (the Free Democrats switched coalitions for economic reasons and because of differences with the SPD on security matters, but also because the steady decline of the SPD in this phase threatened to engulf the FDP, too) it could base its *Ost- und Deutschlandpolitik* on continuity. *Pacta sunt servanda* ('Treaties are there to be kept') Alois Mertes, the CDU's foremost foreign-policy spokesman admonished the Christian Democrats – but for most of the members of the CDU/CSU this was no longer a hurdle of any significance.[35]

The Kohl Government and Reunification

The coalition of CDU/CSU and FDP under Chancellor Helmut Kohl made – to put it very briefly – two significant contributions to prepare the ground for reunification. Firstly, it placed high priority on the extension of personal contacts between East and West Germany. When the figures moved up from 36,000 East German visitors under sixty years of age (for those over 60 years the figure was about 2.7 million) in 1981 to more than one million by 1987 it seemed clear to at least some observers that this was going to have an effect within the GDR – and, indeed, restiveness and dissatisfaction grew among the East's young people.

Secondly, under the leadership of Foreign Minister Hans-Dietrich Genscher, but obviously with the support of and significant contributions from the Chancellor, the Federal Republic fostered its relations with the Soviet Union by trying above all to put across two messages: firstly, that Germany did not pose a threat to the Soviet Union, and secondly, that on the contrary it represented a potential economic partner for the Soviet Union that was capable of helping that country solve its growing difficulties in this field. In both respects the Soviet Union needed to be convinced that Germany's firm integration in the West was not a disadvantage, but could be beneficial from the Soviet point of view, membership in NATO tying down German military power, membership in the European Community giving Germany an important base from which it could offer assistance. Here, indeed, were the arguments that were going to make Germany's integration with the West and reunification compatible – something the SPD was slow to realise.

Of course reunification was not clearly foreseen. However, while the SPD was moving away from the aim of reunification, the CDU was not. It would be incorrect to claim that the short-lived excitement about the reunification issue in the CDU party programme in February 1989 was a sign that even the CDU was beginning to give up the basic principles of reunification in favour of a more pragmatic policy along the lines of the SPD. The programme did emphasise pragmatic steps to improve inner-German relations, but it did not give up the aim of reunification.[36]

Rather, two other changes were occurring. Firstly, many Social Democrats were, in fact, publicly beginning to renounce the aim of reunification in favour of some form of European peace structure, including the two German states.[37] Secondly, within the population as a whole, but also within the CDU/CSU, there was a growing acceptance of the German–Polish boundary as it exists today. This development was carefully encouraged by the government.[38]

When the Wall fell and the SED regime collapsed in East Berlin, Chancellor and Foreign Minister moved boldly. Initially thinking in longer terms (compare Kohl's ten-point plan of November 1989),[39] the government became aware in early 1990 that the pressure exerted by the East German population made it necessary to move much faster. Thus the economic, monetary and social union was introduced on 1 July, reunification was achieved on 3 October, and the first free all-German elections since 1933 were held on 2 December.

What controversies remain? The claim that everything moved too fast is now a moot point – and considering the uncertain development in the Soviet Union even some of those making this claim may want to reconsider. But whatever the assessment may be: the government in fact had had no choice.

A second accusation is levelled by the Opposition: namely, that the costs of reunification had not been fully tallied. This is correct, although in view of the economic chaos in the former GDR, and the lack of reliable records and statistics, it was difficult to assess the costs even at the beginning of 1991.

Many other problems remain and will have to be dealt with: not only the rebuilding of the economy, fundamental reform of the legal and educational systems, the integration of the two armies, the instatement of local government within the five new federal states and so forth, but mainly the mental growing together of the two parts of the population. This, in the long run, is the most important task.

Conclusions

The first conclusion is that despite all the differences over reunification in Germany during the past four decades there has also been a significant degree of agreement and continuity. Up to the eighties, the major differences were differences of practice, not of principle; in the mid-eighties a difference of principle became visible at a time when the practical differences had been eroded.

In particular, it would be wrong to argue that any one party was the sole contributor to the achievement of reunification. Although it is true that Adenauer's policy eventually triumphed – all the criteria that he enunciated turned out to be the correct ones – the 'new *Ostpolitik*' of the SPD–FDP coalition made important contributions in preparing the ground for the ultimate realisation of the Adenauer principles: reunification in freedom and in the Western framework of the EC and the Atlantic Alliance. Obviously, it would be incorrect to claim that reunification is a direct result of SPD–FDP *Ostpolitik*, but it would also be wrong to say that this policy made no contribution at all. Its contribution lay in the relaxation of tensions in Eastern Europe and in the Soviet Union, in breaking down the image of a revanchist and threatening Germany; but it also lay in the easier and intensified contacts which this policy had opened up for Germans in East and West. As Adenauer initially stated and Willy Brandt reiterated in 1969: unless we increased these contacts and hence halted a possible *Entfremdung*, a further growing apart, there would be little to reunite.

Secondly, the aim of reunification – though questioned by some and increasingly losing support among Social Democrats in the seventies and eighties – was never given up by any government or by the population. This is true for both West and East Germany. Although the East German government in the sixties and seventies removed references to one Germany not only from the constitution but from almost all public statements, names and so forth (and did not even any longer permit the singing of the GDR anthem, with its now famous refrain 'Deutschland, einig Vaterland' – 'Germany, united fatherland'), even here there were still occasional references to the concept of a united, socialist Germany as a very long-term aim.

As far as the population is concerned, the desire for unity seemed understandably stronger in East than in West Germany. But in West Germany too all polls indicated that support for the aim of reunification remained consistently high; scepticism was expressed mainly with regard to the realisability of the goal within a foreseeable time-span.[40]

There were, however, those that were willing to give up the goal completely. They were concentrated mainly among the supporters of the Social Democrats and the Greens, but they could also be found elsewhere. There were several differing reasons: a small minority considered reunification undesirable in the first place; most, however, were simply sceptical with regard to its realisability. They felt it better to adapt to 'the realities' and to make the best of the situation. The problem here was that they saw only part of the realities: the realities of power and not those of opposition, of resentment, inefficiency and instability. Indeed, the ultimate dilemma of Social Democratic policy was that it was geared to achieving stability by the acceptance of a status quo that was inherently unstable.

Whereas few of those basically antagonistic towards reunification changed their attitudes in 1990, many of those who had simply been sceptical and had hence accepted the division, 're-adapted' in the course of events and became careful supporters of unification, supporters, but full of reservations about the pace and content. The SPD candidate for Chancellor in 1990, Oskar Lafontaine, was as good an example as any of those holding this position.

Thirdly: what did change in the course of the years, however – and almost imperceptibly – was the attitude to the boundary question and the former Eastern territories. Here the Brandt government's acceptance of the boundaries in substance, i.e. in all but absolutely final legal form, as well as a corresponding statement by the German Protestant Church a few years earlier (which had first sparked an intensive public debate), had prepared the ground.

The lapse of time and the decreasing importance of the refugees as a separate group in German politics were important here (at the end of 1990 there were only eight members of parliament left who contested Kohl's acceptance of the boundaries before the Constitutional Court).[41] But ultimately most important was (let us give credit where it is due) the insight of the German people. Most of them not only understood that reunification would be achieved only if the existing boundaries were accepted, but were also prepared to accept those boundaries in order to achieve reconciliation with Poland and with the new generation of Poles born and now living in those former German territories, where today only a few Germans remain.

Fourthly: did reunification catch us all by surprise? By this I mean the fact of reunification – not the precise date, which no one could foresee.

I do not think that it caught us all by surprise. It caught some by surprise – particularly, of course, those who had given up the aim of German reunification, i.e. many Social Democrats in Germany and at least some of our allies in Britain, France, and other European countries.

But I have always resisted the opinion that the event as such was a surprise, and could under no circumstances have been foreseen.[42] There are three reasons for this. Firstly, overcoming the division of Germany and Europe was always a proclaimed political aim of the West. One can take most NATO communiqués as evidence for this. Though this may have been lip-service to some, it was not lip-service to all. Secondly, the West had always proclaimed that totalitarian systems are inherently unstable, and that they – together with their inefficient centralised economies – must and will collapse sooner or later. And thirdly, the Germans themselves had never – not even the Social Democratic governments – given up the aim of reunification.

Fifthly: what can we learn from this? I believe that we can learn several things. We can learn that even in the fast-moving twentieth century events that do not happen within one legislative period are not necessarily 'unrealistic'. In other words, we should understand again that some things take place in longer periods, and hence we must see them in a long-term perspective and adjust our policies accordingly. This is true for positive as well as negative developments.

From this we may derive a second lesson. While politicians may have to make definitive judgements on the basis of inadequate knowledge, social scientists, I feel, should (occasionally, at least) display a degree of modesty. It is worthwhile taking a look at some of the predictions made by social scientists with regard to the German question in the past ten or twenty years. I am not against prognoses in social science; what I am critical of, however, is the certainty and absoluteness with which some of these predictions are made. A bit more care and a bit more modesty seem in order.

Sixthly: having said that, let me make a prediction. The issue of reunification in German politics, which is still an issue today with regard to its implementation, will cease to be an issue within five to ten years. As in the case of Adenauer – to whose memory the entire political spectrum in Germany today pays respect – in just a few years' time all will claim to have been proponents of reunification and all will claim to have significantly, even decisively, contributed to its coming about. Reunification as an issue in German politics will then be history: partly glorified, partly manipulated and partly – perhaps mainly – forgotten.

Notes

1. Cf. 'Vertrag über die abschließende Regelung in bezug auf Deutschland', in *Bulletin*, Presse- und Informationsamt der Bundesregierung, 14 Sept. 1990, pp. 1153 ff.
2. As I stated in early 1987, cf. Dieter Mahncke, 'Sicherheitspolitik in Westeuropa – Deutsche Interessen und Anliegen zwischen Ost und West, in *Integration*, 1–88, pp. 23–33. This article was also published in English under the title of 'Divided Germany and European Integration – Challenges and Constraints for a Common Security Policy', in Wolfgang Wessels and Elfriede Regelsberger (eds), *The Federal Republic of Germany and the European Community: The Presidency and Beyond*, Bonn, 1988, pp. 169–92.
3. Cf. mainly Konrad Adenauer, *Erinnerungen*, 4 vols, Stuttgart, pp. 1965 ff. Also Klaus Gotto, 'Der Realist als Visionär – Die Wiedervereinigungspolitik Konrad Adenauers', in *Die politische Meinung*, March–April 1990, pp. 6–13 (in English in *German Comments*, June 1990, pp. 30–6); Dieter Mahncke, 'Adenauer und die Sicherheitspolitik der Bundesrepublik', in Helmut Kohl (ed.), *Konrad Adenauer 1876–1976*, Stuttgart

-Zürich, 1976, pp. 87–97; and Hans-Peter Schwarz, 'Das Spiel ist aus und alle Fragen offen, oder: Vermutungen zu Adenauers Wiedervereinigungspolitik', in Kohl (ed.), *Adenauer*, pp. 140–56.

4. Adenauer, *Erinnerungen*, vol. 2, pp. 63 and 65; see also pp. 124 f.

5. Cf. on this his memoirs, and also Horst Osterheld, one of his closest foreign policy advisers, *Ich gehe nicht leichten Herzens . . . Adenauers letzte Kanzlerjahre*, Mainz, 1986.

6. Adenauer, *Erinnerungen*, vol. 2, pp. 63 ff.

7. Ibid., p. 70.

8. Indeed, Adenauer's policy was also controversial within the ranks of Christian and Free Democrats, Jakob Kaiser and Karl-Georg Pfleiderer being among the most important critics of Adenauer's course. Among prominent publicists Paul Sethe should be mentioned.

9. See, for example, Egon Bahr, *NATO und deutsche Einheit schließen sich aus*, dpa (Deutsche Pressengentur), 18.2.1988.

10. Two other factors were important here: the strong support from the United States and from the population in France and Britain, which had few of the reservations their political leadership had (perhaps as a result of the growing together of the European Community?).

11. There were some exceptions in 1966 and 1968; see below.

12. See *Die auswärtige Politik der Bundesrepublik Deutschland*, Auswärtiges Amt, Cologne, 1972, pp. 472 f.

13. Cf., for example, Klaus Erdmenger, *Das folgenschwere Mißverständnis. Bonn und die sowjetische Deutschlandpolitik 1949–1955*, Freiburg im Breisgau, 1967. A refutation of this thesis can be found in Herbert Graml, 'Die Legende von der verpaßten Gelegenheit zur sowjetischen Notenkampagne des Jahres 1952', in *Vierteljahreshefte für Zeitgeschichte*, July 1981, pp. 307–41.

14. *Die auswärtige Politik*, pp. 472 f.

15. This was the time of the 'bridge-building' concept: see Zbigniew Brzezinski, *Alternative to Partition. For a Broader Conception of America's Role in Europe*, New York, 1965.

16. Deutscher Bundestag, *Stenographische Berichte*, 14.6.1961, pp. 9364–7.

17. Efforts had been made to start the process with Hungary, but this failed. It was, indeed, considered somewhat of a disadvantage to have started the process with the Warsaw Pact 'maverick'.

18. Yugoslavia had originally maintained diplomatic relations with the Federal Republic only; when it took up relations with the GDR in 1957, the Federal Republic had broken relations.

19. The Soviet Union had unequivocally demanded recognition of the status quo in Eastern Europe in general and specifically with regard to the GDR (see details on this in Dieter Mahncke, 'Der politische Umbruch in der Bundesrepublik Deutschland', in Karl Kaiser *et. al.* (eds), *Die internationale Politik 1968–1969*, Jahrbücher des Forschungs-

instituts der Deutschen Gesellschaft für Auswärtige Politik, Vienna, 1974, pp. 374–90, specifically pp. 377 f.). It broke off negotiations in July 1968 and published a part of the exchange, whereupon the Federal Republic published all the documents: *Die Politik des Gewaltverzichts. Eine Dokumentation der deutschen und sowjetischen Erklärungen zum Gewaltverzicht 1949 bis Juli 1968*, Presse- und Informationsamt der Bundesregierung, Bonn, 1968.

20. This policy climaxed in treaties between the GDR and Poland, Hungary, Bulgaria and Czechoslovakia. A statement by Communist party leaders, meeting in Karlovy Vary in April 1967, pointed in a similar direction. See on this Mahncke, 'Der politische Umbruch', pp. 376 f.

21. Cambodia took up relations with the GDR on 8.5.1969, declaring that this was not intended as an 'unfriendly act' toward the Federal Republic of Germany.

22. When South Yemen took up diplomatic relations with the GDR on 30.6.1969 the Federal Republic reacted promptly by immediately suspending relations. See on all this in greater detail Mahncke, 'Der politische Umbruch'.

23. Cf. Dieter Mahncke, *Berlin im geteilten Deutschland*, Munich–Vienna, 1973, pp. 48 f.

24. This is the time of what could be called Peter Bender's 'inferiority complex theory'. In his opinion the GDR, isolated and without international recognition, had an inferiority complex which made it very rigid in its attitudes. This would change once the GDR was recognised: see *Zehn Gründe für die Anerkennung der DDR*, Frankfurt, 1968. See also Eberhard Schulz, *An Ulbricht führt kein Weg mehr vorbei*, Hamburg, 1967.

25. Already when Mende was Minister of All-German Affairs before the Grand Coalition came to power he had developed concepts for a more 'mobile Ostpolitik'; cf. Mahncke, 'Der politische Umbruch', p. 385.

26. The election platform of the FDP, accepted at the Nuremberg party congress (23–25.6.1969) rejected formal recognition of the GDR and maintained the aim of German reunification, but spoke of 'two German states' and demanded the abolishment of the *Alleinvertretungsanspruch* and the Hallstein Doctrine. The main aim was to be the practical improvement of relations between the 'two German states'.

27. In 1967 the NPD gained seats in the *Landtage* of Rheinland-Pfalz, Schleswig-Holstein, Niedersachsen and Bremen; in 1968 it gained 9.8 per cent in the *Landtag* elections in Baden-Württemberg. Cf. on this David P. Conradt, *The West German Party System: An Ecological Analysis of Social Structure and Voting Behavior 1961 to 1969*, London–Beverly Hills 1969, p. 9.

28. For a general review see, for example, William Griffith, *The Ostpolitik of the Federal Republic of Germany*, Cambridge, Mass., 1978 and Wolfram Hanrieder, *Germany, America, Europe. Forty years of German Foreign Policy*, New Haven, 1989.

29. Cf. Kurt Plück, 'Das Ringen um das Selbstbestimmungsrecht der Deutschen', in Rainer Barzel (ed.), *Sternstunden des Parlaments*, Heidelberg, 1989, pp. 44–69.

30. See on this Dieter Mahncke, 'Abschluß der Neuordnung der Beziehungen zwischen der Bundesrepublik Deutschland und Osteuropa', in Wolfgang Wagner *et. al.* (eds), *Die internationale Politik 1973–1974*, Jahrbücher der Deutschen Gesellschaft für Auswärtige Politik, Munich–Vienna, 1980, pp. 193–216.

31. On the value of these see Plück, 'Das Ringen', but also the debate by Ludwig Mertes, Rainer Barzel and Konrad Repgen from the CDU as well as Claus Arndt and Egon Bahr from the SPD point of view, in *Frankfurter Allgemeine Zeitung*, 1.8.1990, p. 8, 3.9.1990, p. 8, and 20.9.1990, p. 10.

32. For such statements see Plück, 'Das Ringen'.

33. See on this Mahncke, 'Abschluß der Neuordnung der Beziehungen', pp. 200 ff., with further references. The decision was reprinted in: *Dokumentation der Bayerischen Staatsregierung zur Prüfung der Verfassungsmäßigkeit des Grundvertrags. Urteil des Bundesverfassungsgerichts vom 31.7.1973*, Bayerische Staatskanzlei, Munich, 1973. The decision was widely criticised by members of the SPD.

34. Cf. Mahncke, 'Abschluß'.

35. Cf. Dieter Mahncke, 'Kontinuität und Wandel: Die Ostpolitik der Bundesrepublik Deutschland seit dem Regierungswechsel 1982', in *Politik und Kultur*, 1/1987, pp. 33–50.

36. Three criticisms were levelled at the original draft presented by the then CDU Secretary-General Heiner Geissler: it did not specifically mention reunification, it made German unity 'dependent' on the agreement of all Germany's neighbours, and it stated that German unity could not be achieved in the foreseeable future. At the end of the discussion all of these criticisms were heeded. Cf. 'Unsere Verantwortung in der Welt', CDU-Dokumentation 6/1988 (4.2.1988) and 12/1988 (17–18.4.1988), and also 'Künstlich aufgeblasen', *Süddeutsche Zeitung*, 18.1.1988, 'Aufregung um Bonner Binsenweisheiten', *Neue Zürcher Zeitung*, 19.2.1988, 'Im Deutschland-Disput streiten drei Parteien', *Die Welt*, 19.3.1988, and 'Geisslers Deutschland-Thesen vor Änderungen', *Frankfurter Allgemeine Zeitung*, 23.3.1988.

37. See on this Wilhelm Bruns, 'Von der Deutschlandpolitik zur DDR-Politik? Zur jüngsten Diskussion in der CDU', in *Sozialdemokratischer Pressedienst*, 16.2.1988, pp. 1–2 and Wolfgang Wiener, 'Zweite Phase der Entspannung. Zur Ostpolitik der SPD in der Opposition', in *Deutschland-Archiv*, 1–1986, pp. 37–40.

38. Compare Wolfgang Schäuble, 'Die deutsche Frage im europäischen und weltpolitischen Rahmen', in *Europa-Archiv*, 25.6.1986, pp. 341–8. See also the Chancellor's State of the Nation Message of 1986,

14.3.1986, Deutscher Bundestag, *Stenographische Berichte*, p. 15757, and other speeches (references in Mahncke, 'Kontinuität und Wandel', p. 50). The accusation, often levied against the Chancellor in 1990, that he was in fact not really willing to accept the boundary with Poland was thus both incorrect and irresponsible. What the Chancellor had consistently said was that final acceptance would have to come from a united all-German government, a position finally accepted by everybody in the 2+4 negotiations, including Poland when it participated in the negotiations during the Paris meeting in June 1990.

39. 'Zehn-Punkte-Programm zur Überwindung der Teilung Deutschlands und Europas', Deutscher Bundestag, 28.11.1989, reprinted in *Bulletin*, Presse- und Informationsamt der Bundesregierung, 29.11.1988, pp. 1141–8.

40. See the arguments and references on this in Mahncke, 'Sicherheitspolitik in Westeuropa'.

41. It is worth reminding the reader that West Germany integrated a total of 11 million refugees – a constituency large enough to be ignored only at his peril by any politician.

42. See, for example, Mahncke, 'Sicherheitspolitik in Westeuropa', (written in 1986) in which, at least, I argued that the German question was an unsolved problem and that interest in reunification was high.

HANNELORE HORN

Collapse from Internal Weakness – The GDR from October 1989 to March 1990

The very title of this chapter already anticipates the main finding of my investigations, namely that the collapse of the political system in the German Democratic Republic (GDR) was mainly due to that system's own internal weakness. Yet such a finding may well in itself be seen as a matter for some astonishment, seeing that scholars and politicians have for years been taking a view which would logically have led to a completely contrary conclusion. For in such quarters the opinion that the political system of the GDR could increasingly be characterised as one of internal stability based on a growing consensus has until very recently enjoyed widespread acceptance – an opinion which has been supported by the presumption that tendencies towards a division of power and some sort of rule of law were increasingly influencing the conduct of the system.

And at the same time there has also arisen a foreign-policy-based approach to the explanation of these events which has focused on *perestroika* and its repercussions on and effects in inspiring political developments in Eastern Europe and the GDR. The developments between October 1989 and March 1990 therefore need to be analysed and interpreted by taking into account both internal and external factors; but the analysis here will concentrate on the internal factors.

We are considering an exciting period of German and international history, which lasted only half a year. At the start of that period there was a repressive, communist-orientated, one-party dictatorship in the GDR. At its end, we had free elections leading to a multi-party system and a coalition government.

1. The Strength and Dynamics of the Pressure 'From Below'

The manifold nature of these exceedingly complex events and the way in which they interacted as stimuli or obstacles make it no easy task to pinpoint definite phases and turning-points. This thicket of interdependent events proves that the effective and complete collapse of the Socialist Unity Party's (SED) regime was not the result of a single, sudden death-blow. It was above all the consequence of an ever-present, changing and growing pressure 'from below'. This pressure found expression in the interaction and dynamics of the following three socio-political factors: the mass exodus of East Germans to the Federal Republic; the constantly increasing articulation of public criticism through newly formed opposition groups; and the mass demonstrations.

The fleeing masses, to begin with, represent the outward sign of fundamental changes.[1] They were an overwhelming expression of protest against the political, economic and social living conditions in the GDR. They began on a very large scale in August 1989, when about a hundred GDR fugitives were crossing the Hungarian border into Austria every day. After this the numbers grew. In 1989, until the opening of the Berlin Wall on 9 November, 225,233 East Germans left their country. Almost as many followed in 1990 up until the middle of March. Their 'option' to flee via Hungary, Czechoslovakia or Poland placed a burden on the GDR's relations with its 'brother countries'. Moreover, when the Hungarian border opened on 11 September 1989 and the possibility of emigration was conceded to those swelling masses in Prague and in Warsaw, the SED government suffered extraordinary losses of prestige, not least among its own ranks. It found no plausible explanation for this phenomenon. At first, the explanations remained entrenched within the old patterns: i.e. it was claimed that one could easily do without such 'disloyalists'; and along with this derogatory labelling went a hostile rhetorical campaign against the Federal Republic.

The pressure to act, which emanated from the fugitives, forced Honecker and his followers to yield to the demands of the refugees step by step. They found themselves compelled to reduce their terms more and more, and to make concessions to those wanting to leave the GDR. For instance, those willing to return from Hungary, Czechoslovakia and Poland to the GDR were promised legally issued exit permits without, however, any dates, being initially specified at which this would happen. But in due course the GDR leadership was forced to reduce the processing time for permits to six months (on 26.9.1989), and finally to two weeks.[2]

Likewise, the government agreed to allow those who had already fled to return at any time for the purpose of a visit. This meant a fundamental abandonment of position, particularly in the light of the past practice of demonising those wanting to leave. This was then superseded by the guarantee of return without penalty for all fugitives, i.e. an amnesty (20.10.1989 and 27.10.1989). Under the pressure of events, the exodus problem led to official consent to issue passports and travel visas to all East German citizens (25.10.1989). With this measure, extensive freedom of movement existed for all from the end of October onwards. Yet, the mass exodus to the Federal Republic (FRG) continued with varying rhythms. So on the one hand, until the elections on 18 March 1990, emigration remained a huge expression of mistrust towards the new Modrow government in particular; and on the other, it also dramatically reinforced the pressure upon that government to move towards political change.

A second catalyst of this phase of upheaval, which set the direction for the political developments, was the activities of the initially illegal opposition groups. Here the mass exodus played a stimulating role in their formation and unification. Small opposition groups had existed in the GDR since the mid-1970s, and their number markedly increased in the 1980s. These groups, numbering between 160 and 500,[3] operated essentially under the shelter and protection of sympathising pastors of the Protestant Church. Human and civil rights, as formulated at the Helsinki Conference, strongly determined their list of values, as did an orientation towards another, and a better, form of socialism.[4] The political leadership had for the most part left these groups unmolested until the late 1980s, when some of the groups stepped out from under the church's 'shadow' with political publications and proclamations. In addition to these groups, the 'Initiative for Peace and Human Rights' was formed in 1985–6 outside the formal framework of the Church. This group also experienced persecution later.

In September 1989, in the light of the mass exodus, many of these by no means homogeneous groups united. In Leipzig, the 'New Forum'[5] was created, in Berlin, 'Democracy Now'.[6] They called upon the population to remain in the country and to fight for a better future there. All the groups considered themselves as civil rights movements. Although they initially operated illegally, their political orientation slowly became familiar everywhere.[7] They have earned a place in history for having articulated the latent dissatisfaction of many citizens, thus helping them to free themselves from isolation, anonymity and passivity. In addition, they were often the catalysts for far-reaching political actions, as well as the initiators and organisers of the first massive demonstrations.

In this development, some church representatives provided shelter and confidential protection rather than intellectual and political inspiration and initiative. The Monday 'Prayers for Peace' in the Nikolai Kirche in Leipzig were typical of many similar relations between church and opposition groups. The leadership of the GDR initially met this development with bans and arrests. Under the pressure of protesters and demonstrations it then found itself forced to set those arrested free. Eventually, the leadership under Egon Krenz signalled its readiness to talk, first with the church and then with representatives of the opposition groups. They were then invited to televised interviews and discussions; and finally the groups were legalised.

Eventually, cautious political opposition also arose from the '*bloc* parties', particularly from the Liberal Party. As early as 12 October 1989 this party had urged reform and demanded the legalisation of 'New Forum'. However, these parties cannot be looked upon as a driving force which brought about the fall of the regime. But like the civil rights groups, they too set the stage for the developing pluralism.

Hand in hand with the mass exodus and the formation of oppositional groups operating country-wide went the growing mass demonstrations, which had started early in October (for example, in Leipzig, Magdeburg and Dresden). They were the third and perhaps most important component that brought the SED regime to its knees. At first social-political in nature, orientated towards improving the system and towards democratic reform in general (slogans and banners), they became increasingly specific and political. Their focus changed. The demonstrators' list of demands comprised the abandonment of the leadership role of the party (6.11.1989 in Leipzig); freedom of expression, of the press, and of assembly (10.11.1989); and rapid social changes and the punishment of those responsible for the desperate situation in the GDR (which was finally officially admitted); they also engaged in protest against corruption and the misuse of authority by the SED.[8] Eventually, from the last ten days of November on, the mass demonstrations became more nationally motivated, with the mass movement aiming at the unification of both German states. The successive slogans of the demonstrators: 'We are the People'; 'We are one People'; and finally, 'Germany, United Fatherland', marked the direction of these developments.[9]

In the same way as in the case of the mass exodus, the reaction of the SED leadership to the mass demonstrations showed many signs of retreat. At first, the regime reacted with violence.[10] In the end, the demonstrations were tolerated and accepted as an obvious element of the political culture.[11] Nowhere did it come to the use of firearms.

The combined effect of the mass exodus, the mass demonstrations, and the political activities of the opposition groups proved capable of bringing such strong pressure to bear upon the SED that it finally found itself prepared to abandon the system. Up until the time of the elections in March 1990, the mobilisation of the masses increasingly proved to be the essential element of pressure from below. They were called upon whenever needed and prevented any attempts by the old regime to stabilise the situation.

2. Potential Weaknesses within the SED Regime

This picture of a political leadership retreating in the face of manifold pressures, and that retreat finally leading to the abandonment of the system, fails to answer the question why the leadership did retreat, and did not defend itself with all the methods of power politics that were available to it. The answer is definitely not to be sought or found in a single-cause explanation. In my view, there are primarily four factors which help to explain this retreat of the leadership and the eventual collapse of the system.

(a) The Lack of Political Acceptance of the SED System

The political leadership and legitimacy of the system of the GDR was never accepted by an overwhelming majority of the population. The external aspect of a political system which had had quasi-identical structures for more than four decades gave – superficially considered – an impression of political stability. In fact, however, there existed no form of stability worth mentioning which was based upon consent and consensus between the SED leadership and the population. The denial of human and civil rights, the repressive control of the people's educational and professional development, and the destruction and disregard of customary values, as well as the lack of economic efficiency, all caused dissatisfaction with and rejection of the system. Through the failure to take the measure of consent or rejection through free elections, the political leadership created for itself the room for manoeuvre needed in order to fake the appearance of irrefutable acceptance by the people from which it derived in part the political legitimation of its power. In the history of the GDR this lack of acceptance of the system may have been subject to fluctuations. It increased after the building of the Berlin Wall with the new generations that grew up in its shadow. No longer could active political opponents withdraw through escaping; rather they formed a genuine and growing potential for opposition.[12] In this sense, the building of the Wall proved indeed to be a boomerang.

The political leadership in the GDR was well aware of the discrepancy between verbal appearance and reality. From the beginning of the 1980s the State Security Service had been preparing sport stadiums, arenas, etc., to serve as huge prisons or internment camps for an evidently anticipated growing mass opposition.[13] The massive resistance with which the political leadership was confronted revealed the full extent of dissent. After forty years, the political system of the GDR found among its citizens no nominal consent which would have been capable of guaranteeing its survival. It was the power-structure which had preserved the outward appearance of stability in the past. Nevertheless, when the hitherto enduring certainty of Soviet military support for the system began to fade, the structures which had formerly served as its buttress also began to lose their firmness. Without an external guarantee, the system proved to be feeble because it lacked even nominal acceptance among its people.

(b)   *The Internal Weakness of the SED*

The leadership role of the party, the SED, was of central importance in the ruling power-structures. Its political effectiveness depended on its political homogeneity, in particular within the party leadership. Political uniformity, both internally and externally, is the elixir of life of all ruling communist parties. The very policy of *perestroika*, however, became a particularly heavy burden on the unity which was formally upheld by the inflexible, rigid and superannuated party leadership under Honecker. The political alternative offered by Gorbachev increasingly encountered sympathy at all levels within the SED. Consequently, under the growing pressure of mass opposition the policy of *perestroika* increasingly became a factor of appeasement and a way out of the dilemma at all levels within the SED leadership. The actual swing to implementing elements of *perestroika* under Egon Krenz, however, was only possible at the price of far-reaching changes in the leadership. The full extent of internal division within the SED came to the fore, and tended to weaken the credibility of the new leadership. In keeping with an old communist tradition, the new leaders began by publicly criticising the policies of their predecessors, i.e. their political foster-fathers. They also revealed aspects of their mismanagement.[14] In addition, *glasnost* was allowed to develop its effectiveness in the GDR too, and began to close the gap between appearance and reality in the press and in public discussion. As more and more information about the leaders' élitist and feudal life-styles was made public (hunting-grounds, several cars, houses, etc.), as well as about their falsification of the elections, their misuses of office, their violation of the laws, the old – and soon afterwards the new – leadership became the target of extraordinarily emotional public criticism.

The SED responded, on the one hand, with the introduction of party proceedings against the highest party officials on the grounds of their 'violation of laws' and, on the other, with the rehabilitation of those members innocently accused or expelled from the party. The result was a crisis of inner-party loyalty, with hundreds of thousands leaving the party. Thus, the party lost all credibility, even among its most ardent and sincere followers.[15]

The political inflexibility of a superannuated party leadership, the lack of internal party unity, opportunistic self-destruction and an increased knowledge of the unlawful and irregular behaviour of leading officials weakened the ability of the party to act to such a degree that it fell into a state of paralysis. The effective downfall of the SED meant that the political system lost its central supporting pillar, and thus the crucial transformation of the system occurred. An an organisation, the SED ceased to be the decisive political power. Even the attempt to cast off the burdens of the past through a partial change in name (SED/PDS), which aimed at generating new strength, was unable to retrieve the situation. Nevertheless, SED officials continued to hold influential governmental and social posts. But they could no longer be active as a homogeneous force and were, moreover, compelled to share power with new political forces (for example, at the 'Round Table' as an institution of control and dialogue).

(c)   Loss of Self-assurance in the Security Service

A third factor explaining the retreat of the SED concerns the reliability of the armed organs of the state, in particular, the troops of the Ministry for State Security (Stasi). The membership of the security service and its officer corps was directly connected with the personnel and the structures of the party. Hence the divisive bacillus within the SED infected them too. Here too, there arose doubts as to the correctness of the official party line.[16] These doubts led to irritations which later became evident, for example, when the Stasi did not resist the breaching of the Wall on 9 November 1989.

The Stasi and the People's Police were still following the instructions of their superiors when they, particularly on 7–8 October 1989, took action with great brutality against the peaceful demonstrators in many cities (East Berlin, Leipzig, Dresden, Plauen, Jena, and Potsdam) and broke up the demonstrations.[17] These brutal proceedings sparked increased public criticism. The victims responded with charges and complaints against the conduct of the security forces. An apology for these violent actions was demanded by the church and opposition groups.[18] They demanded a renunciation of violent policies in general, the punishment of the guilty, and the introduction of an independent inquiry commission. A 'China syndrome' was spoken of, and this fostered the continuing mass exodus.[19]

The reaction of the leadership to these extraordinary and publicly voiced demands bore all the characteristics of opportunist retreat. It wished to give the impression of legally correct procedure, and agreed to a thorough investigation of all charges and petitions.[20] The leadership also admitted that innocent bystanders had come to harm through its actions and that there had been 'misuses of authority' and 'unlawful acts' by the security forces against the *Zugeführten* (suspects).[21] It promised that each individual case would be examined by the Prosecutor-General. In addition, the newly created parliamentary Inquiry Commission was ordered to investigate the possible illegality on the part of the 'Protection and Security Organs' (7.11.1989). Finally, Erich Mielke, the long-standing head of State Security, was called to account before the Volkskammer. In his attempt to justify their proceedings, on 13 November 1989, he made a very poor public impression. In the eyes of the State Security Service and all other security forces, these were highly irregular reactions and types of behaviour on the part of the SED leadership and, in addition, extremely embarrassing.

The order to the Inquiry Commission ('Protection and Security Organs') clearly reveals the attempt to put the blame for the attacks on the police force and not on the State Security Service. This intention was soon to be confirmed. Only two days later, the General Prosecutor announced that an indictment had been entered against one police officer and that eight further judicial inquiries had been opened. (In East Berlin alone, 323 petitions and complaints had been lodged).[22] On 24 November it was announced that another police officer had been sentenced for seriously injuring a demonstrator. Prosecutions of Stasi members were not in evidence.

Nevertheless, the protests against the Stasi continued, and the attempt to deflect the blame towards the People's Police did not succeed. When Hans Modrow, the former First Secretary of the SED district party organisation in Dresden, began to form his cabinet as Prime Minister, he responded with the dissolution of the Ministry of State Security. The 'Office for National Security' was formed in its place; but this soon proved to be a caretaker for all the old apparatus.

With the admission of infractions by the security forces and the promise to punish the guilty, the SED leadership had launched a far-reaching policy which could only have the effect of creating alarm among the members of the Stasi. With its admissions and actions, the SED leadership began a policy which the members of the Stasi saw as a threat not only to their authority but also to their security.

In normal times, the Stasi was the most important prop of SED rule. It operated under the latter's direction all the time. Its members were thoroughly inured to performing even unlawful acts for the government and party. In order to divert attention from its own responsibility for the use of violence, the SED leadership now denied the State Security Service its political protection, and thereby presented the Stasi as the real source of violence and illegality. But because of this the Stasi's

reassuring knowledge of the party's ever-present protection, was
lastingly disrupted. The readiness of many members to follow orders
from above blindly was shaken. The resignation of the long-standing
Stasi chief Erich Mielke, together with the official swing of the new
leadership under Krenz in the direction of rather vague policies of
transformation, increasingly advanced the tendency towards
ambivalent behaviour within the security forces. Thus, the SED
gradually destabilised its most powerful and dependable support. As
a result the Stasi's members were no longer reliable partners for the
SED leadership in any attempt to crush demonstrations.

(d)   The 'Socialist Bias' in the Oppositional Civil Rights Groups

The question why the SED retreated cannot be fully
answered without examining the goals of the civil rights groups and
the Protestant Church. These groups orientated themselves in the
first place toward human and civil rights as they were formulated in
the Final Act of the Helsinki Conference, to which the GDR government was itself a signatory. But, in general, for them this meant the
realisation of these rights within the GDR, and, moreover, in a
socialist GDR.[23] What they envisaged was a 'Third Way' for a
separate Socialist German State.

Operating illegally, they obviously developed their ideas in isolation from the mass of the population. And thus they failed to notice
that socialism, of whatever kind, was not what the majority of the
population expected or hoped for. Yet their political positions were
closely akin to, or rather coincided with, some elements of *perestroika*,
and, consequently, with ideas which were met with sympathy within
the SED, even at high levels. Under these circumstances, it was
somewhat difficult for the political leadership to classify these groups
as clearly counter-revolutionary, and thus to fight uncompromis-
ingly against them.[24]

The groups of the civil rights movement were the ones who called
for the first mass demonstrations, and who, at the beginning, set the
agenda. Their call to stay in the GDR ('We are staying here!')
coincided with the interests of the political leadership. They were
also effective in preventing violence by the demonstrators. As a
result, the typical provocations brought about by illegal activities on
the part of the opposition – something that happens in most revolutions – did not occur. And thus the threshold above which it would

have been easy to justify the use of force to suppress these demonstrations as legitimate had been set very high. And when, between 2 October and 8 October, demonstrations throughout the country *were* violently broken up it appears that it was only one part of the old SED leadership which was behind this course and acting on a presumption of the existence of a counter-revolution,[25] and that this presumption was actually considerably at variance with the interpretations of another set of leading SED officials and members.[26] So that when, on 9 October, the crucial Monday Demonstration in Leipzig was *not* violently broken up, that fact can – among other things – be attributed to the influence of the latter element in this constellation of opinion within the SED. This is also what explains the successful co-operation of three district party Secretaries of the SED with prominent local citizens.[27] Together they formulated principles with which they made an appeal for peaceful behaviour at the coming mass demonstration. These principles also included the promise to hold dialogues with the government over the future of socialism in the country.

The events of 9 October 1989 in Leipzig marked the Copernican revolution in the process leading to the collapse of the GDR. In that context the SED leaders apparently came to the view that they would abandon the use of violence in future.[28] After that, there was no more violent repression from the state. There may have been a number of reasons for renouncing violence. Among them there are the socialist tendencies in most important civil rights movements and in the Protestant Church. This factor weakened the unity and readiness of the political leadership to resist. The whole process would surely not have been so peaceful and lacking in bloodshed, if the end of socialism or the unification of Germany had been dominant on the banners of the demonstrators from the start. When these demands emerged toward the end of November, there was no longer any united political power that could have compelled a retreat from them.

The lack of acceptance of the SED system had been a weakening factor throughout the forty years of its history – a weakness which had to be compensated for by a policy of repression. It amounted to a delayed-action guillotine permanently suspended above the political system of the GDR, which finally descended and brought about its death. The internal weakness of the SED and the gradual loss of confidence on the part of the security forces, as well as the specific embarrassments which proceded from the socialist orientation of the opposition groups, can be seen as short-term operating forces. Only under the influence of specific historical conditions and constellations of events were they able to develop the disintegrating mechanisms with which they weakened the political leadership. These historical conditions and constellations were essentially of an external nature: the change in the policies of the Soviet Union and the developments in the GDR's erstwhile 'brother countries'.

3. The Revolutionary Nature of the Collapse

In the meantime a discussion has begun among scholars as to the nature of the political collapse in the GDR. This discussion revolves around the question: was it a revolution, or does the nature of the actual experience go against the use of this term? Various answers are possible. To a great extent the answer depends upon the definition of the term 'revolution'.

This term means – first of all – the fundamental transformation of an existing condition. With reference to the realm of politics, it means a fundamental transformation of the existing political and social order. The origin and course of the transformation can indeed have highly different features. Its driving force may be the masses ('People's Revolution') or élitist social groups ('Revolution from above'), and it may succeed through peaceful or through violent means. The process of change can proceed either quickly or slowly. Thus the decisive feature of a revolution is a fundamental political and social transformation.

In this respect, there has been a partial revolution in the GDR, resulting in democratic government. But a distinguishing feature is that the communist government itself in essence took, or tolerated, steps towards the political collapse (the guarantee of freedom and human rights, pluralism, and free elections). It did so by no means voluntarily, but rather under the pressure of an articulate mass opposition, as well as the activities of the members of the 'Round Table'.[29] What is typical of many revolutions – an overthrow of the old system immediately sweeping its representatives from their offices – did not occur in the GDR. This revolution proceeded peacefully and without bloodshed. As a People's Revolution it brought about a change by expressing opposition on a massive scale.

The question of who – 'technically' speaking – started this process of change is, therefore, of secondary importance.

This also applies to the peaceful nature of the change. Violence or the extent of the bloodshed determine the degrees of escalation known to most revolutions. They definitely accelerate the pace of governmental change. However, they are not necessarily an essential element of a revolution, as the 'Glorious Revolution' should have taught us. Likewise, of course, the physical annihilation of the former ruling class would considerably facilitate the desired transformation. Nevertheless, the establishment of a new social and political order – the goal and result of the upheaval – need not necessarily fail in the absence of violence on the part of the revolutionaries.

The success of a peaceful revolution depends indeed to a particularly high degree upon the existence, co-operation and activities of a new socio-political élite. In almost all the countries governed by communist parties, there is a marked lack of such an independent 'counter-élite'. Through its specific recruitment practices the SED bound to itself the majority of those best suited for leading positions in government and society, whereas citizens suspected of opposition, for ideological reasons or because of their actual behaviour were barred from any chances of promotion. As a consequence of this and of the 'brain-drain' caused by flight there developed in the GDR a politically highly precarious lack of potential governmental personnel outside the SED. The lack of radicalism in the revolutionary process and the dearth of personnel alternatives ultimately resulted in an extensive number of SED executives and sympathisers remaining in office. In this context it is worth mentioning that Modrow helped to keep secret the political practices and crimes of the old system by allowing the destruction of Stasi records and the manipulation of personal files.[30] Moreover, all those who profited from the old regime were given the opportunity of providing for themselves. A change in power in favour of the new class at the expense of the old one could therefore take place only to a limited extent.

The degree of resistance on the part of long-standing and convinced communists is very difficult to ascertain. The old powers and their networks (*Seilschaften*) are able to promote, tolerate, or – through obstruction – prevent the transformation process to the limits of their individual positions of power. In sum all these factors burden the process of change. They are perfectly capable of prolonging the duration of the process, but not of preventing it. The German

Revolution of 1989 also bears the characteristic of a national revolution, providing additional forces in favour of an upheaval.

The duration of the transformation process is of no great importance if one wants to determine whether it is a revolution or not. The Russian Revolution, for example, required many years for a total social change, whereas the act of seizing power in October 1917 bore all the signs of a *coup d'état*. The French Revolution of 1789 was of a similar type. Rosenstock-Huessy, a German scholar and an authority on revolutions, found that authentic revolutions take many years.[31] According to him, a revolution is a crisis, a melting-down process, in which all the ideas, individual traits and customs of a people become incandescent. It means a conversion, threatening the people with madness. 'Madness' was one of the terms most frequently used of this period in the GDR.

Thus upheaval between October 1989 and March 1990 in the GDR can in effect be seen as a revolution resulting essentially from internal weakness. At the political level the revolution achieved its aims; at the social level, however, it remained – of necessity – still incomplete.

How to evaluate this German Revolution in the entire spectrum of the revolutions of history is quite a different matter. It has to be viewed in the context of the changes within the Soviet Union and of the other revolutions in Eastern Europe. In this respect it also bears the sign of a so-called *Lehnrevolution*[32] – i.e. an adopted revolution which lacks originality and independence. Nevertheless, the German Revolution helped to end an epoch of European or even world history, and contributed to the vision of a new order.

Notes

1. For a survey of the flow of refugees since 1961, see Volker Ronge, Loyalty, Voice of Exit?, in *Die fluchtbewegung als Anstoß und Problem der Erneuerung in der DDR*, ed. Werner Göttrik, Opladen, 1990, pp. 29–46.
2. For all data without specific references see *Chronik der Ereignisse in der DDR*, eds. Ilse Spittmann and Gisela Helwig, Edition Deutschland Archiv, 4th edn, Köln, 1990, and *Neue Chronik DDR* – Berichte, Fotos, Dokumente, eds. Zeno and Sabine Zimmerling, Berlin, 1990, Ser. 1–3, 7 August 1989 – 18 March 1990 (cited hereafter as *Neue Chronik*).

3. Stasi estimate 160 groups, see A. Mitter and S. Walle (eds.), *Ich liebe Euch doch alle, Befehle und Lageberichte der MfS Jan. – Nov. 1989*, East Berlin, 1990, pp. 46–8; 500 groups are named by Thomas Ammer, Anfänge eines demokratischen Parteiensystems in der DDR, in *Außenpolitik* (April 1990), p. 377.

4. On the political orientations of such groups: 'Mit Vordenkern und Akteuren der Wende im Gespräch', *Deutschland Archiv* (December 1990), pp. 1935–41; Eckhard Jesse, ' "Wir sind das Volk", Neues Selbstbewuß tsein, Vielfältigkeit und Gefährdungen der Opposition', in *DDR*, ed. Göttrik Werner, pp. 47–68; Stephan Bickhardt (ed.), *Recht ströme wie Wasser*. Christen in der DDR für Absage an Praxis und Prinzip der Abgrenzung. Ein Arbeitsbuch, Berlin, 1988; Timothy Garton Ash, *Ein Jahrhundert wird abgewählt* (translation), Munich–Vienna, 1990, pp. 390–8; Th. Ammer, 'Anfänge' pp. 377–8; *Neue Chronik*, ser. 1, 19 October – 23 November 1989.

5. Founded 12 September 1989, officially registered on 11 November 1989. Among the signatories: Bärbel Bohley, Rolf Hendrich, Jens Reich, Katja Havemann.

6. Founded 12 September 1989. Signatories: K. Weiß, H.-J. Fischbeck, L. Mehlhorn.

7. For example small-scale demonstrations at Pentecost (East Berlin) on 13 August 1987; on the anniversary of Rosa Luxemburg's and Karl Liebknecht's deaths on 18 January 1988; on the occasion of the exposure of vote-riggings in local elections on 7 May 1989.

8. According to Stasi sources the number of demonstrators and demonstrations steadily rose from October to November. For example they reached a peak of 210 demonstrations, with 1.3 million participants, from 10 October to 5 November 1989. On 4 November half a million people took part in Berlin alone. See A. Mitter and S. Walle (eds.), *Ich liebe Euch doch alle*, p. 249.

9. Wolfgang Schneider, *Leipziger Demontagebuch* (Leipzig and Weimar, 1990) conveys a vivid impression of the slogans and watchwords on the banners; similarly Charles Schüddekopf (ed.), *Wir sind das Volk. Flugschriften, Aufrufe, Texte einer deutschen Revolution*, Reinbek bei Hamburg, 1990; and T. G. Ash, *Ein Jahrhundert*, pp. 394–5. 'Deutschland, einig Vaterland' is a quotation from the national anthem of the GDR, but from a passage whose use had officially been dropped.

10. Especially on 7 and 8 October 1989 in many towns and parts of the country.

11. The First Secretary of the SED in the region of Berlin, Günter Schabowski, on 29 October in Berlin.

12. Until the building of the Wall 3.4 million people fled the GDR; almost a million between 1961 and 1989 (959,909 legal or illegal emigrants).

13. J. von Flocken, E. Jurtschitsch, and M. Klomowsky, 'Bekannte Per-

70 Hannelore Horn

14. For example national debts of 130,000 million East Marks.
15. On 8 November and 2 December 1989 thousands of SED members gathered in front of the building of the Central Committee in East Berlin. Among other things they demanded 'a party leadership that listens to the people'. A similar gathering of 10,000 SED members took place in Leipzig on 31 October 1989: see Spittmann, Ilse, 'Runderneuert. Die PDS, Die Partei des Demokratischen Sozialismus', *Deutschland Archiv*, 23, 4/1990 pp. 508–11.
16. See for example Markus Wolf, *Troika*, Berlin, 1989; Georg Reuth, 'Die Idee vom reformierten Sozialismus', *Frankfurter Allgemeine Zeitung* (2 February 1991), p. 14; Karl Wilhelm Fricke, 'Die Erblast der DDR-Staatssicherheit', *Außenpolitik* (4/1990), pp. 403–11.
17. G. Wendland, Prosecutor General of the GDR reported on 3456 'Zugeführten' to the Volkskammer (the GDR parliament), *Neues Deutschland* (hereafter cited as *ND*) 20 November 1989.
18. For example, the letter of the Protestant Church (Bishop Forck) to the head of the government, Willi Stoph, on 13 October 1989, made public on 22 October 1989 and Bishop J. Hempel's demand at a church meeting in Dresden (21.10.1989); likewise the protest of the group 'Demokratischer Aufbruch' (21.10.1989) and the meeting of reform groups in East Berlin on 23 October 1989.
19. Bishop Demke spoke of a 'China syndrome' to the Synod of Saxony on 5 November 1989.
20. The First Deputy Prosecutor General and the First Deputy Head of People's Policy in East Berlin, *ND*, 21–2 October 1989, p. 2.
21. Wolfgang Herder, Chairman of the Volkskammer Committee for National Defence, before the Staatsrat on 24 October 1989, *ND* (25 October 1989), pp. 1 and 3.
22. Friedhelm Rausch, Head of Policy in East Berlin on 15 November 1989, *ND*, 17 November 1989, p. 8.
23. Rein, Gerhard (ed.), *Die Opposition in der DDR. Entwürfe für einen anderen Sozialismus*, (Berlin, 1989; Hubertus Knabe (ed.), *Aufbruch in eine andere DDR. Reformer und Oppositionelle zur Zukunft ihres Landes*, Reinbek bei Hamburg, 1989; Georg Reuth, 'Die Idee'; T. G. Ash, *Ein Jahrhundert*, p. 396. Bishop Forck in the Gethsemane-Church read out a proclamation of leading members of the diocese Berlin–Brandenburg in which a *demokratische, rechtsstaatliche, sozialistische Perspektive* ('a democratic, law-abiding, socialist outlook' was postulated (9.10.1989): Cf. also *Für unser Vaterland* ('For our fatherland'), a proclamation by GDR artists, signed by high-ranking representatives of the Protestant Church (General-superintendent Krusche and Bishop Demke) on 28 November 1989.
24. E. G. B.-Bohley and R. Hendrich were not arrested: Jesse, ' "Wir sind das Volk" ', pp. 54–5: Reuth, 'Die Idee'.

25. Christa Wolf to a parliamentary inquiry commission with reference to former President of the Volkskammer, Horst Sindermann (15.11.1989).

26. See Bernd Okun, *Deutschland-Archiv*, December 1990, p. 1938; Hannes Bahrmann and Christoph Links, *Wir sind das Volk. Die DDR zwischen Okt. und 17. Dec. 1989. Eine Chronik*, Weimar und Wuppertal 1990, pp. 15–20.

27. Kurt Masur, Conductor of the Gewandhaus Orchestra Leipzig, pastor Peter Zimmermann, and satirist Bernd Lutz; their proclamation was made public on radio and TV. For the development in Leipzig cf. Ash, *Ein Jahrhundert*, pp. 390–4.

28. See 'Parteirechenschaftsbericht' in Günter Schabowski, *Das Politbüro* Reinbek bei Hamburg, 1990– p. 191.

29. Meeting for the first time 7 December 1989, the Round Table's discussions, something completely unknown up to then in the GDR (arguments instead of polemics) were televised for hours at a time. On the development and activities of the 'Round Table' see Uwe Thaysen, *Der Runde Tisch. Oder: Wo blieb das Volk?*, Opladen, 1990.

30. Fricke, 'Die Erblast', p. 409; idem, 'Entmachtung und Erblast des MfS', *Deutschland Archiv*, 12/1990, pp. 1881–90. Thaysen, *Der Runde Tisch*, pp. 163–72.

31. Rosenstock-Huessy, *Die europäischen Revolutionen und der Charakter der Nationen*, Stuttgart, 1961, 3rd edn, p. 22.

32. Ibid., p. 6.

UWE THAYSEN

The GDR on Its Way to Democracy[1]

Prehistory

You will have read a great deal about the prehistory of the GDR's revolution from my colleagues Mahnke and Horn in the preceding chapters. So I can now concentrate on setting out the *axioms of my argument*. Frau Horn has explained the collapse of the GDR as a collapse caused by internal weakness. With this I agree. Today, as the economic and ecological disaster becomes more and more visible, we are almost surprised that the GDR reached the year 1989 at all. It was *external* factors, however, which triggered the internal collapse of the GDR.

The most important external factor was the (internal) situation of the Soviet Union. The reason for the comparatively late arrival of *glasnost* and *perestroika* in the GDR lay, I believe, in the weakness of *both* the government (viz. its inflexibility, as a result of biological and ideological ossification) *and* the opposition (viz. its lack of concepts and personalities, and the inability of those who finally stood up to organise themselves effectively).

Have we witnessed a revolution at all? Certainly we have, inasmuch as from Plato via de Tocqueville to Marx, Engels, Lenin and Trotsky the total collapse of the old regime is made the crucial precondition of fundamental change. These thinkers might have had quite differing ideas about the decisive conditions, the course and the consequences: yet none of them would have disagreed that in the GDR a system *collapsed*. Nevertheless, the term 'revolution' is increasingly used rather hesitantly by former GDR citizens. On the one hand, the 'victors' have no wish to pay posthumous tribute to the Marxist view of history, even less to Trotskyite revolutionary romanticism: to them, change – and that means change *back* to an essentially bourgeois society (*'bürgerliche' Gesellschaft*) – has not been radical enough to justify talk about a 'revolution'. Everywhere in administration and society they suspect *die alten Seilschaften* ('the old networks') of obstructing democratisation and the development of a bourgeois market economy.

On the other hand, we have those protagonists of the autumn of 1989 who still subscribed (and subscribe) to the Marxist view of history. While they, too, may have welcomed the *Einschlafen* ('falling asleep') of the GDR as a state, to use Engel's phrase, they do not regard the introduction of the Western-type formations of democracy and society into the GDR as *progress*. Thus, to them, the title of 'revolution' seems unjustified as well. These disenchanted idealists are found primarily in the *Bürgerbewegungen*, the citizens' movements. I have usually sensed strange embarrassment among these people whenever they were praised as 'revolutionaries'.

The Formation and Organisation of Opposition

However, the first steps of the GDR towards democracy had been in the revolutionary mood, so to speak, that is to say they had been conspiratorial. Opposition groups were formed that aimed, where this seemed possible, at an *open* contest with the anachronistic regime of old men. For specific reasons there was no East German revolutionary élite, no German Dubček, none of the Prague window-cleaners, nothing of the Czech or Polish political counter-culture in general. Political organisation of systematic resistance in the GDR only began after the Hungarians had made the first hole in the iron curtain.

(In order not to give a wrong impression: West German intellectuals, including political scientists and specifically students of the GDR, in a way helped the East German intelligentsia to avoid the realisation that the system in the GDR was a totalitarian one.)

The most important opposition groups which were founded in 1989 were (see Diagram 1):

74   *Uwe Thaysen*

Diagram 1: The Initial Formation of the Political Forces at the East
German Central Round Table at the Inaugurating Session
on 7 December 1989

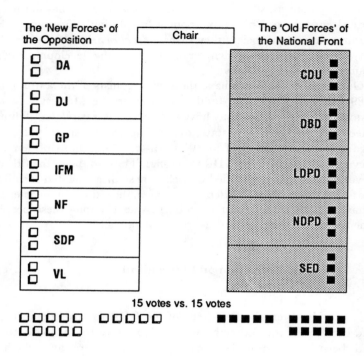

15 votes vs. 15 votes

This initial formation was sought and achieved by the 'Contact Group' (Kontakt-gruppe) of the oppositional 'New Forces' which had aimed at a public confronta-tion with the SED-regime from 4 October 1989. The different groups are listed in alphabetical order: Democratic Awakening (DA), Democracy Now (DJ), Green Party (GP), Initiative for Peace and Human Rights (IFM), New Forum (NF), the Social Democratic Party of the GDR (SDP, later SPD), United Left (VL) on one side, the Christian-Democratic Union of the GDR (CDU), the Democratic Farmers' Party (DBD), the Liberal Democratic Party of Germany (LDPD, later LDP), the National Democratic Party of Germany (NDPD) and the Socialist Unity Party of Germany (SED, later renamed SED-PDS and eventually Party of Democratic Socialism, PDS) on the other.

DIAGRAM 1: THE GROUPS OF THE GDR-OPPOSITION AT THE CENTRAL ROUND TABLE

- Initiative für Frieden und Menschenrechte ['Initiative for Peace and Human Rights'] (IFM, founded 1985, published appeal for joint action 11 March 1989)
- Neues Forum ['New Forum']
  (NF, founded 11 September)
- Demokratie Jetzt ['Democracy Now']
  (DJ, founded in 1987, 'Appeal for intervention on our own behalf' published 12 September 1989)
- Demokratischer Aufbruch ['Democratic Awakening']
  (first activities in June 1989, founded 2 October)
- Sozialdemokratische Partei ['Social Democratic Party']
  (SDP, later SPD. First steps towards foundation since 24 June 1989, formally established 7 October)
- Grüne Partei ['Green Party']
  (GP, grew out of the 'Green-Ecological Network Ark', first steps towards forming a party since 5 November, founded 24 November)
- Vereinigte Linke ['United Left']
  (VL, founded November 1989)

These groups met in October–November 1989 under conspiratorial circumstances. Conspiratorial because they had not been licensed, because quite generally the SED at the centre and in most regions was not yet ready for dialogue – even though this dialogue had started in some areas as early as the beginning of October 1989, for instance in Dresden.

All seven groups, from the start, had *no* intention of colluding or even collaborating with the government, as had happened – to some extent – in Poland. They rejected the approach of a *Zirkularperspektive* ('all-round perspective'); instead they were bent on confronting the rulers, those responsible for the misery and the suppression in the GDR. This approach led to the constellation depicted in Diagram 2.

The initial basic formation of forces in this confrontation was cleverly devised by the opposition groups (not by reform-minded SED-functionaries!). To ensure eventual success for the opposition at the Round Table it was necessary to clearly differentiate old from new and opposition from those holding responsibility, without

Diagram 2: Seats and Votes at the East German Central Round Table since the Second Session (18 December 1989)

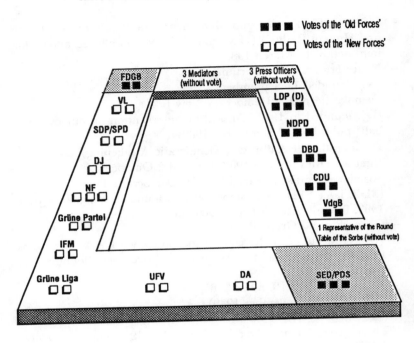

Legend:
The arrangement depicted here was the order of seating from the second session on 18 December 1989 until the final session on 12 March 1989. Thus, because of the late admittance of some groups and the room situation, the physical order of seating ceased to represent the political front-line between 'Old Forces' and 'New Forces' as it had done in the first session (7 December 1989, Diagram 2). Politically, the FDGB would have had to be seated close to the SED, while the representative of the Sorbs belonged to the Opposition.

precluding the possibility of a switching of sides by some groups of the National Front later in the process.

The invitation to Round Table talks was issued both by the opposition groups and by the Church. The sessions were also chaired in turn by three churchmen. Likewise, the press officers were clergymen. The church was thus performing an extremely delicate balancing act: while it strongly supported the case of the opposition groups, its representatives at the Round Table were simultaneously mediators within this mediating institution. Regrettably, I do not have the space to go into the role of the churches in detail here – that would take a chapter of its own, if not a whole book.

The opposition groups were keen that none of the despised mass organisations of the SED, for instance the official trade union FDGB, would be allowed to sit at the Round Table – although the mass organisations, too, were members of the Volkskammer, the GDR's legislature. The *bloc*-parties of the National Front, on the other hand, had been transmission belts of the SED, just like the other mass-organisations, but could not be excluded from the talks. For this reason, seven opposition groups of what I call the 'New Forces' faced five parties that made up the 'Old Forces'.

By giving the opposition groups two votes each (except for New Forum, which was the largest group, and got three) and three votes to each group of the Old Forces, a balance of fifteen votes for each side was agreed upon (see Diagram 2).

This was the constellation of forces when the Round Table met for its first session on 7 December 1989. In the early stages, the SED tried to destroy this parity by trying to introduce two of its stooges, the FDGB and the VdgB (the Farmers' Association), to the Round Table. While the SED succeeded in doing this, the New Forces compensated for this imbalance by asking two new groups to join the Round Table: the 'Independent Women's Association' (UFV), founded only four days earlier, and the 'Green League' (GL), which up to that point had not in fact yet been officially founded. Each of the four new member organisations was given two votes, so that the final constellation was 19 vs. 19 votes (see Diagram 3).

Note that a representative of the Sorbs, an ethnic minority in Saxony, was also admitted, but not granted the right to vote. Also, from the beginning of 1990, the proceedings of the Round Table were broadcast live and uncensored on TV.

The 'Old Power-Struggle'

Both sides were now ready for a confrontation that I have termed the 'Old Power-Struggle'. By this I understand the over-throwing of the SED and its security apparatus. Only after this had been achieved did the 'New Power-Struggle' begin. The 'New Power-Struggle' is what I call the emerging competition for votes in

78 *Uwe Thaysen*

Diagram 3: The Political Front-line at the East German Central Round Table from the Second Session on 18 December 1989

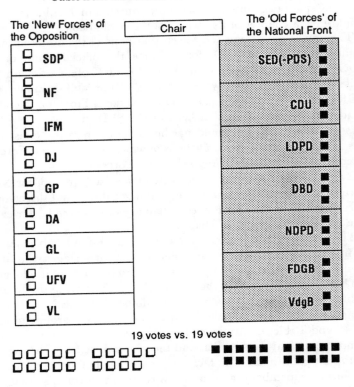

19 votes vs. 19 votes

Diagram 3 depicts the political confrontation in the early stages of the Round Table talks. The ranking tries to reflect the relative political importance of the different groups in the first phase (until 8 January 1989), although competence and impact of the groups/parties greatly differed from issue to issue. On the side of the 'Old Forces' this ranking was clearly predetermined by the system of the National Front. 'New Forces': Social Democratic Party of the GDR (SDP, later SPD), New Forum (NF), Initiative for Peace and Human Rights (IFM), Democracy Now (DJ), Green Party (GP), Democratic Awakening (DA), the Green League (GL), Independent Women's Association (UFV), United Left (VL). 'Old Forces': Socialist Unity Party of Germany (SED, later renamed SED-PDS and eventually Party of Democratic Socialism, PDS), Christian-Democratic Union of the GDR (CDU), Liberal Democratic Party of Germany (LDPD, later LDP), Democratic Farmers' Party (DBD), National Democratic Party of Germany (NDPD), Free German Trade Unions Association (FDGB) and the Farmers' Association for Mutual Assistance (VdgB).

the first free elections among the new as well as the old parties of the GDR.

It is important to record that the SED had lost out long *before* the Round Table talks commenced. In addition to the great *internal* weaknesses to which Professor Horn has referred, the dynamics of change were exacerbated by a number of external factors and circumstances, of which I will only mention the most crucial:

1. The politics of *détente* following the CSCE Helsinki agreement of 1975 gave East European dissent a moral and legal foundation. The developments of the last fifteen years have shown that, contrary to Marx's foreword to his *Critique of Political Economy* 'to be is to do', and not – at least not only – vice versa.[2] This philosophical statement can also be restated in legal terms: to adapt the famous formula of German jurisprudence of *die normative Kraft des Faktischen* ('the normative power of the fact'), the breakdown of the Marxist–Leninist system demonstrated die *normative Kraft des Normativen* (the 'normative power of regulative ideas'). In view of the recent war in the Gulf there is something consoling to me in this statement, because the fifteen years of the CSCE agreement have demonstrated the explosiveness of the idea of human rights and of the right to self-determination as formulated in basket III of the CSCE. To latent dissidents this agreement became a crucial encouragement to *be political* and to become part of the political process, despite often very differing views. Since about 1983, this general development also led to slightly more organised demands for reform in the GDR, concentrated on issues such as peace, ecology, and the economy.

2. As liberalisation began to spread around Eastern Europe towards the end of the 1980s the SED regime became more and more isolated, thus dramatically worsening the lack of perspective for GDR citizens. Particularly among young East Germans the courage of desperation grew rapidly. The narrowing of individual options for the future generated the well-known *mass flight* from East Germany – it in fact continues even today. This mass flight saw, to use Lenin's phrase, people 'vote with their feet' against the GDR. It also, to refer to Marx this time, made the petrified conditions in the GDR dance, and kept them dancing. Simultaneously, *mass demonstrations* started which gave the necessary vigour to the emerging systematic attempts to organise the demands for democratisation.

3. On 2 May 1989, Hungarian border guards cut a first hole into the
   iron curtain, which was officially opened on 10 September 1989.
   The Czechs opened their part early in October. On 9 November
   the German communists were forced to open the last and longest
   section of the iron curtain. In retrospect one could argue that the
   GDR's path to democracy was already traced out from this
   moment. But certainly the question whether there would be an
   East German or an all-German democracy had not yet been
   settled. The opposition groups and the parties of the *ancien régime*
   were in accord when they jointly proclaimed the 'independence'
   and 'long-term development' of the GDR at the beginning of the
   Round Table talks in early December 1989.

In order to create a (more) democratic GDR it was the first
imperative to overcome the most important instrument of the SED's
power, the State Security Service, the *Staatssicherheitsdienst* ('Stasi').
The Stasi's assignment was to act as 'shield and sword' of the party,
and even the SED reform government of Hans Modrow had no
intention of relinquishing this instrument of repression. Thus, at
some point in the winter of 1989–90, party and Stasi changed roles:
the party became the 'shield' of the Stasi, and covered the security
service's retreat. I have called Hans Modrow the 'champion of
orderly retreat'. On the eve of 1990 it was by no means clear whether
Modrow's government in East Berlin might be able to maintain, or
even fully restore, communist power. Only by issuing an ultimatum
(on 8 January) which culminated in mass demonstrations outside
the Volkskammer (11.–12.1.1990) and the 'storming' of the Stasi's
headquarters by demonstrators (15.1.1990), did the opposition groups
force Modrow to abandon his plans for a new security service (to be
named the *Verfassungsschutz*, like its counterpart in West Germany). The
hydra-headed Stasi had been comprehensively decapitated.
    From this very moment, the Modrow regime totally changed its
strategy. It should be stressed that there was a clear link between
this change in strategy and the regime's realisation of the defeat of
the Stasi. From now on the Modrow–De Maizière government
aimed at incorporating the opposition groups by offering each of
them a ministerial post, though without portfolio. After nerve-
racking negotiations between 22 and 28 January the SPD, which
had initially been most reluctant to compromise its political vir-
ginity in not having collaborated with the SED (its prime asset),
agreed to join a 'government of national responsibility'. Ironically,

this concession was extracted from the SPD in the very same room in which the forced amalgamation of the Communist and Social-Democratic parties into the SED had taken place in 1946.

With Gorbachev's decision to admit the issue of German reunification to the agenda of history the cards were reshuffled. The parties and groups of the Round Table had to make up their minds how to react to the demands for reunification voiced in the streets. Moreover, the continuing – even worsening – mass flight after the opening of the wall on 9 November 1989 threatened to sap the human resources of the GDR mortally, with two to three thousand departures everyday.

All the parties to the Round Table (except for the 'United Left', VL) now wanted reunification; but a number of decisions made it clear that the Round Table was intent on preserving some specific aspects of a GDR 'identity'. The Round Table came to stand for a slow, conscious, reflected merger on equal terms and with a constitutional assembly (i.e. on the basis of Article 146 of the West German Basic Law); while the demonstrators and those leaving the country represented the desire for a quick and unconditional take-over of the East by the Federal Republic (that is, they preferred an accession of the GDR to the Federal Republic according to Article 23 of the *Grundgesetz*.

The opposition groups have complained that the winners of the first free election of 18 March 1990 and the West German government in Bonn consciously accelerated the speed of unification at the expense of the people in the GDR (and to the detriment of alternative political concepts, particularly of elements of direct democracy, the creation of a new constitution, and of a new political culture quite generally). In reality, it was they themselves who advanced the date for the elections (which had initially been scheduled for 6 May 1990 in the first session) to 18 March 1990. This rescheduling had largely been the responsibility of the then SPD leader, Ibrahim Böhme, and Hans Modrow. Their deal not only surprised the *Bürgerbewegungen*, the citizens' movements, but also most members of the SPD. For the former, this date came much too early to organise a campaign effectively (lack of money, photocopiers, paper; loose, inefficient, network-type structure; no aid from Western 'sister-parties'); for the latter, though, an early election seemed advantageous, since all election polls – wrongly, as we now know – expected the SPD to win by a wide margin.

For the social scientists among us, particularly those engaged in electoral research, one major reason for the SPD's exaggerated expectations will be interesting: the fault lay in the methodology of the research institute INFAS hired by the SPD.

The Parties Under the Spell of the March Elections

Until well into February, the SPD saw itself as the probable winner of the imminent election. This error was grounded in the party's misinterpretation of two crucial developments: on the one hand, the Social Democrats underestimated the success of the 'repositioning' process of the old party system. This, on the other hand, was partly due to a total misjudgement of the dynamics of reunification. The consequences of the now realistic option of reunification for the party system were seen in a much clearer light by the old *bloc*-parties, even by the PDS, than by the SPD and the citizens' movements. The Eastern CDU, without doubt, had superior access to information via the chairman of the Western CDU, Chancellor Helmut Kohl. The Eastern SPD, by comparison, was poorly advised by the candidate of the Western SPD, Oskar Lafontaine.

I have been able to take a look at the minutes of the last session of the 'Democratic Bloc' on 28 November 1989. In this session the chairman of the Eastern CDU, Lothar de Maizière, gave notice of the termination of the CDU's membership of the *bloc*. This occurred behind closed doors. Officially, the CDU and the Eastern Liberals did not leave the bloc until 4 December 1989. But even this occurred *before* the first gathering at the Round Table (on 7 December).

The party system had come under strong influence from external processes while it was still struggling with its internal ruptures; and so the political forces regrouped under the spell of the forthcoming Volkskammer election of 18 March 1990. But this dynamism was hardly noticed; it occurred below the surface of public perception. Even the Social Democrats failed to realise what was going on. Their attention remained fixed on the Council of Ministers, the Round Table, and Berlin in general.

At the Round Table, that is to say in their public image, both the CDU and the LDPD (Liberals) remained in large part on the side of the 'reconstructed' SED(–PDS). The SPD thus believed that the stigmatisation of these two parties as collaborators during forty years of SED rule would preclude any significant electoral success on the part of the CDU and/or LDPD.

In January 1990 it was still not clear whether the Western CDU would eventually be willing to support the Eastern CDU, in view of the corruption of the latter during the previous forty years. For quite some time the Western CDU believed that 'Democratic Awakening' (Demokratischer Aufbruch, DA) would be its only acceptable potential partner in the East. Only on 5 February 1990 (i.e. four days after the Soviet acceptance of reunification) was an electoral pact consisting of the East German CDU, the DA, and the DSU founded under the name of 'Alliance for Germany'. The DSU (German Social Union), which limited its activities to the Southern GDR on the model of the Bavarian CSU (Christian Social Union), had not been founded until 20 January 1990. Despite the fact that the DSU and, similarly, the liberal Forum Party, could probably claim more support than some of the citizens' movements at the Round Table, both (and many more) were denied places at the Round Table.

The Round Table and the Problem of its Legitimation

Legitimation was the biggest problem of the Round Table. Its members had not been elected, and their official objective was to make free elections in the GDR possible. For this reason, the Round Table initially agreed that it would not make any far-reaching political decisions. Indeed, the Round Table restricted itself until the end of January 1990 to vetoing government decisions (see Diagram 4). Only after Prime Minister Modrow had managed to draw the opposition members into his government, where they shared responsibility with ministers from the former *bloc* parties, did the Round Table became a steering instrument for GDR politics. This started on 28 January 1990, and this date might also be seen as the political end of the Round Table, although it continued to meet and produce legislation. This was, in any case, the view of one of Modrow's closest advisers, who wrote that on this very day, the Round Table had become 'superfluous, without noticing the fact itself'.[3]

Under the influence of Modrow, the Round Table increasingly moved towards a confrontation with the West German government in Bonn. On 5 February it voted against allowing West German speakers to take part in East German campaign rallies; on 12 February it demanded a 'solidarity-contribution' of DM 15 billion 'immediately' – in other words before true democracy had been

Diagram 4: Periods and Functions in the History of the East German Central Round Table

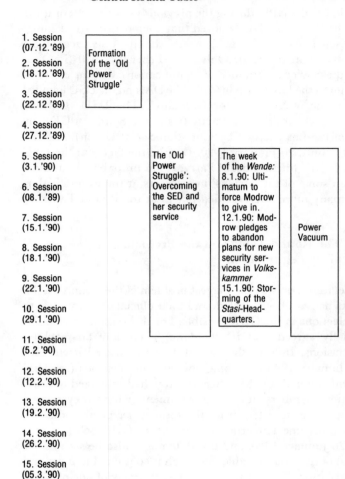

1. Session
(07.12.'89)

2. Session
(18.12.'89)

3. Session
(22.12.'89)

4. Session
(27.12.'89)

5. Session
(3.1.'90)

6. Session
(08.1.'89)

7. Session
(15.1.'90)

8. Session
(18.1.'90)

9. Session
(22.1.'90)

10. Session
(29.1.'90)

11. Session
(5.2.'90)

12. Session
(12.2.'90)

13. Session
(19.2.'90)

14. Session
(26.2.'90)

15. Session
(05.3.'90)

16. Session
(12.3.'90)

Formation of the 'Old Power Struggle'

The 'Old Power Struggle': Overcoming the SED and her security service

The week of the *Wende*: 8.1.90: Ultimatum to force Modrow to give in. 12.1.90: Modrow pledges to abandon plans for new security services in *Volkskammer* 15.1.90: Storming of the *Stasi*-Headquarters.

Power Vacuum

From the coalition to the 'Government of National Responsibility' or from veto organ to steering instrument

An overview over the different phases of the brief history of the East German Central Round Table. Unavoidable simplifications may help to increase awareness for the essentials. In view of the broad spectrum of the tasks the Round Tables tackled in each session, even a periodisation concentrating on the main issues will lead to some overlapping.

Formation of the 'Government of National Responsibility'	
Steering-instrument or integration of the opposition into the 'Government of National Responsibility'	
Arena for the 'New Power Struggle' (campaign forum)	Decision against Western campaign speakers
Symbol for a new/old East German identity?	'Points' for Modrow's visit to Bonn
	Charter of Social Rights
	New GDR constitution

1. Session (07.12.'89)
2. Session (18.12.'89)
3. Session (22.12.'89)
4. Session (27.12.'89)
5. Session (3.1.'90)
6. Session (08.1.'89)
7. Session (15.1.'90)
8. Session (18.1.'90)
9. Session (22.1.'90)
10. Session (29.1.'90)
11. Session (5.2.'90)
12. Session (12.2.'90)
13. Session (19.2.'90)
14. Session (26.2.'90)
15. Session (05.3.'90)
16. Session (12.3.'90)

established in free elections; in February–March it demanded the preservation of the (supposed) social 'achievements' of the GDR; and in its last session on 12 March it approved a new constitution[4] for the new German state. Most important of all, the Round Table opted for the 'slow' path to reunification according to Article 146 of the Basic Law. This slow mode, it was argued, would be more gentle. Implicitly, this was thus an argument to abide by the old ways. This was the Modrow option.

The Answer of the People

In the first (and last) free election in the GDR, East German voters decided against this course, i.e. in favour of the Kohl option. The Round Table's legitimation problem was thus answered. The elections confirmed that the most effective actors in the GDR's struggle for democracy could be found on the streets – i.e. in the demonstrations, leaving the country, in the polling booth – and not at the Round Table. Thus one can conclude that, by the standard of democratic principles, it is a myth that the East German revolution was 'expropriated' or 'raped' (to quote some terms that have been used).[5]

It was the SED which created the GDR state as its power-base.[6] The brutal experiment of a socialist state in half a nation with its foundation mainly in the power-ambitions of the SED came to its end at the moment of the collapse of the twin internal and external pillars of its existence: the Soviet Union and the Stasi.

We experienced a revolution in so far as we could trace a real collapse, a breakdown of the efficiency of Leninist centralism. Compared to all other East European countries the change has also been radical enough to speak of a revolution, although it really was – and is – an importing and replacing rather than an overturning process.

Almost everywhere in the world the East German revolution has been welcomed as a signal for two experiences hitherto not generally associated with German politics: Germans behaved both peacefully and pragmatically. The masses took to the streets for democracy and the rule of law and they proved able to handle their problems without the superstructure of a state, at Round Tables and in citizens' committees.

Nevertheless, it is a myth to claim that the events of 1989/90 could in a way make up for a lacking revolutionary tradition in Germany, or compensate for the missing opposition against the Nazi tyranny. Myths like that are dangerous political romanticism. Fortunately this does not seem to be a real danger at the moment. What one can observe, however, is an alarming contrast between the peaceful developments of 1989/90 on the one hand, and an irresponsible and short-sighted willingness on the part of some Germans to sell arms on the other. The message of 1989/90 was a different one, and it may well be that this message is responsible for the present reluctance of the greater Germany to abandon its accustomed (and generally welcomed) position, forty-five years on, of institutionalised harmlessness.

The East German revolution could stay peaceful because it carefully avoided unmasking *completely* the totalitarian character of the regime, and the responsibility of the SED–PDS for this regime. This is why I refuse to speak of a 'negotiated' revolution (as Rudolf Tökes has done with respect to the developments in Hungary).[7] In this, we may detect some paradigmatic aspects for models of peaceful transition from tyranny to democracy. The price for peacefulness is an alarming silence about questions of guilt and responsibility for the principles and mechanisms of suppression. In my opinion this silence will be a severe burden for Germany's future; and this again is a reason for research in, and discussion of, our topic.

Notes

1. This chapter is based on Uwe Thaysen, *Der Runde Tisch. Oder: Wo blieb das Volk. Der Weg der DDR in die Demokratie*, Opladen, 1990.
2. 'Es ist nicht das Bewußtsein der Menschen, das ihr Sein, sondern umgekehrt ihr gesellschaftliches Sein, das ihr Bewußtsein bestimmt.'
3. Karl-Heinz Arnold, *Die ersten hundert Tage des Hans Modrow*, Berlin, 1990, p. 76.
4. For the development of the draft, compare Thaysen, *Der Runde Tisch*, pp. 143 ff.; for the ensuing discussion *Kritische Justiz*, No. 4, 1990.
5. Cf. for example Michael Schneider, *Die abgetriebene Revolution*, Berlin, 1990.
6. See Dietrich Staritz, 'Die SED, Stalin und die Gründung der DDR', *Aus Politik und Zeitgeschichte*, 15, 1991, 25.1.1991, pp. 3 ff., who presents new source-material proving that Grotewohl *et al.* pressed for the establishment of a separate socialist German state with Stalin, who was reluctant, from 1947 on.
7. Rudolf L. Tökes, *The Negotiated Revolution*: Economic Reforms, *Social Change and Political Succession in Hungary 1986–1990* (forthcoming).

WOLFGANG BERGSDORF

West Germany's Political System under Stress: Decision-Making Processes in Bonn 1990

I would like to divide up my tentative remarks on the political events that took place in Germany during the year 1990 into four chronological parts. The first part is dedicated to the People's Chamber (Volkskammer) election on 18 March, resulting in the first freely elected parliament in the GDR. A second part will deal with the period from March until economic, monetary and social Union between the Federal Republic of Germany and the GDR went into effect on 1 July. The third phase of political developments in Germany in 1990 was the negotiation of the unification treaty and establishment of the necessary foreign policy prerequisites on the basis of the Two-Plus-Four process, formally concluded by German unification on 3 October. The fourth part is dedicated to the election campaign and the results of the election held on 2 December, from which the tasks for the future can be defined.

The fact that Chancellor Helmut Kohl plays a key role in the subject I am dealing with, both as a person and as a political leader, will also come as no surprise to you. This is a result of my interest in analysing an assertion made by a colleague in Freiburg, Wolfgang Jaeger. He maintains that the German 'chancellor democracy' characteristic of the initial years of the Bonn republic under Konrad Adenauer has, since then, developed into a 'co-ordination democracy', in which an omnipresent need for co-ordination makes political leadership almost impossible. In his book *Normative und institutionelle Ordnungsprobleme des modernen Staates* (Paderborn, 1990), which would translate into something like 'normative and institutional regulatory problems in modern government', Jaeger made a strong statement in favour of what he refers to as the 'chancellor election club'. He sees in the enormous expansion of party structures an important reason for their loss of credibility and for a functional loss on the part of the entire system of government. Jaeger feels that with the modernisation of their structures and the expansion of their functions the parties in Germany have taken things much too far, and recommends more modesty as a therapy.

I.

Modesty is the first point I would like to deal with, modesty that has grown up out of our amazement in view of the revolutionary events that have taken place in Eastern Europe and the former GDR. The Poles needed ten years to eliminate communist rule gradually and by means of very complicated procedures, ten years before the first freely elected post-war prime minister was able to take office. It took the Hungarians around ten months to achieve more or less the same results. The Germans in the former GDR managed to overthrow an inflexible communist regime without a civil war. The Czechs and Slovaks succeeded in freeing themselves from the stranglehold of the all-knowing and all-powerful communist party in ten days. In Romania the decision against totalitarianism was taken in little more than ten hours.

This time-comparison shows the accelerating speed with which the infectious and dynamic nature of freedom enabled it to prevail over its only seemingly omnipotent suppressors. To this extent the year 1989 marks the end of European totalitarianism. It also stands for the correctness of a key assumption in political thinking, an assumption fewer and fewer people continued to share the longer the peoples of Central and Eastern Europe were enclosed by monopoly party structures: in other words the assumption that the desire for freedom can only be suppressed by force for a limited period of time. The year 1989 will go down in European history as the year of self-liberation.

The implosion of the communist system in Central and Eastern Europe placed the subject of German unity on the political agenda,

both in Germany and in the international community – not over-
night by any means, but ineluctably over a period of months. The
fall of the Honecker regime and the opening of the Brandenburg
Gate were preceded by key events. The most important prerequisite
was Gorbachev's dropping of the Brezhnev Doctrine, a fact that
received little attention initially. This motivated the American
ambassador in Germany, Vernon Walters, on taking up his post in
April 1989 to predict that Germany would be reunited during his
time in Bonn.

During the summer thousands of GDR citizens made use of their
holidays to occupy the German embassies in Prague, Budapest and
Warsaw with a view to persuading the authorities to let them go to
the Federal Republic of Germany. The Hungarian head of government, Nemeth, then announced the first test of a totally new policy
to Chancellor Kohl during a secret meeting held in August. He
agreed to open Hungary's borders early in September. When this
happened, at midnight on 10 September 1989, a refugee flow began
that resulted in more than 340,000 people from the GDR, most of
them young, moving to the Federal Republic of Germany by the end
of 1989. Mass demonstrations brought about the collapse of the
Honecker regime and the opening of the German–German border
on 9 November by his successor, Krenz.

On 11 November 1989 Chancellor Kohl conducted two telephone
conversations that provided him with information on potential resources and necessary preconditions for his future policy on Germany. His first interlocutor was Egon Krenz, who had been elected
General Secretary of the SED on 8 November. In this conversation,
which was later published, the two sides advocated a strengthening
of co-operation. Kohl asked Krenz what fundamental changes he
intended to make. The new SED boss responded diffusely and
evasively. Afterwards Chancellor Kohl had a telephone conversation with Soviet General Secretary Gorbachev, in which he told him
about the conversation with Krenz. Kohl informed Gorbachev of his
assessment that Krenz had no chance of succeeding as long as he
was not willing to institute genuine reforms. Gorbachev did not
contradict this forecast. Shortly before that, on 10 November, Gorbachev had sent Kohl a message expressing his concern regarding
the safety of the Red Army in the GDR. In this way the Soviet
General Secretary indicated to Kohl that the Red Army would
remain in its barracks, regardless of what might happen.

The 'Ten-Point Programme for Overcoming the Division of Germany and Europe' which the Chancellor presented in his policy statement to the German Bundestag on 28 November 1989 was a logical consequence of the events that had taken place in the previous weeks. Since the summer the Bonn government had been able to assume that German unity would become a focus of German and international policy. The Chancellor, the Foreign Minister and all leading politicians in the government coalition made use of international meetings and contacts to promote the prospect of gradually overcoming the division of Germany and to request support for this. Kohl included in his ten-point plan all those elements, including 'federal structures', which had been recurrent in talks he had held at the international level. The idea for the ten-point programme arose on 23 November in an evening discussion with his closest advisers. On that particular evening the view prevailed that the time-frame for implementing the ten-point plan would extend into the year 1993.

This was also the thinking that was predominant both in the Bonn coalition and in the opposition on the length of time that would be needed. The Chancellor was the first to be faced with the fact that this time-frame did not correspond to the actual course of events. This was on 19 December 1989, when he travelled to Dresden for a meeting with the new prime minister of the GDR, Hans Modrow. At the time, hundreds of thousands of people lined the streets from the airport to the meeting-place in a demonstration in favour of German unity. At the later by that evening, when he made his speech to the people of Dresden, Kohl had understood that the desire being shown by the people of the GDR to achieve unity as rapidly as possible would obviate any and all schedules for a gradual merger of the two parts of Germany. The German political agenda for the year 1990 could thus only be that of bringing about unification as rapidly as necessary and in as orderly a manner as possible.

II.

The year 1990 began with mass demonstrations in the GDR in support of German unity. The autumn chant of 'We are the people' was modified, and the definite article was replaced by an adjective that now expressed a call for unity: 'We are *one* people.' All attempts undertaken in the autumn by the SED or by the democracy movement to legitimise the idea of maintaining two states in Germany by asserting separate cultural or social identities had failed.

This led to a uniquely rapid change in attitudes towards the German question among opinion leaders in the Federal Republic of Germany. With very few exceptions, journalists who had still pleaded in favour of two separate states in November and December altered their stance and advocated German unity. The same is true of opposition leaders, who, except for the Greens, thus paid tribute to the popular will that was clearly recognisable in the mass demonstrations.

The undiminished flow of resettlers from East to West Germany made it evident that it would be necessary to bring the process of unification to a rapid conclusion. Here it becomes clear that the people in the former GDR played a leading role in the political decision-making processes of the year 1990, as was the case already in the autumn of the previous year, and that the political leaders in West and East Germany attempted with varying degrees of skill to steer this popular will.

As a result of the disastrous situation the East German economy was in, the Bonn government was forced to deal, first of all, with economic and financial matters. In January the German–German Economic Commission met for the first time, in East Berlin. The West German government offered the GDR six billion marks in additional low-interest loans for the support of small- and medium-sized businesses. At an initial German–German entrepreneurial conference in Hanover 200 economic experts discussed potentials for co-operation. The cabinet committee on German unity, established by the Chancellor on 7 February, was to focus its activities primarily on the economic challenge. At the time Kohl proposed to the Modrow government that negotiations on a monetary union should be initiated immediately, the prerequisite for which would have been a fundamental economic reform. Since Modrow refused to accept this condition, he failed during his visit to Bonn to gain support for his request for financial assistance amounting to 16 billion marks.

The Bonn government made use of all the options available to it to gain foreign policy support for its unification policy. On 10 February in Moscow Kohl and Genscher received assurances from Gorbachev that Moscow would not stand in the way of German unity. A few days later the United States and the Soviet Union agreed on reducing their forces in Central Europe to a level of 195,000 men each. In Ottawa the foreign ministers of the four Second World War Allies and the two German states agreed on a series of conferences referred to as the 'Two-Plus-Four' process, with a view to eliminating Allied rights over Germany as a whole. On 24 and 25 February President Bush and Chancellor Kohl expressed their support of NATO membership for a unified Germany.

Kohl was in constant contact with President Bush and President Gorbachev, as well as with his European counterparts in London, Paris, Brussels, Rome and elsewhere, in all phases of the unification process. Personal meetings at conferences and reciprocal visits were supplemented by numerous contacts by letter and telephone. At the same time, Foreign Minister Genscher travelled incessantly in Europe, as well as back and forth across the Atlantic, and, in doing so, pulled the Americans, the Soviets and the Europeans closer together. The Chancellor and his Foreign Minister succeeded in achieving the necessary amount of consensus during those decisive months. The opposition failed to spark dissent in the government coalition on the objective, the approaches and the speed of the unification process. During this period of time at least one co-ordination meeting a week was held by the chairmen of the coalition parties together with the parliamentary group chairmen and the parliamentary group secretaries. The individual MPs, the parliament as a whole and the parties were to be kept fully informed and to be involved in this phase, dominated by an executive government active for the most part in the foreign-policy area.

Meetings with the opposition were less frequent. The reason for this was the onset of the People's Chamber election campaign. The Greens viewed policy on Germany with unrelenting suspicion. The SPD, initially in two minds about objectives and policy approaches, finally expressed its clear support of unity as an objective on 7 March, inspired to do so by Willy Brandt. Its schedule for German unity provided for the accession of the GDR to the Federal Republic under Article 23 of the Basic Law. However, the SPD openly expressed its preference for a referendum and a new constitution.

The SPD was the first of the major parties to provide massive support for the newly founded SPD organisation in East Germany. The CDU found this a great deal more difficult, since its East German counterpart had collaborated with the SED for decades. It was not until a fundamental change in personnel at all party levels had taken place, and the 'Alliance for Germany' had been formed on 5 February, that the CDU party chairman gave the go-ahead for wide-ranging election-campaign support. At the urging of Helmut Kohl the CDU in the GDR, the German Social Union (DSU), supported by the CSU, and the Democratic Awakening (Demokratischer Aufbruch, DA) group, a product of the autumn revolution, joined forces in this alliance.

The result of the People's Chamber election contradicted all the predictions that had been made by the polls and the media. The 'Alliance for Germany' emerged from the election as the clear winner, with a total of 48.1 per cent of the vote. The CDU alone received more than 40 per cent, making it nearly twice as strong as the SPD, the party that had gone into the race as the favourite. This election result posthumously acquitted Konrad Adenauer of a serious charge. During his lifetime critics had accused him of showing insufficient interest in reunification, and based this accusation on his fear of what would probably have been an SPD-dominated eastern part of Germany. The first phase on the road to German unity had been completed. In the GDR a free election had set the stage for a government that took on the task of bringing about unity, and in doing so, making itself superfluous.

III.

The Grand Coalition government, including the FDP, under Prime Minister Lothar de Maizière, took up its work on 12 April 1990. It committed itself to the objective of following an orderly path to German unity and seeing to it that the interests and potentials of GDR citizens were taken into account in the process.

The Bonn government began engaging in an effort to achieve what it had always refused earlier GDR governments. The objective now was to gain as much international support for East Berlin as possible. On 21 April EC foreign ministers agreed to a three-stage plan aimed at integrating the GDR into the European Community. On 28 April the EC heads of state and government agreed to German unification as a policy objective. A few days later Foreign Minister Genscher opened the first ministerial round of the Two-Plus-Four talks in Bonn, the most important topic of which was the Alliance membership of a united Germany. On 3 June President Bush and Soviet President Gorbachev declared in a joint press conference that the Alliance preferences of a united Germany could be decided by the Germans themselves. Shortly thereafter Lothar de Maizière became the first GDR Prime Minister to visit the United States, and was received in Washington by President Bush. A group of German banks granted the Soviet Union a five billion mark loan, for which the Bonn government provided a guarantee.

The close and continuous co-operation between Bonn and Washington proved to be of particular value in this phase of the unification process. With his willingness to engage in disarmament President Bush contributed in large measure to Gorbachev's no longer seeing a 'Western threat' and accepting a strategic withdrawal from Central Europe. Bush calmed the Western European capitals whenever fears were expressed regarding an excessively large or unpredictable Germany. He helped to develop the Two-Plus-Four formula and, by doing so, to limit the negotiations on German unity to their 'external aspects'. With a large measure of diplomacy he helped to ward off demands expressed by other European countries to take part in the negotiations. In particular he sought support in Warsaw, based on German assurances of a definitive recognition of the Oder–Neisse border.

From the outset, President Bush and his administration supported the German unification process actively and without reservation, leaving no doubt as to the fact that the reunification pledge of earlier years continued to be valid in the new situation. The close personal relationship between Bush and Kohl did not leave the slightest doubt as to the sincerity of mutual assurances. Chancellor Kohl did not doubt for a second that the American president would stand by his obligations based on the Bonn Convention. Conversely, the American president could be sure that the German government would under no circumstances entertain the idea of leaving the Atlantic Alliance. The American president backed the German Chancellor in this very important phase of ensuring the success of the unification process in foreign-policy terms.

In Washington at the end of May President Bush succeeded in convincing President Gorbachev that the United States had no intention at all of taking advantage of the internal problems being experienced by the Soviet Union to gain advantages for itself. This certainty was an important prerequisite for the reorientation of Soviet policy in the German question.

In these few months domestic political activities were focused primarily on preparing for economic and monetary union. In this the Federal Government enjoyed the full support of the German National Bank. Thus, the Federal Chancellor's invitation of 7 February to the GDR to participate in the negotiations over the introduction of the FRG's currency to the GDR was loyally endorsed by the Bank's expert council. Also, the conversion rate which was finally negotiated between the two German Governments at the beginning of May was agreed by the currency authorities, since it by and large corresponded to their own recommendation at the end of March of 2 East Marks: 1 Western DM. However, the Federal Bank's recommendation was leaked through indiscretion to the public on 1 April, thereby causing considerable disquiet in the GDR. The political forces in the GDR formed a common front against this. The new rate which was then worked out with the GDR was on average 1.83:1.

As a result of a decision taken by the Chancellor, wages, salaries, rents, pensions and scholarships were converted at a rate of one to one. Savings and cash were converted at various rates, depending on social needs. On 18 May the German–German Treaty on Economic, Monetary and Social Union was signed in Bonn. It was approved by both German parliaments on 21 June. At the same time, the two parliaments approved the definitive recognition of Poland's western border.

The decision of the Bundestag and the People's Chamber about the final confirmation of the Oder–Neisse line as the inviolate Western border of Poland with a united Germany, achieved a foreign policy aim of the reunification process on a central point, painful for Germany but conducive to the peaceful future of Europe. The common decisions of the freely elected, democratically legitimate parliaments thereby expressed the political will of the German people to achieve the unity of the nation again, at the cost of finally renouncing the territory beyond the Oder–Neisse line. The treaty about the existing border between Germany and Poland, which was later signed on 14 November (ratified in mid-1991 by the first all-German parliament), finally confirmed the Chancellor's consistently clear and internationally legal view, that only a freely elected all-German sovereign body would have the power to give a firm guarantee about the inviolability of the Oder–Neisse line.

This decision had been preceded by a decades-long debate, in which Helmut Kohl, even during his time as Minister-President of the Rhineland Palatinate, had expounded the view that Germany could only give legal recognition to the Oder–Neisse line in return for achieving its own unity. During the discussion of the Warsaw Treaty in 1972, he had already defined an earlier recognition of this border by Germany as externally problematic and internally risky. For this would be the unique key to achieving Polish agreement to German unity. Internally, only the practical combination of border recognition and unity would assure a lasting acceptance of this territorial renunciation by the German people.

The Bundesrat approved the two Bundestag resolutions on 22 June. Only the SPD-governed states of Lower Saxony and the Saarland rejected the German–German Treaty, which thus took effect from 1 July 1990. At this time the GDR transferred its sovereignty regarding financial and monetary policy matters to the Bonn government and to the Bundesbank in Frankfurt.

Thus the executive and legislative powers in the two German states travelled a key part of the road to German unity together. This presupposed intensive co-operation between the governments in Bonn and East Berlin at all levels, as well as close co-ordination between the two parliaments. The fact that the telephone lines between East Berlin and Bonn as well as the transport system between the two capitals did not collapse under the overload was only attributable to improvisation on the part of the German Post Office and the Federal Armed Forces.

IV.

A few days after 1 July negotiations began in East Berlin on the second German–German treaty, the Unification Treaty, the conditions and implications of which were to be the predominant domestic policy issue in the weeks to come. Within a very limited period of time agreements had to be reached on all areas of public life, aimed at overcoming the discrepancies that had arisen between regulations in the Federal Republic of Germany and those in the GDR in the forty years the country was divided. At the same time it was necessary to create transitional arrangements in those areas in which the automatic extension of West German regulations to the East would have led to unacceptable situations and injustices for the people in the GDR.

During the first half of the year the Bonn government was more strongly absorbed by foreign-policy activities than by domestic problems. This situation changed when negotiations began on the unification treaty, which required SPD approval.

It was not the very difficult questions connected with privatisation that triggered a public controversy between the parties in the government coalition and between the government and the opposition. Instead, it was differences of opinion on the provisions of the law governing abortions. Chancellor Kohl invited the chairmen of the coalition parties and the SPD as well as other leading politicians of these parties to the Chancellery for late-night meetings on a number of occasions to discuss and clarify these and other controversial issues in the Unification Treaty. The SPD chancellor candidate was involved in these intensive talks between the government and the SPD. As prime minister of the Saarland he had refused to approve the first German–German treaty in the Bundesrat.

In these nightly sessions the CDU chairman succeeded, with the help of the West German negotiation leader, Interior Minister Wolfgang Schäuble, in achieving a consensus in the coalition and compromises between the coalition and the SPD on the controversial elements of the Unification Treaty. All major problems and controversial points are dealt with on a thousand pages of typed script and in hundreds of pages of annexes. The Unification Treaty was signed on 31 August by Wolfgang Schäuble and the East Berlin negotiator, Parliamentary State Secretary Günther Krause. On 20 September the Bundestag and the People's Chamber approved the treaty with the necessary majority, opposed only by the votes of the PDS and the Greens. A day later it was approved by the Bundesrat. Two days later it was signed into law by the Federal President.

In this third phase of the German unification process there was practical and purposeful co-operation between the Government on the one hand and the Bundestag and Bundesrat on the other. Parliament and the State Governments of the West German Länder, as well as the Opposition in Bonn, were included in the unification process from the beginning, without thereby diluting the responsibility of the executive. Only two and a half weeks after the opening of the internal German border, the Chancellor made a first Government statement to the Bundestag on 28 November 1989. This was followed throughout the first half of 1990 by further Government statements and debates about German political questions. The budgetary committee of the Bundestag was kept continually informed from the end of 1989. Also the Länder were kept fully informed by means of discussions with the Heads of State and of the Senate offices, as well as with the Heads of the Länder governments. On 24 April 1990, when Chancellor Kohl gave GDR Prime Minister de Maizière a working paper in the form of a draft treaty about currency, economic and social union, the Opposition received the draft the same day and the Länder the next. During the ratification process the Bundestag and the Bundesrat were in any case intensively involved with the State Treaty question.

The formation of the Bundestag committee for German unity,

which first sat on 11 May 1990, created in addition to the already existing technical committees a special parliamentary body, which the government used for the further integration of the legislature into the unification process. The committee met twenty times, and not only kept itself informed by the Government about the progress of the negotiations with the GDR, but played a leading role in the parliamentary ratification process for the unification and electoral treaties. In addition, the Federal Interior Minister used the West German part of the committee as a helpful advisory organ before the individual rounds of the negotiation with the GDR.

In East Berlin, on the other hand, co-operation among the parties became increasingly difficult as the day of German unity drew closer. In July the Liberals left the de Maizière government, since no agreement could be reached in the East Berlin coalition on the election mode to be used. In August the Social Democrats withdrew from the East Berlin government, denying de Maizière the necessary parliamentary majority.

Domestic policy issues dominated in this phase. However, it was also in this phase that the foreign-policy activities required to safeguard the unification were completed. Chancellor Kohl achieved a breakthrough during his meeting with Gorbachev in the Caucasus Mountains. There Gorbachev assured him that a united Germany would be granted full sovereignty, and after that would be able to decide freely on its own alliance membership. This success of German diplomacy was preceded by a NATO special summit in early July at which NATO extended a 'hand in friendship' to the Warsaw Pact, and all NATO members welcomed German unification and expressed their wish for German membership of NATO.

Gorbachev noted the Chancellor's commitment, together with that of President Mitterrand, to advocating economic and financial co-operation between the Western industrial countries and the Soviet Union, which had been shown at the EC summit in Dublin and again at the economic summit in Houston, Texas. On this basis the Soviet leadership could see that constructive relations between the United States and Germany would not result in a disadvantage for the Soviet Union, and that German unity in freedom would create a European partner for the Soviet Union on whose predictability and co-operativeness it could rely. The Two-Plus-Four process was concluded in Moscow on 12 September. Fourteen days later East Berlin and Moscow agreed that as of 3 October 1990 the GDR would no longer be a member of the Warsaw Pact.

The smooth timing of domestic and foreign-policy activities, the huge volume of regulatory requirements and the time-pressure created by the people in the GDR demanded a maximum of concentration, improvisation and imagination from the decision-makers in Bonn and East Berlin, whether politicians, diplomats or senior ministerial officials. The result attained is rewarding enough. The German dream of living united and free was fulfilled on 3 October 1990.

In addition to political and diplomatic activities, the German government was involved during 1990 in a broad-scale public information campaign. Doubtless the largest challenge facing the German government in 1990 was that of calming domestic and foreign fears regarding potential negative effects of the German unification process on stability in Europe. A reunited Germany, with a population of around 80 million, its economic strength, its established political weight, its past, its regaining of full sovereignty understandably triggered fears as to its future course. These fears appeared in the United Kingdom during the Ridley affair, among other instances. In response, the German government focused its communication efforts on the confidence the Bonn democracy had built up over the past forty years as a reliable and predictable partner. The Chancellor, the Foreign Minister, and, with them, the entire government and the political forces behind them, dared not and did not cease to present the argument that overcoming the division of Germany needed to be seen as overcoming the division of Europe, and that German unification and the European integration process were two sides of the same coin.

Since Europeans have good memories there was a need in all formal and informal talks to clarify the differences between German unification in 1990 and that of 1871:

1. In 1871 unification was a process imposed 'from above', even though it was welcomed by the people. Today, unity is the result of the first successful revolutionary process in Germany to be initiated by the people themselves.
2. In 1871 a unified Germany was founded after wars against Austria (in 1866) and France (in 1870–1). Today, unity is the result of the peaceful self-liberation of West Germans' fellow-citizens in the former GDR, whose courageous mass demonstrations toppled the communist regime.
3. More than a century ago Germany's European neighbours

viewed German unification with anything from scepticism to rejection. In particular, the French loss of Alsace–Lorraine made the reclaiming of lost territories a central theme of French foreign policy and, as such, made the Franco-German conflict a constant which all European powers had to reckon with. In 1990 German unity was achieved with the approval and support of all Europeans, and Franco-German friendship is rightly seen as one of the chief driving-forces for European integration.

4. The annexation of Alsace–Lorraine had a restrictive effect on the foreign policy of the German Reich. By contrast, united Germany's recognition of all its borders, including that formed by the Oder and Neisse rivers, creates additional latitude that is of benefit to the European integration process.

5. The unification of Germany in 1871 resulted in the formation of a classic nation-state in the form of a constitutional monarchy, to which imperial designs were attributed, despite the assurances that were given that this was not the case. The united Germany of 1990 is a country in the form of a federally structured parliamentary republic. It cannot be compared with the nation-state of the nineteenth century, in that it is willing to transfer a large part of the sovereignty it has regained to transnational institutions in Europe.

6. In 1871 the foreign policy future of a united Germany depended on the ability and willingness of the country's political leaders to maintain a balance of power between Germany and the other major European powers: France, Britain, Austria–Hungary and Russia. Maintaining this balance of power led to recurrent crises, and failed completely when Bismarck was no longer at the helm of the ship of state. Today united Germany is firmly anchored in a Western community based on shared values as well as on common economic and defence interests, a situation that makes a separate national course for the 80 million Germans absolutely impossible. The Germany of today sees its destiny in Europe, and European integration as the German *Staatsraison*.

7. As a result of the change in power-structures caused by the 1871 unification of Germany there was a wave of militarisation throughout Europe that exerted a strong influence on public life in general. Today overcoming the East–West conflict, as a prerequisite for German unity as well as for European unification, is making possible a process of demilitarisation that is unprecedented in history, both in quantitative and in qualitative terms.

The fact that the German government and the Germans in general succeeded in making these fundamental differences clear to their partners and to all Europeans in the course of the Two-Plus-Four process was not just a measure of the success of the German communication effort but also a key prerequisite for unification. This message gained credibility on 3 October 1990, when foreign journalists and governments were able to see for themselves that the Germans by no means entered into a state of national fervour, but rather simply celebrated their regained unity and afterwards dedicated themselves soberly to dealing with the problems caused by forty years of division and to expressing their political interests in an election campaign.

V.

When the smoke from the verbal barrages had cleared after the election, the winners and the losers returned to political business as usual, familiar and yet so new, since German unification has brought with it a vast range of new problems. However, it is worth taking a look at the first all-German election to be held since 1932 and the result it produced, giving the Bonn government coalition a viable majority of nearly 55 per cent of the vote. Foreign commentators rightly described this landslide victory for the Kohl government as a plebiscite on German unity and its architect, Helmut Kohl.

The election campaign in December 1990 showed a number of differences compared with past election campaigns. The first of these differences, from which all the others derive, was the fact, known to the voters, that the election on 2 December constituted the first free general election held in the whole of Germany in the post-war period. It was an election that stood out from other, more ordinary elections. It was the legitimating conclusion to a process that began in the autumn of the previous year on the streets of East Berlin, Leipzig, Dresden and elsewhere, causing the communist dictatorship to crumble. As such, it is understandable that this most recent election campaign was monothematic in nature. No issue other than German unity had a chance of exerting a decisive influence in the election. The dominant position of this theme degraded all other issues to problems, the importance of which was determined by the dominant issue of German unity.

A second difference in comparison with other election campaigns manifested itself in the fact that the electorate sensed that it knew early on who was going to win. Already in the summer half the electorate was fairly sure that the Bonn coalition would succeed in getting its government mandate renewed. By November four out of five voters shared this view. This public forecast led to signs of resignation in the opposition that were increased by the general lack of response to campaign issues that diverged from the main German theme.

The most difficult problem the opposition faced in terms of communication was its inability to eliminate doubt as to its support of the German unification process. We need only remember the SPD's initial support of the Chancellor's ten-point plan, which was soon made obsolete by events in the former GDR. This support was rapidly withdrawn and replaced by criticism of the objectives and of the course being taken by the unification process, something that many people understood or misunderstood as a definitive 'no'. The SPD's declaration of support for the unification process came too late to be able to eliminate fully the doubts created by its earlier position.

A third difference, and a very important one in comparison with earlier election campaigns, was the fact that all the parties involved in the campaign had to focus on two separate publics, the people constituting the population of West Germany, who had to be told that the burdens facing them as a consequence of unity could be dealt with without any substantial reduction in their standard of living, and the people in the newly created German states, who needed to be encouraged to accept and solve the problems that had arisen and would continue to arise in the process of economic restructuring.

For this reason the main interest for both German publics was economic competence – a further difference in comparison with earlier election campaigns. The monothematic character of the election campaign meant that a single competence dominated all the others, and that foreign- and security-policy issues declined in importance by comparison. This explains the conspicuous lack of polarisation in the campaign.

German unity also changed the general conditions that obtain for elections. In 1990 a total of 23 parties and voter groups stood for office. The last time an election had taken place involving a similar number of parties was in 1949. In 1990 a Federal Constitutional Court ruling resulted in a similarity between the 1949 election and the first all-German Bundestag election. It was decided to apply the 5 per cent rule for parliamentary representation separately for the new German states, so that the authors of the peaceful revolution in the former GDR would not be deprived of the opportunities they deserved as a result of the need to acquire a fairly large percentage of the vote. In 1949 there were also separate 5 per cent rules for every state, the intention being to ensure variety and a lively atmosphere in the Bundestag.

At the polls the people decided to maintain the stability of the established system of parties under the new conditions in united Germany: 88.7 per cent of the votes were cast for the traditional parties, the CDU/CSU, the SPD and the FDP. This was only 2 per cent less than in the 1987 Bundestag election in the smaller Federal Republic of Germany. The result of the election on 2 December 1990 resulted in two further important changes. The only new party to enjoy political success in the past ten years, the Greens, were relegated to extra-parliamentary status. Only the Greens elected in the Eastern German states were permitted representation in the Bundestag, in the framework of the Alliance '90 group. Thanks to the separate application of the 5 per cent rule, the party succeeding the SED, the PDS, which received 9.9 per cent of the vote in the new German states, gained access to the new parliament, even though it received only 2.4 per cent of the all-German vote. The other new party founded in the western part of Germany, the Republicans, also failed to make it into the Bundestag. With 2.1 per cent of the all-German vote, they did considerably worse than the Greens. For the first time in a long time the German party spectrum has elements of almost equal strength on the left and on the right, although only one such element is represented in parliament.

The most important result of the election in December 1990 is the fact that 20 million voters supported the policies of the centre–right government and gave it their mandate for the future. The CDU/CSU won 43.8 per cent of the overall vote. This is not better than the results of all past elections in the former Federal Republic. However – and this is of more than just historical interest – it had achieved the best result any party has ever had in a free election in the whole of Germany.

The details of the overall election result are of interest. The CDU (without the CSU) emerged from this election stronger than the SPD. The last time the CDU alone did better than the SPD was in 1957. The last time the SPD had an election result worse than the one in 1990 was also in 1957.

Overall, the election result shows that the electorate, despite a growing trend towards swing voting, will vote for a policy able to generate a climate of confidence based on clearly defined objectives and constancy. The road leading to this election result was difficult, strewn with obstacles and full of risks. Sixteen months before this election took place no professional political analyst would have ever assumed that the decline the government coalition was in at the time could have been overcome in the way it has been. Chancellor Kohl's determination and perseverance in steering, accelerating and mastering the unification course, despite resistance and obstacles, has led to success and created a broad basis of confidence for his government's future policies. In retrospect, even critics concede that the pace Helmut Kohl set in the unification process was correct and necessary. The words of warning Soviet Foreign Minister Shevardnadze issued in connection with his resignation on 20 December 1990 and the critical developments in the world political situation since then make Chancellor Kohl's energetic use of the opportunities provided appear more than justified in the circumstances.

German political decision processes in 1990, their tempo, system and method, the mastery of the external and internal political dimensions, the presentation of a functioning federalism, and also – despite all party-political confrontation – the co-operation between the major parties, completely confounded the critics of an apparently fragmented, clumsy political system, which was supposed to be almost incapable of decision-making. Domestic and foreign observers of democracy in Bonn have seen in the decision-making processes during 1989–90 a shining example of the possibilities for political leadership of a 'co-ordination democracy' under less than easy conditions. That such a result could be achieved is above all due to the overriding importance of the theme of German reunification, which was nationally and internationally recognised as coming about as a result of overcoming East–West confrontation. However, it is also due to the historical achievement of Chancellor Kohl, who was the first to recognise the opportunity and know how to exploit it, despite domestic and international resistance, through the courage of his own convictions. In this respect his friendly relations with the American and Soviet Presidents, as well as with the heads of European states and governments, stood him in good stead.

The result of the election on 2 December 1990 shows that political leadership is possible, and will be rewarded by the electorate even under the difficult conditions that obtain in a 'co-ordination democracy'.

Still, this observation by no means disproves Jaeger's sceptical thesis regarding overextension of the system of government and losses of function for the parties. It could be argued that the extraordinary challenge constituted by the opportunity to achieve German unity and the stress this brought about, referred to by Professor Grosser in the title given to this chapter, led to an enormous effort on the part of the government and the party system that temporarily compensated for and concealed negative trends. Jaeger's assertions will have to be examined in the light of day-to-day political activities in the all-German situation. The December election also showed that the German electorate tends to avoid unpredictable risks, prefers concentration and continuity in the political system, and likes to see its politicians work to their full physical and mental capacity.

In summarising my remarks I would like to say that the German unification process can be diagnosed as having constituted a challenging 'eu-stress' – a label the doctors have devised for situations which, though stressful, stimulate and strengthen the vitality of the human organism in coping with future challenges – for the German political system, and that the political system has stood the test – at least as far as the German electorate is concerned.

The German government is now faced with other tasks of considerable magnitude, which will also constitute 'eu-stress' challenges. It will be necessary to move ahead with the process of merging the two parts of Germany. In this context, the cultural and psychological problems that exist in the new German states as a result of nearly sixty years of dictatorship will probably be more difficult to eliminate than the material differences between Eastern and Western Germany. It will also be necessary to use Germany's newly-won unity to accelerate the European unification process. All the prospects one can conceive of for European unification and supranational European structures will leave no room for major-power ambitions on the part of a united Germany. They will require of the German government that it invest imagination and energy in a new architecture for European politics, in which the Germans will become less and less sovereign and more and more an integral part of a new community. The *Staatsraison* of a united Germany is its integration in Europe. It is only in this way that it will find its identity. It is only in this way that it will draw the necessary conclusions from its history. Finally, it is only in this way that Europe will exert a strong influence in the coming century.

UWE ANDERSEN

Economic Unification

The German economic unification process is a topic which is fascinating and dangerous at the same time:

— fascinating, because the task of economic unification means integrating two antagonistic economic systems in a very short time, an experiment in political economy without precedent in modern history;
— dangerous, because we are in the middle of the process of integration, the outcome is still open and it is far too early to give a balanced, thorough and empirically backed analysis.

Nevertheless, I will try to give an overview. In what follows I will (1) develop a comparative framework; (2) analyse the starting position and alternative strategies for economic unification; (3) discuss the implementation of the chosen strategy and the main problems involved; and (4) provisionally take stock.

1. Analytical Framework

If one looks at the controversial discussion on German economic unification, it is interesting to note that some observers explicitly or implicitly use a comparative perspective. As I think such a comparative perspective and framework is useful, I will mention three possibilities:

1. One may compare the ongoing experiment with the radical change in West Germany after the Second World War. In the

economic sphere the latter started with a radical monetary reform in 1948; then there followed the introduction of the special
German model of the Social Market Economy; and finally this
resulted in the so-called 'economic miracle' in the fifties and
sixties. Some people look at this process as a possible model for
the development in East Germany, and ask what can be learned
from this former German experiment for the current task.

2. Other people look to the attempts in the different East European
    countries to change their socialist, centrally planned economies
    into market-oriented systems, and ask whether the German ex-
    periment could be helpful for their case.

3. And last, but not least, some observers compare the economic
    integration of East and West Germany with the integration pro-
    cess of different member countries within the European Com-
    munity (EC), especially with the current and ambitious task of
    Economic and Monetary Union (EMU). This is a comparative
    perspective, which I think is of special interest, and I would like
    to take it up later on.

In both the German and the EC integration case, the following
triangle can be used as a fruitful analytical framework:

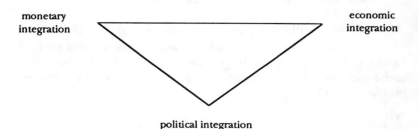

monetary   economic
integration   integration

political integration

The most interesting question is, what dependencies or inter-
dependencies exist between the apexes of this triangle, especially if
one takes into account different degrees of integration in the three
corner systems, and what this means for the choice of integration
strategy, including different timetables.

2. Starting Position and Alternative Strategies

Although the German Democratic Republic (GDR) was looked upon as the most efficient economic system among the socialist East European countries, it showed a very poor performance compared with West Germany. Table 1 gives an overview of important indicators for the last 'normal' year 1988.

To mention just a few features, which characterised the old system of the GDR:

— an overcentralised, party-dominated structure of decision-making in the political and economic system with virtually no freedom for the individual firms, which had been integrated into bureaucratic superstructures, the so-called *Kombinate*;
— a distorted price-system with little relationship to shortages, being subordinated to the central planning system;
— public, or more precisely state ownership of the overwhelming bulk of the economy (surviving small private companies accounted only for about 5 per cent of the workforce);
— inefficient investment and an over-aged capital stock;
— according to the communist ideology, nearly full employment, with an extraordinary 83 per cent female employment, but at the price of greatly overstaffed companies, low individual incentives for the employees and poor productivity;
— a centralised system of planned foreign trade, mostly — about two-thirds — with the socialist countries (nearly 40 per cent with the Soviet Union alone);
— a non-convertible currency.

The basic weaknesses of the East German economic system have long been evident, and were well-known within the GDR. It should be mentioned that in the sixties the GDR tried a wide-ranging reform called the *Neues Ökonomisches System* ('New Economic System') to decentralise its economic system and give its individual firms more leeway in decision-making. At that time the GDR was at the forefront of the economic reform developments in Eastern Europe,

Table 1 Federal Republic of Germany and German Democratic Republic: Comparison of Selected Economic and Social Indicators in 1988

	Federal Republic of Germany	German Democratic Republic
Area and Population		
Area (*1,000 sq. km.*)	249	108
Population (*millions*)	61.4	16.7
(*By percent of population*)		
Of working age	67.0[1]	65.0
Pensioners	18.5[1]	16.0
Employment		
Total employed (*millions*)	27.4	9.0
(*By percent of population*)	44.5	53.9
Female employment (*in percent of total employment*)	38.1[1]	48.6
Employment by sector		
(*By percent of total*)		
Agriculture and forestry	4.0	10.8
Mining, manufacturing, and construction	39.8	47.1
Other sectors	56.2	42.1
Household Income, Consumption, and Saving		
Average monthly gross earnings (*DM/M*)	3,850	1,270
Household saving (*by percent of disposable income*)	12.8	7.1
Households with:		
(*By percent of total*)		
Automobiles	97	52
Colour television	94	52
Telephone	98	7[2]
Production, Investment, and Prices		
(*Annual real growth rate, 1980–88*)		
GNP/NMP	1.7	4.2
Gross fixed investment	0.7	2.0
Of which: Machinery and equipment	2.4	5.0
Consumer prices (*annual percent rate of change, 1980–88*)	2.9	—

Table 1 cont.

	Federal Republic of Germany	German Democratic Republic
External Trade in Goods		
(By percent of total exports)		
Exports to state-trading countries	4.4	69.5
Imports from state-trading countries	4.7	68.7
Trade balance		
(By percent of GNP/NMP)	6.0	1.0
Of which: State-trading countries	0.2	1.0
Monetary Accounts of Households		
Household financial assets[3] *(billions DM/M)*	1,196.6	167.2
Velocity of money[4]	1.11	0.97

Source: Leslie Lipschitz, Donogh McDonald (Eds): *German Unification, Economic Issues*, Occasional Paper 75, International Monetary Fund, Washington, DC, 1990; p. xv.
[1] 1987.
[2] 1985.
[3] Currency and bank deposits. Year-end for the FRG and year average for the GDR.
[4] Private disposable income divided by household financial assets.

and some West German observers saw it as at the brink of a socialist market economy with state ownership. The reform experiment, however, failed, primarily because the leadership of the communist party – the *Sozialistische Einheitspartei* (SED) – retreated from the main reform aspects. They feared the erosion of their power-base if the party were to loosen its control over the economy. The result was a recentralisation of the economy, aggravating its structural defects. In the eighties the characteristic feature of the East German economy was stagnation, and by the end of the decade the economy was living more and more on its capital. If one takes into account the economic turmoil in COMECON in combination with the deteriorating economic situation within the GDR, even without the political revolution an economic crisis lurked around the corner.

Under these conditions the economic relationship with West Germany was of special importance to the GDR.

In its most significant structural aspects the West German economic system was nearly the opposite of the GDR model. For political reasons the government of the Federal Republic of Germany (FRG) had always tried to strengthen economic ties with East Germany, and had even been ready to pay a high financial price for doing so. A growing part of this 'inner German' trade was financed by interest-free credit, and the FRG government paid out large amounts for inner-German travel, for the improvement of transit highways, and even for the release of political prisoners in the GDR. Most valuable for the East German economy was its 'hidden' membership of the EC, in so far as its exports into the EC were treated like West German goods and could cross borders without the normal barriers to non-members. In the negotiations leading to the European Economic Community in 1957 the FRG government had insisted on this special status for the GDR economy, because it did not regard the GDR as a foreign country.

A special feature of the GDR in its final stage was the superior position of the DM, the currency of the western class enemy. The citizens of the GDR were allowed to hold amounts in DM with special East German banks and to buy goods normally not available for home currency – including East German export goods – in special 'Exquisite Shops' with DM. Ideologically it certainly was a blow, and a dangerous demonstration to the population that for ordinary citizens the most valuable goods were available only if they managed to get West German currency, normally by close contacts with West German relatives or friends. The result was a peculiar class society, with the major dividing-line drawn between privileged DM-holders and holders of second-class eastern money.

After the peaceful revolution in the GDR in autumn 1989 and the sudden opening of the iron curtain dividing Germany, the reformed, but still SED-dominated Modrow government was aiming at a political solution with some sort of political independence within a weak German confederation. In the economic system the Modrow government was looking for a third way between a socialist and a market economy, although with economic and financial support demanded from the FRG. In February 1990 Chancellor Kohl, who formally had suggested a Ten Point Plan for an inner German reconciliation in a medium-term perspective, reacted to the accelerating developments with a surprising step. He offered negotiations on a quick monetary union, with the perspective of political union. In the first free election in the GDR in March 1990 the CDU-led 'Alliance for Germany' gained an astonishing victory. The overwhelming majority of the population voted for German unification, including monetary and economic unification. Quick negotiations as to the details of the unification process followed. Partner in the negotiations was the new de Maizière government of the GDR, which was backed by a Grand Coalition consisting mainly of the Christian Democrats, the Social Democrats and the Liberal Free Democrats.

From an abstract academic point of view there were still different options for a strategy of integration. Most economists favoured the so-called crowning approach, with integration steps starting in the field of economic policy followed and crowned by steps in the monetary field. It was obvious that the necessary transformation of the GDR economy into a market economy with competition from the outside would reveal the socialist inefficiencies and the poor competitiveness of most products and firms, with a corresponding risk of high unemployment at least in the short run. By postponing full monetary integration the adaptation of the exchange-rate of the East German currency could be used as a shock-absorber to facilitate the transformation process. With low exchange-rates the companies of the GDR would have a better chance to compete. However, there were two important, mainly political, arguments against such a strategy, one internal, one external:

1. Internally one had to take into account the high expectations of the East German population, especially their strong desire for 'real' money, that is the West German DM. These expectations were combined with the 'exit option' – voting with one's feet. A famous dictum of that period was: 'If the DM does not come to us, we will go west to the DM.' The rising inner German East–West migration, however, caused more and more problems in both parts of Germany – housing problems and growing conflicts in the West, and a loss of the most flexible part of the population, and thereby worsening economic prospects, in the East.
2. Externally the instability of the international political situation, especially within the Soviet Union, was a decisive factor. In this perspective a quick monetary union seemed an instrument to push on with political integration until it reached a point of no return.

So the decision in favour of quick monetary union was a genuinely political one, taken by the Kohl government in the course of trying to seize a rare historical chance for German unification, with a conscious evaluation of the political, economic and monetary risks involved. At the same time this decision was meant as a signal of hope for the East German population. It has to be stressed that the timing for economic and monetary risk-taking was nearly optimal, because the West German economy was in an excellent condition, the currency strong and the inflation rate low, the government finances in good order, and – after a tax reduction – private savings especially high.

In the negotiations between the two German governments the dominating Western side tried to reduce the monetary, economic and financial risks. The Bundesbank, the West German central bank, which is a very strong and politically independent actor in econ-omic policy, had reacted cautiously to the government's political decision for quick monetary union. It became strongly involved in the negotiation process. Chancellor Kohl took a prudent tactical step in choosing Hans Tietmeyer, a Bundesbank director and former state secretary in the Ministry of Finance, as chief negotiator on the West German side. The result of the negotiations was a state treaty on German economic, monetary and social union ('GEMSU'), which included as the fourth aim environmental union.

In its timing the monetary integration was one step ahead. One can interpret this as a special example of the 'motor approach', using monetary integration as a motor for economic integration. Starting from 1 July the West German DM became the only Ger-man legal tender, and the Bundesbank the only central bank re-sponsible for monetary policy in the two still-existing German states. But a 'parallel approach' with simultaneous progress in monetary and economic integration was at least aimed at, in so far as the treaty obliged the East German government to adapt its economic framework as soon as possible to the Social Market Economy of West Germany. Financial aid from the FRG was to support the difficult transition process, and especially to strengthen the social net. Unforeseen budget deficits in the GDR could be financed by credit only with the explicit consent of the West German Ministry of Finance. These examples make it abundantly clear that, although two German states still existed, the GDR had fully lost its monetary and economic sovereignty.

This far-reaching monetary and economic integration was closely connected – a point which needs to be stressed – with the declared aim of the treaty of reaching full political integration as soon as the consent of the four Allied powers had been obtained. When the unification of Germany was reluctantly approved even by the Soviet Union, formal political integration was quickly completed on 3 October, when the former GDR joined the FRG. In December, in the first all-German election, the old West German coalition government of Christian and Free Democrats was backed by the voters in East and West Germany. The main issue of the election campaign had been the unification strategy, and the costs and problems it would involve. Although most of the Social Democrats finally had reluctantly approved the two state treaties between the FRG and GDR, Lafontaine, the Social Democratic challenger to Chancellor Kohl, had been one of the harshest critics of quick monetary union. His main problem was that he could not offer a feasible alternative. However, he strongly emphasised the social consequences of monetary union in the East and the high costs, including tax increases, which it would involve for the West German population. Partly in reaction to these attacks, the coalition government went so far as to rule out tax increases, arguing that the booming West German economy in combination with a modest debt increase would be sufficient to finance the unification process. This certainly was a dangerous position, if one takes into account the uncertainties of the integration process which lay ahead. The special feature of the integration experiment of the two German states which should be stressed is the GDR's one-sided and complete borrowing of the existing model of the FRG in its political, monetary and economic dimension (including its legal framework and institutional structure) over a very short period of time.

3. Implementation of the Strategy – Main Problems

In general, the situation in East Germany has been worse than expected, and this in nearly all its aspects. The old SED government had systematically given a false picture of the state of the economy, and even the scientific publications in the West had been far too optimistic.[1] For a recalculation of the development of GNP per caput in both parts of Germany see Fig. 1.

If one looks at the monetary union in a technical sense, it has been

Figure 1: Gross Domestic Product per caput from 1950 to 1989

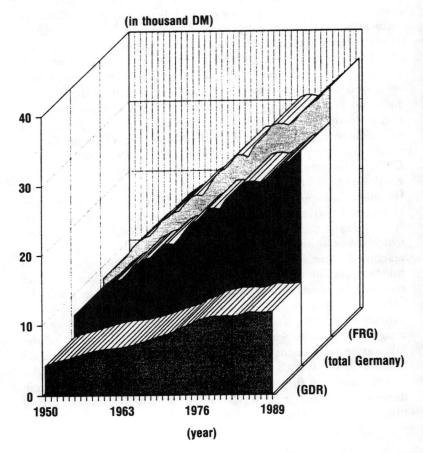

Source: Merkel, Wilma; Wahl, Stefanie: Das geplünderte Deutschland. Die wirtschaftliche Entwicklung im östlichen Teil Deutschland von 1949 bis 1989. Schriften des Instituts für Wirtschaft und Gesellschaft. Bonn 1991; p. 57.

successful. On 1 July 1990 the GDR gave up its monetary sovereignty, and all state power in this field was transferred to the Deutsche Bundesbank, which, without any institutional merging and compromising with former GDR monetary institutions, was given sole responsibility for monetary policy in Germany as a whole. At the same time the DM became the only German legal tender. The first difficult task to be faced was therefore to decide on an adequate conversion rate for the exchange of the former GDR currency into DM. This decision had been taken formally in the state treaty on GEMSU, but the decision-making process had demonstrated the highly sensitive character of the issue. In a study for the government the Deutsche Bundesbank had suggested a highly differentiated formula, with different conversion rates for financial stocks and flows in particular.

When through indiscretion the Bundesbank suggestion leaked to the public all differentiations vanished, and the discussion centred on a 1:2 conversion rate for wages, neglecting all the compensation elements inherent in the Bundesbank formula. The outcry from the East German population at this was so marked that politically the Bundesbank proposal soon turned into a dead duck. The result was a political decision which on the whole was very favourable for the East Germans. On average the conversion rate for financial assets amounted to 1:1.8, which is far better than the calculated exchange-rate of 1:4.2 in the former GDR planning system. It also stands in marked contrast to the monetary reform of 1948. Different conversion rates were used chiefly for social reasons. Smaller savings of private citizens, for example, were converted at the rate of 1:1.

On the whole, the average conversion rate for financial assets of 1:1.8 was only slightly better than the suggestion of the Deutsche Bundesbank. The main difference between the actual reform and the Bundesbank proposal was the 1:1 conversion rate for financial flows, and the consequences this was to have for the competitiveness of the East German economy in the future.[2]

One of the fears connected with monetary integration in Germany was that it would lead to inflation, because the East German consumers would spend all their converted savings on the new goods of high quality now available to them. Such a sudden surge in demand would certainly have endangered the aim of price stability. One has to take into account, however, the different size of the East and West German economies. The GNP of the GDR was only about 1/11 that of the FRG, and the total converted savings of the East German population were smaller then the savings of the West German population in the year 1990 alone. The money supply (M 3) went up by about DM 160 billion, which was roughly 1/8 of the West German amount (M 3 = 1220 billion). As parts of the converted amounts were expected to go into longer-term interest-bearing assets, the increase of the money supply seemed to be roughly in line with the increase in productive capacity brought about by the absorption of the East German economy. Even if one suspected some monetary surplus in the GDR, it has been low compared with that in other East European countries. If one further takes into account what have in general been reasonable spending patterns on the part of the East Germans and a prudent monetary policy on the part of the Bundesbank, one has the main factors that explain why reasonable price stability has been obtained, at least up to February 1990. Also the apprehension that under the new circumstances the DM would be considered to have become a weak currency has so far proved to be greatly exaggerated.

It should be mentioned that monetary reform has been facilitated because the financial sector has become the earliest and most strongly integrated sector of the economy. The two-tier banking system of the West was rapidly adopted in East Germany, not only in respect of the Deutsche Bundesbank and its central banking system, but in the private banking system, too. The big West German banks expanded quickly into the eastern territory, partly by taking over former GDR banks. Two good examples of a strong commitment in East Germany are the two leading German banks, the Deutsche Bank and the Dresdener Bank, the latter taking the opportunity to return to the city of its origin – Dresden.

Monetary integration in Germany will carry important and potentially far-reaching institutional consequences for the Deutsche Bundesbank, too. Although the direction of adaptation is a highly controversial question right now, according to the state treaty the decision has to be taken in 1991. The Bundesbank mirrors the federal structure of the FRG, in so far as its main decision-making body – the *Zentralbankrat* – consists of up to eight directors of the centre in Frankfurt, nominated by the central government, and the directors of the Bundesbank branches in each West German state, nominated by the state government. To follow this old pattern under new conditions would mean building up a new Bundesbank branch in each of the five new states (Länder) in East Germany, and expanding the size of the Zentralbankrat correspondingly. The majority of the Zentralbankrat has voted against a reorganisation along these lines, as it would make the Zentralbankrat too big as a decision-making body, and would further reduce the relative weight of the centre in Frankfurt. Instead it has recommended reducing the number of the state branches (*Landeszentralbanken*) to obtain a more balanced model, which is to be achieved by giving some branches responsibility for the territory of more than one of the smaller states, as is the case in the Federal Reserve System of the United States of America. The fierce resistance of the smaller states, which would loose their own *Landeszentralbank*, can be partly explained by the fear that such a reform of the structure of the Bundesbank would stimulate the discussion of a reform of the federal structure in general, which some bigger states are demanding anyway.

Looking to economic integration, one gets a more sinister picture. At the moment the economic situation is divided. There is a still-booming western economy, not least because of integration, and a deteriorating eastern element. The 1:1 conversion rate combined with a generally free price system – the main exception being housing – really was a harsh way of undertaking change. It brought the serious distortions in the economy, the extremely poor condition of the capital stock, the hidden unemployment, and the low competitiveness in the East out into the open. Industrial production in East Germany has fallen by more than half, a trend in part accelerated by an excessive tendency to buy only western goods and a reduction of orders from the traditional East European markets by about two-thirds – a virtual breakdown. The smaller agricultural sector is in severe crisis; and the service sector has not expanded as quickly as had been hoped. Against this general background, in what follows I will take up some of the main outstanding problems, which are hotly debated in public, and which confront decision-makers with difficult options.

Property Rights and Handling of State-Owned Companies

Part of the former GDR system was its often arbitrary use of expropriation, and, more generally, its disrespect of private property, especially that of political opponents. Therefore many people who had lost their property under communist rule expected to get it back after German unification. As the loss of property rights had taken place up to 45 years ago, and in the meantime there has been scope for many changes, even a reconstruction of the developments in an individual case is often difficult. Especially in the housing sector, many East Germans feared that the claims of former owners or their heirs would be prejudicial to their interests and bring about new injustices. From the economic point of view the uncertainty of the situation with regard to property rights, especially those to real estate, has become a serious obstacle to new investments and new enterprises.

In the negotiations on German unity the Soviet Union as one of the former Allied victors of the Second World War insisted that its decisions as an occupying power, especially on expropriation, should be upheld. As the Soviet Union made this point a precondition for its consent to German unification, the German government acquiesced. But after unification some former owners argued that this clause violated the *Grundgesetz*, the West German constitution, and brought this question before the courts. In spring 1991, in a very important decision, the powerful Bundesverfassungsgericht, the German supreme court, accepted the position of the government, but obliged the State to devise some sort of system of compensation.

Expropriations by the formerly sovereign state of the GDR are a different case. In the state treaties on German unity it is the right of restitution which first and foremost is granted to former owners. Only if restitution proves to be impossible does compensation take place. Experience has shown that this regulation has gone too far in protecting the rights of former owners, to the detriment of the economic interests of the East German population in general. It also added to the uncertainties and hesitations of people contemplating economic involvements in East Germany. So in spring 1991 the government reassessed its position, and legislation was passed which qualified the priority of restitution over compensation. Now, if within the next two years investment and economic development are at stake, real estate or a state company may be sold to potential investors rather than restored to the former owners; and in such a case, the owners can only retain a claim to compensation. Critics argue that the new legislation is still inadequate, because it is too complicated and time-consuming.[3] Much will depend on the readiness of the various administrative decision-makers to make resolute use of their new legal opportunities.

One of the extraordinary tasks that have to be faced in rebuilding the East German economy is to split up the monstrous *Kombinate* and take into private ownership as many companies as possible. Whereas this basic philosophy is generally accepted, the concrete strategy of privatisation and its implications are heatedly discussed. The extremely difficult job of privatising about 11,000 companies has been given to the *Treuhandanstalt*. This state trust agency had already been founded by the Modrow government, which staffed it mostly

with functionaries of the SED. In the meantime the Treuhandanstalt has been reorganized, and western managers experienced in
directing private companies have assumed the leadership of it. Formally the Treuhandanstalt is acting under the responsibility of the
Federal Ministry of Finance. The new Minister of the Economy,
Möllemann, tried in vain to get this responsibility for his depart-
ment, arguing that the Treuhandanstalt is an important instrument
in economic policy. The coalition government has deliberately
passed the direct leadership and responsibility for decision-making
to experienced managers, in order that difficult decisions concerning
the future of thousands of eastern companies should not be dominated by immediate political considerations and pressures. The management of the Treuhandanstalt has decentralised its organisation.
The headquarters in Berlin remains responsible for the big companies, but the branch offices alone are in charge of companies of
only regional or local importance.

Experience has shown that the task of privatisation is much more
complicated and time-consuming than had been hoped. The interest
of western companies and business people in taking over former
state companies of the GDR was not as great as had been expected.
At the end of the first quarter of 1991 about 1,300 companies had
been privatised. Most of them had gone to new owners in West
Germany, although the government is very much interested in involving companies from other western industrialised countries (up
to early 1991 non-German companies have acquired only about 5
per cent of the privatised firms). The Treuhandanstalt has to take
into account very different and sometimes conflicting aims. On the
one hand it has to look for new owners as quickly as possible,
bearing in mind the prospects for economic development. On the
other hand it has to be careful not to waste public capital, i.e. to get
a fair price. Furthermore, it has to consider the consequences for
competition in special markets. One well-known example of how
things can go wrong is the former GDR airline *Interflug*. The West
German airline *Lufthansa* was interested in taking over *Interflug*, but
this idea was rejected with the argument that *Lufthansa* would thus
acquire too dominating a position in the German air-traffic market.
When other interested parties such as British Airways withdrew, the
end of this unhappy saga was that *Interflug* had to go out of business.

As the Treuhandanstalt not only has to look for new owners for
the former state companies, but in the meantime also has to finance
them, it often faces a difficult choice. In the absence of potential

purchasers, in each particular case it has to decide whether a company will have a good chance to stay alive in competitive markets, and, therefore, should be reorganised with financial and other support from the Treuhandanstalt, or whether it should stop operations, with the result that all its employees will lose their jobs. Up to early 1991 only a small proportion of the companies have gone out of business. In a situation of high and still-growing unemployment any decision to wind up a company faces increasing opposition and political pressure. The Treuhandanstalt has already become one of the most hated institutions in East Germany. The assassination of its first president, the respected top manager Detlev Rohwedder, by the terrorist group RAF (Red Army Faction) can only be interpreted as an attempt to exploit such sentiments in a search for popular support. Although such a calculation will fail, there are increasing political pressures to use the Treuhandanstalt as an instrument of industrial and regional economic policy, by supporting companies with taxpayers' money in an effort to protect jobs against market forces. In reaction to this development the *Sachverständigenrat zur Begutachtung der gesamtwirtschaftlichen Entwicklung*, the German Council of Economic Advisers, which is a stronghold of market-oriented economists, has firmly advised the government and the public to stick to a course relying on market forces in restructuring the East German economy, and warned against a resort to statist policies for shaping industrial and regional structures.[4] In this context it has pointed to a similar cycle of public sentiments after the monetary reform of 1948, and warned against impatience.[5]

The Treuhandanstalt has to strike a delicate balance. On the one hand, it is clearly no acceptable solution to wind up the operations of all companies for which new private owners cannot be found in a relatively short space of time. On the other hand, there is certainly a danger that under the pressure of unemployment, growing unrest within the East German population, and mounting pressures from regional political figures within the Treuhandanstalt hard decisions may be avoided. This could mean that many companies, which have no real chance of survival on their own merits, are supported for political reasons, thereby burdening the state with ever-increasing subsidies and darkening future economic prospects.

It has to be mentioned that the financial value of the state companies in East Germany has been grossly overestimated. The state treaty provides that the returns on privatisation shall be used for the restructuring of the economy and that the East German population shall share out any remainder. The experience of the Treuhandan-stalt already shows that the latter clause is an illusion, and that the greater part of the budget of the Treuhandanstalt has to be financed by the Ministry of Finance. From the budget of DM 37 billion in 1991 only DM 14 billion are expected to accrue from privatisation.

Unemployment

From the point of view of the East German population unemployment is certainly the main problem in the process of recon-struction. As open unemployment was no problem in the old GDR, the population was not psychologically prepared for this novel situation, especially since the expectations of a rapid and rather painless integra-tion into the western economy were greatly exaggerated. With quickly rising unemployment the mood changed radically, and the govern-ment was confronted with massive protest demonstrations, organ-ised in part by trade unions. It is certainly necessary to bear in mind that unemployment not only has financial consequences for the individual (though these are smoothed by the strong social net in Germany), but fundamentally changes the whole life situation, and may change political perspectives and behaviour, too.

In May 1991 842,000 people were officially registered as unem-ployed in East Germany, which is 9.5 per cent of the work force, and some 4 percentage points above the West German rate. For a realistic picture, however, one has to consider the extremely high number of about 2 million short-time employees. Short-time workers get 90 per cent of their salaries, financed mainly by state subsidies, some without working as much as a single hour. The majority of short-time employees are busy less than 50 per cent of the normal work time. Their abundant free time has not yet been used to acquire qualifications and skills to the necessary degree, some critics argue because of the relatively high pay that is available without the need to work. There have been deficiencies on the demand side – in interest, the demand for information and motivation – and on the supply side – in the quantity and quality of training programmes available – which have to be corrected. As the favourable special conditions for short-time workers in East Germany formally run out in the middle of 1991, there are risks of mounting unemployment and corresponding demands for measures to fight this foreseeable development. There is still a negative difference between newly created jobs and the old uncompetitive ones which are lost. The

Figure 2: Labour Market in May 1991

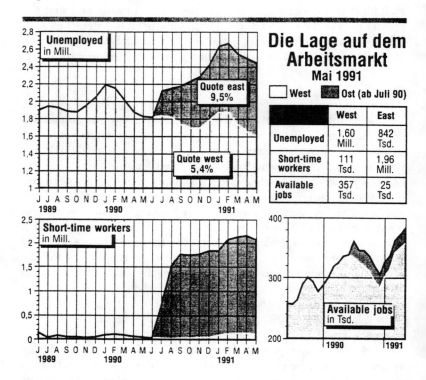

Source: *Süddeutsche Zeitung*, 7 June 1991, p. 25.

Sachverständigenrat, for example, forecasts 1.7 million unemployed (nearly a quarter of the work force) and still about 2 million short-time workers by the end of 1991.[6] Under these circumstances the special conditions for short-time workers will probably be prolonged, but only for those who are ready to take part in courses leading to qualifications. At the moment discussions center on *Beschäftigungs- und Qualifizierungsgesellschaften*, special work and training companies, designed to avoid the stigma of unemployment and use up the free time as productively as possible in terms of gaining qualifications. But in general, the qualified work force is still seen as one of the strong points in the East German economy, especially in the industrial sector.

In contrast to the situation in East Germany, employment in

West Germany has strongly increased in 1990. Nearly 700,000 new jobs have been created, a number which was last attained in the 1950s. About 300,000 migrants from East Germany have found new jobs in West Germany. On the one hand this migration has reduced the pressure on the labour market in East Germany; but on the other hand it can be seen as a brain-drain that will be detrimental to the restructuring process in East Germany. A growing number of people, especially in the frontier districts, accept long hours of commuting between the work place in the West and their living-quarters in the East.

Wages.

At the start of GEMSU the productivity of East German companies was estimated at only roughly one third of that of their western competitors; but the same was true of wages. However, wages in East Germany showed little differentiation, and in the meantime have much increased. Wage policy is confronted with a real dilemma. Wages in East and West will have to be brought much closer together in the medium term. A situation such as one finds for example in Berlin, where an equally qualified garbage-man or electrician in the western part earns about twice the salary of his eastern colleague a mile away, is not tolerable for long within one country. However, eastern companies can afford to pay higher wages only if their productivity rises roughly in line with the wages. This difficult situation would be eased if trade unions and employers would try new methods of collective bargaining,[7] especially those involving employees' participating in risks and profits; but that has not been the case up to now. Instead the West German trade unions, which have absorbed their former eastern counterparts, stick to their traditional methods in seeking to implement a strategy aimed at a rapid harmonisation of wage levels.

The *IG-Metall*, the biggest German trade union, has reached an agreement for its metal-workers' branch which will pave the way for other branches, too. Starting from a level of 60 per cent of western wages on 1 April 1991 it will bring up eastern wages to 100 per cent within three years. Although the *Sachverständigenrat* has welcomed the idea of a multi-year agreement as providing companies with the sort of basis for long-term economic calculations that they need, it has strongly criticised the projected pattern of wage-equalisation as being too rapid to be capable of being matched by productivity gains, so that it would become a counter-productive factor in the struggle to reduce unemployment.[8] Others have defended such a strategy, mainly because otherwise a migration of such a new order of magnitude may be initiated that neither the western nor the eastern half of Germany could sustain it. In addition it has been argued that a speedy equalisation would also promote the transfer of employees in a West–East direction – a transfer which is indispensable in the case of certain types of specialist workers. However, formally tying eastern wages to those in the western part of the country also means that collective bargaining in West Germany becomes a determining factor for the chances of restructuring the eastern economy. Big wage increases, such as those of 6 to 7 per cent in 1991, set the target for the productivity gains necessary to keep eastern companies afloat still higher. Even the former Social Democratic Chancellor Helmut Schmidt has stressed the negative implications of the western-oriented wage policy, and has criticised the trade unions for their lack of solidarity.[9]

Private Investment

Private investment is regarded as a key to a successful reconstruction of the East German economy, and especially as a precondition for higher productivity and a successful fight against unemployment. Since the savings rate in West Germany is high (12–13 per cent), as are the profits of the western companies – partly because of the higher consumer demand in East Germany – in general there is no shortage of private capital. Some observers have criticised the western companies for being too reluctant to invest in production in East Germany, and for only using it as a market for their products. According to a poll carried out by the IFO research institute 20 per cent of West German industrial companies plan to invest in East Germany this year, as do 50 per cent of the bigger companies. But western managers point to a list of important handicaps for private investment, especially:

- a poor infrastructure;
- difficulties in acquiring adequate real estate for production and business purposes, partly because of legal uncertainties concerning the claims of former owners;
- administrative barriers, mainly delays in getting the necessary permits;

- the uncertain financial consequences for the new owners that may arise from damage inflicted on the environment earlier, if the eastern companies responsible for it are now taken over;
- rapid increases in wages; and
- uncertainties concerning the development of East European markets.

Often these handicaps are not adequately compensated for even by the powerful investment incentives made available by the state. These tax incentives and other subsidies have been steadily, but unsystematically, increased, so that at the moment up to 50 per cent of the investment costs are covered in the first year. Critics such as the distinguished former Minister of the Economy Karl Schiller have pointed to the complexity and lack of transparency of these diverse measures, and demanded that the government should simplify as well as intensify the tax incentives for a limited time-period.

Infrastructure

The deplorable state of the infrastructure comprises two main elements. Firstly the physical infrastrusture, for example the transport and communication network, has been run down. Moreover, the environment in general is in an alarming condition. In a study by the IFO research institute financial resources for necessary environmental protection up to the year 2000 are estimated at more than DM 200 billion, more than 50 per cent of this sum being needed for water protection alone. Public investment in business-oriented infrastructure will be an important state contribution to economic reconstruction in East Germany. The *Sachverständigenrat* estimates this investment at DM 30 billion in 1991, including that for the state-owned postal – improvement of the communication net – and railway systems. This sum is considerably higher per caput than in West Germany. High public investments in the infrastructure, however, are not only an element that is complementary to private investment, but an important demand push for the East German economy, especially the building industry. In West Germany big traffic projects, for example new national highways, require a planning period of ten to twenty years. Highly complicated and perfectionist laws and regulations give interested parties much scope to delay projects by going to different courts. As such a delay is unacceptable under East German circumstances a special law is under way to allow short cuts for specially important projects. Even more difficult are public investments in the infrastructure at a local level, mainly for parallel reasons.

Secondly the administrative infrastructure has to be built up almost completely anew. The East German experiment shows how important capable administrators are for creating the necessary framework for private business and for protecting the environment. Here once more we have a personnel and a financial bottleneck in East Germany. The local administration especially is at the same time overstaffed and understaffed, in as much as the number of administrators is much higher compared with that found in West German municipalities, but qualified and experienced administrators able to cope with the new tasks and challenges are missing. Apart from measures to improve qualifications and skills, personnel support from the western part of the country is indispensable in the short run. The same is true for staffs in the newly established East German states. As administration in the FRG is mainly the responsibility of the states, administrative aid, particularly in the shape of the transfer of experts, primarily has to come from them, not from the federal government. There are special partnerships between particular pairs of western and eastern states, for example between Baden-Württemberg and Saxony or North Rhine-Westphalia and Brandenburg; but the West German states vary in their eagerness to help their eastern counterparts, and so do individual administrators.

Financing

From the outset of the German unification process it has been clear that the reconstruction of East Germany will require not only private investment, but large public transfers from the West as well. The necessary volume of such transfers was controversial and in the public debate about it the difficulty of making an accurate estimate was compounded by the effect of party politics. When at the beginning of 1991 it became more and more clear that the economic and financial situation of East Germany was worse than expected, and that a transfer of more than DM 100 billion a year would be needed for the next few years, the federal government was confronted with difficult options for financing. Although the tax revenues were higher than expected because of the still-booming West German economy, they were not sufficient. Under these circumstances there were three principal options: (1) to increase the public debt; (2) to

Figure 3: General Government Finances

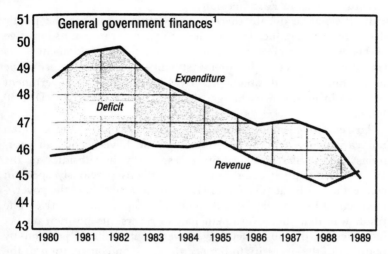

Source: Leslie Lipschitz, Donogh McDonald (Editors): German Unifica-
        tion. Economic Issues. Occasional Paper 75. International Monetary
        Fund, Washington, DC, 1990; p. 3.

[1] National accounts basis: in percent of GNP.

cut expenditure, especially subsidies in West Germany; and (3) to
raise taxes.

   In 1990 the cost of German unification was financed primarily by
higher public borrowing. The general government deficit rose to
DM 90 billion (or, taking into account the surplus in the social
security system, to a public deficit of DM 74 billion) from only DM
21 billion (DM 8 billion) in 1989. The starting position in 1989 had
however been comfortable, inasmuch as the government had successfully reduced the fiscal deficit during the eighties.

   In 1991 the highest public deficit so far – nearly DM 70 billion at
the federal level, and 70–90 billion at the state and municipality
level – is expected. This amounts to a public deficit of about 4 per
cent of the GNP. Although such a percentage is not excessive in
terms of international comparisons, it is extremely high compared
with German tradition since the Second World War. It has to be
stressed that German fiscal policy in the last two years has certainly
backed the economic boom by 'deficit spending'. However, this
Keynesian mechanism was used in a very un-Keynesian situation,

characterised not by a shortage of demand, but by an extreme structural crisis in East Germany.

In the public debate there is wide agreement that the public deficit has to be reduced in the medium term because of its negative effects on the interest rate and on economic development – its crowding-out effect on private investment – as well as because of the future burden on the budget.[10] By 1994 the federal government plans to bring down its budget deficit by more than half (DM 30 billion).

To keep its election promise not to raise taxes to fund German unification the coalition government would have needed an enormous cut in current expenditure, especially in subsidies in the West.[11] Although it could save some billions previously spent in connection with the division of Germany, on the whole the government failed in achieving this difficult, but important objective. The result was that the government had to reverse its position on tax increases. It did so reluctantly, covering its shift of position by pointing to the necessity to finance the German contribution to the Gulf War. In spring 1991 the coalition decided to raise income tax – 7.5 per cent of the tax amount, limited to one year only – oil tax and other taxes on special goods. This decision had become unavoidable under the new circumstances; but the coalition had to pay a high political price for its 'tax lie'. It lost a few elections in various states, and the control of the Bundesrat, the second chamber consisting of members of the state governments, went to the Social Democrats. As the consent of the Bundesrat is needed for most important laws, including tax laws, political decision-making in the FRG has become even more difficult.

One further issue is the kind of tax to be raised, and especially what its effects on distribution and growth will be. The coalition has terminated the income-tax increase because of its suspected negative impact on investment and economic growth, and plans to replace it in 1992 by an increase in turnover tax. This is opposed by the Social Democrats, mainly with the argument that the resulting burden-sharing would be unjust, because it would mainly hit lower income groups.

A highly controversial area is the extent of the burden-sharing not only among different groups of citizens, but also between the different political levels in the federal state. In general, the old West German states have tried to secure their privileged financial position relative to the eastern newcomers, and to shift the burden of German unity to the federal government. In a first compromise in 1990 a

'German Unity Fund' was created for the period 1990–1994, with a total endowment of DM 115 billion. It is financed primarily by additional public borrowing – DM 95 billion, of which one half has to be raised by the West German states, and the other half by the Federal Government; and to a smaller extent – DM 20 billion – by the reduced costs of the division of Germany in the federal budget. One element in establishing the German Unity Fund was an agreement that the new East German states up to 1994 would not participate in the compensation scheme between richer and poorer states in West Germany, and that the federal government would undertake any further financial risks arising from the German unification process. So in the first stage the West German states successfully resisted paying their due share of the costs of the unification process.[12] However, politically this was a short-sighted position, because it divided the western and eastern states, and forced the latter to back the central government in the balance of power within the federal system. When it became obvious that the transfer of public finance to East Germany had to be much bigger than the German Unity Fund had provided for, the West German states reacted along almost exactly the same lines as had the federal government over the tax issue. Reluctantly and under the pressure of public opinion the West German states retreated from their selfish position of defending the status quo and agreed to a new compromise on burden-sharing with the federal government. The financing of the German unity can be looked at as an interesting test of the viability of the federal system in its present form. Since the main decisions as to the future financial system will have to be taken in the next few years, its outcome is still open.

Moreover, not only the raising of funds, but also their expenditure has been criticised. It has been argued that the use of the transferred finances in East Germany – in 1990 about DM 140 billion – is too heavily oriented towards consumption, to the detriment of necessary investment in the future.

External Repercussions

Outside Germany the economic effects of the German integration process on the world economy are of special interest. One positive effect has been that the demand push in East Germany has not only backed the boom in the West German economy, but also strongly increased German imports, and has, therefore, been a counterforce to the recession in other countries. This locomotive function has been praised world-wide, as has the effect on the German balance of payments – viz. the drastic reduction of its formerly extreme surplus. On the other hand, there have been very critical comments on the financing of the German unification process, and especially on its international consequences for interest rates. It is unavoidable, however, that whenever Germany needs a larger share of its extensive savings for internal purposes, less will be available to be channelled into the network of the international capital markets. This reduced supply of capital then tends to push interest rates up. Since the German government has financed the widening public deficit primarily by borrowing on the capital market, the Bundesbank has given a signal, by raising interest rates, which the United States as well as some other European countries have seen as detrimental to their own economic situation. However, IMF staff members have argued that, according to simulations with the IMF model MULTIMOD, the overall increase in long-term real interest rates would be limited to 0.75 per cent. An alternative tax policy – increasing value added tax by about 2 percentage points – would lead to only slightly lower real interest rates, but to a higher inflation rate for a few years to come. All in all, the quantitative economic effects of German unification on other industrial countries would not be large. 'Again, other studies surveyed reach similar conclusions, as the negative demand effects of higher interest rates and positive stimulus from higher imports of Eastern Germany roughly offset.'[13]

4. Conclusion

In my view the German monetary and economic unification strategy really has been a rough ride; but no other choice was politically feasible. In the short run, there are considerable difficulties and risks. The integration process, which aims at basically similar economic conditions and quality of life in all parts of Germany, will need more time and more public financing from the western side than was hoped for. One may doubt whether the main political actors in economic and financial policy have yet fully mastered the unique challenge of German unity to date. Although one can point to certain defects – a strong political orientation towards the status quo, dangerous political promises and fixations, and time-lags in adapting to new information and changed circumstances – the basic strategy seems to be adequate, and the political actors have proved their capacity to learn, even if reluctantly. However, the danger still exists that under the pressure of current and political problems, especially high unemployment in East Germany, the political actors may try stopgap measures which deviate from the necessary orientation towards market-led reconstruction, and thus cloud future prospects. But generally in the longer run there are great opportunities, and a good chance that the German economic unification will be a success, too.

In comparative perspective one should stress that the radical transformation of the former socialist economy in East Germany cannot be a blueprint for other East European countries, simply because the 'big brother', with his proven model of the Social Market Economy and its effective institutional setting, as well as his economic and financial resources, is missing. For the ambitious EC project of EMU the main lesson should be caution concerning preconditions and timing. If a common currency is created prematurely, before the necessary approximation in basic economic indicators among participating members has been reached, the loss of policy-adjustment options expressed via the exchange-rates will put a heavy burden on the economies with lower competitiveness. This will lead to demands for higher financial transfers and compensations. However, I seriously doubt that the population in the richer countries of the EC is ready to finance a much higher transfer to the poorer members. Even within Germany the transfer issue has been and still is politically sensitive. I cannot imagine the necessary political support for a similar transfer generally within the EC, at least in the near future. Another point has to be underlined: a common currency and a common, uniform monetary policy are only feasible in the perspective of a political integration which cannot lag too far behind it.

There is in my view one direct political link between German unification and the EC integration process. As the German government was ready to take a considerable risk in the shape of GEMSU, it is under pressure to take a certain risk in the shape of EMU, as well. I would guess that the German government in the end will bow to this pressure, although it is to be hoped that the institutional setting – the Bundesbank – and public opinion in Germany will manage to secure that the necessary compromise will not sacrifice monetary stability.

Notes

1. See Wilma Merkel and Stefanie Wahl, *Das geplünderte Deutschland. Die wirtschaftliche Entwicklung im östlichen Teil Deutschlands von 1949 bis 1989*, Bonn, 1991, p. 11.
2. For a detailed account of the monetary reform in East Germany see Deutsche Bundesbank, *Monatsberichte*, July 1990. Frankfurt am Main, 1990, pp. 14–29.
3. See for example Deutsches Institut für Wirtschaftsforschung (DIW)/ Institut für Weltwirtschaft an der Universität Kiel: *Gesamtwirtschaftliche und unternehmerische Anpassungsprozesse in Ostdeutschland, Bericht 1*, (Kiel Discussion Papers, 168), Kiel, 1991, p. 31.
4. See Sachverständigenrat zur Begutachtung der gesamtwirtschaftlichen Entwicklung, *Marktwirtschaftlichen Kurs halten. Zur Wirtschaftspolitik für die neuen Bundesländer*, n.p., 1991, p. 31. For a similar line of argument by the IMF staff see Leslie Lipschitz, 'Introduction and Overview', in Lipschitz, Leslie and McDonald, Donogh (eds.), *German Unification. Economic Issues*, Washington, DC, 1990, pp. 1–16. A critical position towards the recommendations of the Sachverständigenrat is taken by Arbeitsgruppe Alternative Wirtschaftspolitik, *Memorandum '91. Gegen Massenarbeitslosigkeit und Chaos – Aufbaupolitik in Ostdeutschland*, Cologne, 1991, pp. 194–205.
5. See Sachverständigenrat zur Begutachtung der gesamtwirtschaftlichen Entwicklung, *Marktwirtschaftlichen Kurs halten. Zur Wirtschaftspolitik für die neuen Bundesländer*, n.p., 1991, p. 31.
6. Ibid., p. 23.
7. See for example Frankfurter Institut für wirtschaftspolitische Forschung e.V., *Wirtschaftspolitik für das geeinte Deutschland*, (Schriftenreihe Band 22), Bad Homburg, 1990.
8. See Sachverständigenrat, *Marktwirtschaftlichen Kurs halten*, pp. 23–5.
9. See Helmut Schmidt, 'Uns Deutsche kann der Teufel holen. Was not tut, damit die Verschmelzung der Deutschen gelingt – ein Acht-Punkte-Programm', *Die Zeit*, No. 21, 17 May 1991. p. 3.
10. The Bundesbank, which has strongly demanded a far lower fiscal deficit in the medium term, has additionally emphasised the negative impact on its monetary policy. Deutsche Bundesbank, *Geschäftsbericht für das Jahr 1990*, Frankfurt am Main, 1991, p. 32.
11. For a recent discussion of the volume of subsidies and its potential for funding German integration see Deutsches Institut für Wirtschaftsforschung (DIW), 'Subventionsabbau als Instrument zur "Finanzierung" des deutschen Integrationsprozesses?', in *Wochenbericht*, 51/2, 1990, pp. 703–14.
12. The Bundesbank estimates that in 1990 the states *in toto* did profit

financially by German unification. See Deutsche Bundesbank, *Geschäfts-bericht 1990*, p. 28.

13. Paul R. Masson and Guy Meredith, 'Domestic and International Macroeconomic Consequences of German Unification', in Lipschitz, Leslie and McDonald, Donogh (eds.), *German Unification. Economic Issues*, Washington DC, 1990, p. 108.

BEATE NEUSS

The European Community: How to Counterbalance the Germans

The year 1990 marked the end of an epoch not only for Germany, but for Europe. Up to then, 'Europe' had become the designation for the countries in Western Europe, if not actually for the EC as a unit.[1] The changes in Eastern Europe place the task of creating the architecture of the whole continent in the hands of the Europeans. Since the crumbling of the Berlin Wall in November 1989 overall attention has been focused on Germany, whose behaviour was considered a crucial factor in the potential for success of the new structures.

The most important questions resulting from this upheaval are the following: How is Germany to be anchored in the West? How can it be kept from a policy of vacillation between West and East? And, last but not least, how can the balance of power be restored between the European nations?

It was not surprising that German unification in 1990 touched off some gloomy predictions about the German role in the future. In the first half of 1990, the newspapers were full of discussions of the supposed military strength of a united Germany – just as they had been forty years previously, when the subject had been the Western half of the then divided Germany. In the 'Two plus Four' negotiations Germany consented to reduce the numbers of its military forces to a modest 370,000. This voluntary surrender of military sovereignty – for that what it was – appeased most of its critics, but redirected attention to the more serious question of economic dominance.

136

The 'old' Federal Republic of Germany played an important role in Europe. In recent years, Germany was the world's largest trading nation, and even the *Land* of Bavaria ranked twelfth world-wide, a fact proudly proclaimed by its Prime Minister. Within the EC, the Federal Republic accounted for less than 19 per cent of the population, but contributed over 26 per cent of the EC's gross product.[2] The strength of Germany's economy led to the Deutsche Mark's world-wide adoption as a reserve currency. Europe became a D-mark zone.

Today Germany is the country with the largest population in Western Europe. With its 78 million inhabitants it comes second in Europe only to Russia. Germany always had comparatively strong trade relations with Eastern Europe. The 'new' Germany inherited the GDR's large-scale economic interchange with the East. It will be much in demand as a partner for the newly reformed Eastern and Russian states and the CIS.

Most analysts predict a harsh time for the German economy for some years to come, because of the burden of revitalising the run-down economy of the former GDR. But in about ten to fifteen years, after the development of a new *Wirtschaftswunder* the weight and therefore the influence of the German economy is expected to be larger than ever before. Does this mean that Nicholas Ridley, a member of Margaret Thatcher's cabinet, was right in his prediction that the EC will be taken over by the Germans?[3] How have the governments in the EC reacted to the new challenge?

The uneasiness about Germany's new role in Europe probably extended to every European capital. The catch-phrase 'Fourth Reich' enjoyed a brief popularity in the newspapers, although most governments were careful to express themselves in more neutral terms.

Paris obviously felt uncertain about its own position. In starting the *Entente Elementaire* with Bonn in the 1960s it had assumed itself to be the dominant partner. During the last two and a half decades it had taken the view that the Franco-German relationship was well balanced. While Germany's economy was weightier, France's political influence in international affairs and in the EC was stronger. As a permanent member of the UN Security Council, as a nuclear power, and as one of the four victorious countries of the Second World War it felt well able to cope with German strength. Today, the last two aspects have lost much of their significance or vanished altogether. With the centre of gravity of the EC moving eastward,

Paris is apprehensive that its role is becoming a marginal one. The French government has therefore had to begin rethinking its political strategy.

Thus in the first half of 1990 President Mitterrand was unsure how to react to the emerging new Germany. He tried various policies, but was wrong-footed by the dynamism and speed of international developments. First he tried to stabilise the GDR as a second German State, and then adopted a pincers policy, which led to his meeting with President Gorbachev in Kiev. Since last summer, however, the Franco-German axis seems to be restored.

Great Britain appeared to be caught even more off-balance than France. The former Prime Minister Margaret Thatcher had a hard time accepting the speed of German reunification. The findings of the Prime Minister's seminar at Chequers in March 1990, as they were summarised in the controversial report of one of her officials, as well as Mr Ridley's 'flattering' words about Germany, have to be taken seriously: they demonstrate how the shift in the balance of power in Europe, caused by German unification, was perceived by the British political élite. France, although probably holding similar views, showed more self-restraint.

Both these countries as well as the other EC members were therefore confronted with the same problem: to find means to neutralise German influence. Yet their answers were different – as could have been predicted from history. For ever since the late 1940s France and Great Britain have differed widely in their proposals for dealing with 'the powerhouse of Europe', as Dean Acheson dubbed their partner nation Germany as early as 1948.

Many aspects of the situation at that time were comparable to those of the present day. A new architecture for Europe had to be created. The United States, as the chief architect, sought for a structure 'in which Germany can be contained, in which Germany can play a peaceful, constructive, but not dictatorial role'.[4] They were convinced that 'there is no solution of the German problem in terms of Germany, there is only a solution in terms of Europe'.[5] Washington tried to foster European integration with the Marshall Plan and the OEEC. Secretary of State Dean Acheson painstakingly tried to persuade the British government to accept the leading role in integrating the Western half of Europe, since France was thought to be far too weak for that undertaking. London refused. So Washington reluctantly accepted that Great Britain was oriented towards its Commonwealth of Nations and the United States, with

Europe ranking only third. The United Kingdom saw in its special relationship with the United States a guarantee of a balance of power. Therefore Acheson concluded: 'The key to progress towards integration is in French hands ... Even with the closest possible relationship of the US and the UK to the continent, France and France alone can take the decisive leadership in integrating West Germany into Western Europe.'[6]

And France did accept this mandate, by proposing the Schuman Plan. Great Britain stayed away, anxious to maintain its sovereignty and only prepared to join after success had proved that it was not in its interest to stay out. The key to Monnet's concept was the demand for the surrender of sovereignty to a European institution before the start of negotiations. Pragmatic co-operation would not have resulted in the close, irrevocably linked community which is today's EC, but probably in a non-committal, weak organisation similar to the OEEC or the West European Union.

The concept of the European Community has indeed been able to weld together the core of Europe during the last forty years more than any of its founding fathers may have expected. And it was able to counterbalance Germany. Should not this remedy against German hegemony and European dissolution be tried again in the present situation?

It was Jacques Delors, the President of the EC Commission who first followed in Monnet's footsteps. He immediately attempted to anchor Germany in the EC. Only weeks after the iron curtain had gone up, he invited East Germany to join the EC as soon as possible, calling the GDR an 'exceptional case'. It would be accepted as a member, he said, irrespective of other countries' applying for membership. He argued that the GDR was 'part of the family'.[7] Of course, Mr Delors understood very well that the alternative could have been West Germany's breaking with the Community and searching for unity and national greatness outside the EC, dashing the once-stable European structure to pieces. He argued in February 1990, perceiving the trend towards unification, that there should not be two Germanies holding EC membership, but only a united one. Jacques Delors knew, of course, that at that time the East German state was already absolutely dependent on West German financial aid, and thus would only double the German weight in the EC's decision-making process.

At the same time the President of the Commission stepped up the timetable for integration. Jacques Delors fully understands that the

core of any national sovereignty is an autonomous monetary policy.
A monetary union and a single currency for Europe will bring about
a definitive and qualitative change in the present system of sovereign
states. At the Rome summit in October 1990 he was successful in
persuading all governments but Great Britain to agree to fix the
starting date for the second stage of European Monetary Union at
1994. In addition the Community members consented to establish
two intergovernmental conferences, one on Monetary Union and
one on *Political* Union. Until 1990 this term was taboo, and called
forth vehement opposition from Great Britain and others. Suddenly
it had become possible to call things by their proper names. Suddenly it even became necessary to press for reforms beyond the
single European Market. For the second time, Germany had been
the catalyst for European integration.

As far as the structure of the whole of Europe is concerned, Mr
Delors envisions a 'Europe of Concentric Circles'. The EC is to be
closely linked to the first circle, the European Free Trade Association. That organisation will be tied to the EC by a treaty concerning
a European Economic Space. The second circle, the reformed Eastern European countries, will be linked to the EC by individually
formulated treaties of association ('European Agreements'), with or
without the option of later membership. Countries with non-market
economies and with democratic regimes of doubtful character, such
as Bulgaria and Romania and Russia have the possibility of nego-
tiating trade and co-operation treaties with the EC, thus forming the
third circle.

So much for the far-reaching ideas of the EC Commission. What
about the member states?

The German government acted according to tradition. Bom-
barded by expressions of mistrust by its friends and neighbours from
the very first changes in Eastern Germany, it had recourse to Konrad Adenauer's policy of using integration as a means of reassuring
its partners. On 28 November 1989 Helmut Kohl declared in his
then-sensational Ten-Point Programme to overcome the division of
Germany: 'the development of inner-German relations remains an
integral part of the pan-European process . . . The future structure
of Germany must fit into the future of Europe as a whole. The
attraction and the image of the European Community is and remains a constant feature in the pan-European development. We
want to strengthen this further.'[8] And in summer 1990 he allowed
himself to be persuaded to fix the date for the second stage of

European Monetary Union (EMU), despite the warnings of Karl-Otto Pöhl, the powerful President of Germany's independent Bundesbank. As a return for his yielding on this issue Kohl proposed an acceleration of political integration as well.

At the time of the Dublin meeting of the European Council in June 1990 President Mitterrand had decided to continue along the tried-and-tested path of the Franco-German *Entente Elementaire* in the context of the EC. In Dublin 'Kohlerrand', as Kohl and Mitterrand are dubbed in Brussels, again put the EC on the road to further integration, as the two countries had done so often before. The decision to open two intergovernmental conferences, one on Monetary Union and one on Political Union, was an attempt by the EC members to counterbalance Germany by taking the all-in-all successful road of building an organised and integrated core within Europe.

Consensus on the general direction of the EC for the future, although not about the details involved, had been astonishingly broad in Dublin. The British Prime Minister, Mrs Thatcher, however, very much disliked the move toward closer European integration.[9] She tried to manage the new European situation by a traditional British approach. Afraid of a 'European super-state' she kept to her 'first guiding principle: . . . willing and active *co-operation* between independent sovereign states' as 'the best way to build a successful European Community'.[10] She saw no need to speed up integration. On the contrary: the democratic development in the East European states provided a welcome chance to invite those countries to join the EC. This policy, which bore the characteristics of the nineteenth century, although it was supposed to solve the problems of the twenty-first, reminds me of the British arguments rejecting the invitation to join a supranationally organised Europe in 1950 and 1955.

By enlarging the EC, Mrs Thatcher tried to kill two birds with one stone. First, Germany's relative weight in the bargaining processes of a Community with 15, 18 or even more members would be substantially reduced. Second, a European Community of this size, enlarged before it had been deepened, would not be the EC we know today. Its means of decision-making as well as its policies would be seriously disrupted by the divergency of its members. The wave of migration to Western Europe and the breakdown of the EC's financial system would necessarily destroy the EC. In this way the Community would probably be reduced to a kind of EFTA, possibly with a single European market, but without the EC's political implications. This position would be very much to the tastes of the former British Prime Minister and of the Tories' right wing.

The British Government could have achieved another aim in pursuing this policy, namely that of not surrendering any more sovereignty in any other area to Brussels. Although none of Britain's European partners is transferring sovereignty to the EC swiftly, London's obsession with this principle is not easily understood in continental Europe. Living so closely together, the other West European nations are well aware that the sovereignty of a nation state has become only relative in many aspects. It could, and can, no longer provide for the main objective, the security – and thus culture and wealth – of a people. From the beginning of European integration, the participating states saw their identities better served by transferring part of their sovereignties, which had become an empty shell, to European institutions.

The merely relative value of sovereignty as a principle is most obvious in questions of environmental protection, drug traffic, and international terrorism. Even in the realm of economic and monetary policy governments are being shorn of the power to set their own rules. Margaret Thatcher used to equate sovereignty with the national identity of a people. Germans, with their experience of a federal state and with a kind of hierarchy of identities, have no problems in being for instance Bavarian, German and European. Usually, they do not feel schizophrenic in the least.

The United Kingdom has since acquired a new government. Is its attitude towards Europe different? John Major got a warm welcome at the Rome summit in December 1990. It was the first time in a long while that the United Kingdom was not singled out for condemnation. Mr Major's colleagues certainly appreciate his less rigorous style. But whether his position is much different from that of his predecessor remains to be seen. Shortly after taking office he declared, according to *The Economist*, that 'there is no need to surrender any more sovereignty to Europe' and he 'also shares Mrs Thatcher's views that extra countries should rapidly be recruited to the European Community, so slowing the momentum for a federal union'.[11] It is still too early to assess his policy. In any case, the new Prime Minister needs time to bring the right wing of the Conservative Party to a more relaxed attitude towards Europe. The progress made in the intergovernmental conferences will indicate the British government's stance.

These, then, are the two main possibilities for further development in Europe: the continental one which seeks to provide an anchor for Germany and for Eastern Europe by further integrating the community economically as well as politically; and the British one, which tries to counterbalance German influence by close intergovernmental co-operation among all democratic European states.

Certainly, both routes lead to a balance of power. One does it by reducing the significance of national states, though without eliminating them. It has created a remarkable stability. The other route, traditional, but often leading to uncertainly and instability, has not exactly been a success story hitherto. Thus one has to ask which of the two concepts is more appropriate in dealing with the German problem, with the European situation in the aftermath of the cold war, and with the economic challenges of the present time?

The majority of EC members have their courses set towards integration. They agree that any move in the direction of a more federal Europe helps to create a viable, vigorous economy. They agree that the lack of a single currency is the ultimate barrier to the Single Market. And they share the view that the Eastern European countries are better served by providing a stable core to which they can hold fast than by a more loosely organised Europe. And they are obviously convinced that a Europe based primarily on intergovernmental structures, with most of the sovereignty resting with the nation states, would make Germany the dominant power in Eastern Europe – because of its geographic situation and its economic strength. Then, and only then, would Mr Ridley be right: Germany would become the new leading power of Europe.

Therefore, in December 1990 the European heads of states and governments agreed on guide-lines for two intergovernmental conferences which started work in Rome on 15 December 1990. These conferences will reconfigure the power within the Community in the direction of a more federal structure. This will help to prevent German hegemony.

The conference on monetary union is well prepared, and is certain to result in a treaty in 1991. Unless its outcome experiences the same fate as earlier plans for monetary union did in the 1970s, Europe will enter the second stage of the EMU in 1994. Now, as a member of the European exchange-rate mechanism, Great Britain has a far better chance of influencing the negotiations than before. The future alone will show whether or not Britain's entry into the system was a means to slow down the process. The Bundesbank will certainly be the model for a European Central Bank, and monetary stability will be its prime task; but this will probably not be given as clear a priority as it has been in Germany. Whether Mr Major's plan for a 'hard ECU' as a thirteenth currency will be included remains to be seen. Although the British Prime Minister's concept is widely criticised by central bankers as impracticable, the prejudice that the 'hard ECU' is only a political instrument to avoid monetary union altogether has disappeared.

The differences between the British concept and the continental European proposals have some similarities to those concerning the Schuman Plan and the foundation of the EEC. The continental Europeans set the final goal – in this case monetary union – and then ask how to get there. This has been the underlying pattern of the process of European integration: the development of the EC has been charted by *political* decisions, and the economy was then called upon to find adequate ways of achieving those goals. Great Britain, however, would prefer to enhance economic convergence in the EC without prejudging the final goal, as had been the case in past decades.[12] Of course the EMU means a merging of sovereignties. But 'in respect to EMU sovereignty means the right to let the currency inflate', which is not an appropriate policy goal in any case.[13] Eleven members of the EC consider monetary union to be a more successful method of reducing the predominance of the Bundesbank: Germany will no longer be able to pursue its own objectives independent of external constraints. This would be a far less certain result with the open-ended approach of the British Government.

In Spring 1991 the outcome of the negotiations on political union was harder to predict because of the awkwardly large number of proposals on the table. Before 15 January the outlook for a *European* foreign policy was quite good. In Dublin the European Council decided to move on from primarily economic integration and from mere intergovernmental co-operation on foreign-policy issues to-wards a political union, including a common foreign and security policy.[14] The intergovernmental conference in Rome will have to talk about the different options of making the EC's foreign policy more efficient, either by improving its existing intergovernmental structure, by integrating it into the EC's policy-making process, or – most probably – by finding a symbiosis between the EPC (European Political Cooperation) and EC mechanisms.[15]

There is no question that it is necessary to adapt to Europe's new situation. And there is also a definite need for a common security policy. It is quite obvious that the US military presence will be drastically reduced by the end of 1991. Neither soldiers nor equipment withdrawn for the Gulf War will be restationed in Europe. Germany will come under strong political pressure from Russia, as Moscow certainly expects Bonn to demonstrate its gratitude to the Kremlin for a long time to come.

Not only Germany but Europe too has to look after itself more, to take more care of the new democracies in the East and the stability of its hinterland. These problems cannot be solved by the nation states themselves unless Europe wishes to run the risk that the pressures – for instance in the case of Germany – or the immensity of the tasks involved might result in severe damage to European stability and indeed to the very fabric of the European institutions.

Moreover, the war with Iraq showed the necessity for Europeans to participate in defending their interests with both political and military means. The Franco-German proposal for a political union seeks to link the EC to the West European Union until 1996, as a European pillar inside Nato.[16] Kohl and Mitterrand are obviously thinking about incorporating article 5 of the West European Union into the EC treaty. In December 1990 the United States also signalled its interest in these ideas.

But the first casualty of the Gulf War was the idea that the European Community could act as a unified power. Indeed the behaviour of the European governments differed widely. On 2 August Margaret Thatcher found herself at the side of George Bush in Aspen, Colorado. It was a welcome opportunity to prove that Great Britain is still America's staunchest ally and that it still makes sense for the United States to care for special relationship with Great Britain. France, on the contrary, offered peace proposals until the clock struck twelve on 15 January.

Germany reacted like a larger version of Switzerland, although Chancellor Kohl had promised on the eve of German unification that the new Germany would live up to its responsibilities. But this was soon forgotten. Germany was occupied with organising its first all-German elections, and then with the difficult task of forming a new government. Bonn had obviously ruled out the possibility of war. It remained silent during the first days of the war, and left all the arguments to be developed by the peace movement on the streets. The Chancellor and his Foreign Minister Genscher

worsened the situation when they allowed a discussion to begin on
Bonn's pre-conditions for defending their fellow NATO member
Turkey. Any action both before and after 15 January was taken
under pressure from abroad.

Criticism from Britain and America was very strong. Both
countries seem to have expected that – less than half a year after
unification – Germany would behave as normally as any state of
that size. This could clearly not be the case. Firstly, the weight and
the responsibility of a united Germany is not yet on the mental
maps of its politicians and citizens. Secondly, Charles Krauthammer's argument concerning the United States seems to fit Germany as well: 'Except for revolution, nothing changes a country
more than war. Great wars define the psyche and sensibilities of a
people for decades.'[17] Germany has started two wars during this
century. Neither war can be described as 'just'. The enormous loss
of life, the air-raids and the destruction of the last one still persist in
the collective memory. The war was lost, and Germany was divided
and re-educated. In mid-1990 Germany's neighbours feared unity
would revive its belligerence. For better or worse the Germans
have proved otherwise. Re-education had been unexpectedly
successful. Yet then as now, Germany was seen as a threat, then for
its presumed bellicosity, and now for its presumed pacifism. The
cheque-book politics of the united Germany were vilified and
scorned.

The British government sees in the Community's ineffectual
answer to the Gulf War, and in German behaviour especially, proof
that the EC is not ready for a common foreign policy. The intensity
of British criticism – there was virtually none from France or the
other countries – gives the impression that recent German policy is a
welcome excuse to block progress towards a more supranationally
organised foreign policy, or indeed towards political union
altogether. Instead, the pitiful result of the EPC in the Iraq crisis has
to be taken as a challenge to develop a more coherent European
foreign policy. The EC was pushed ahead not exactly because
everything was moving smoothly, but because shortcomings had to
be acknowledged. International situations demonstrating Europe's
powerlessness have often borne fruit – the list is an extensive one.

And the EC cannot afford the aloofness of its largest member
state, nor this state's decision to go its own way, which could be
damaging to European interests. The present German government
is not interested in a *Sonderweg* (separate path), either in economics

or in foreign policy. It knows what the long-term price of such a move would be.

Another important question concerning the intergovernmental conference on political union in Rome is the transformation of the institutional system. The reform will not result in a greater role for the new Germany, as the weight of the German vote in the Council of Ministers will not be changed. The 'Big Three', Great Britain, France and Germany, want to increase the impact of the European Council, although Italy and the smaller countries prefer to see the Commission and the European Parliament taking a larger role. This would reduce the weight of the larger countries – Germany included. Jacques Delors proposed to reduce the Commission to only one member per country; but the new tasks of the EC are not consistent with a reduction in the number of members. Only for the European Parliament is a more proportional distribution of seats under discussion. But this also would not result in German predominance, because of a non-proportional distribution of seats to smaller countries.

If the EC is to accept the bolder but more forward-looking alternative of deepening integration first and enlarging the Community later, it will have to keep its structure flexible. It is counterproductive to force Great Britain and other more reluctant partners into a political and economic structure they are not able to tolerate. Far from being an appropriate means of keeping organisations or states together, pressure is rather a way of driving them apart. Enlightened self-interest, which brought the EC together, was the driving force behind the EC's development, not compulsion.

Considering some of the EC members – neutral Ireland for instance, and Austria, a probable new member – membership in the West European Union poses a problem. The same sort of problems may arise with a full membership of Great Britain, Greece and Portugal in the EMU. Therefore the EC will not only have to fix the principle of subsidiarity in the new treaty – a German principle which is much-loved in the United Kingdom – but also leave chances open for opting-out on special issues and under prescribed conditions. The EC in the future will be as it has indeed been since 1973: a two-track community.

The EC should be flexible enough to be open to co-operation with the Eastern European countries, not in political core issues, but in spheres of minor importance which nevertheless will accustom them to the style and procedures of West European politics. Suitable areas for participation would be technological research projects, environmental policy, etc. – all those EC programmes which today already include West European non-EC members. A good example for a specially shaped programme helping Eastern Europe to close ranks with the West is PHARE. It provides financial and technological aid for the transformation of the former socialist economies.

Majority voting wherever possible, opting-out where absolutely necessary: this should be in the enlightened self-interest of the EC. But no country should have the chance to block the overall development against the will of the majority. Margaret Thatcher was adamant in her: 'No, no, no.' John Major does not want to isolate his country. And Great Britain's full participation is necessary to counterbalance the Franco-German special relationship. Britain contributed immensely to the Single Market programme and to the reform of the agricultural policy, and it will make substantial contributions in the future. But Great Britain has to understand that the EC is an undertaking which, from the very beginning, meant far more than mere economic integration.

Western Europe seems to be heading for a thorough reform of the EC to counterbalance Germany and to prepare for the challenges ahead. The process towards integration will be as messy as ever, with no final date ahead. But the increasing importance of informal flows of people and goods, of similar economic and social trends is transforming the shape of Western Europe, with Germany as a catalyst and Eastern Europe dragged along in its wake. Opinion polls in the EC have shown a significant shift in the attitude towards Europe during the last decades, both in Great Britain and elsewhere.[18] Politics will have to adjust to transformations already taking place.[19] Europe's manifest destiny is integration.

Notes

1. William Wallace, *The Transformation of Western Europe* London, 1990.
2. Europäische Gemeinschaft, *Eurostat, Statistische Grundzahlen der Gemeinschaft*, Luxemburg, 1990.
3. For Mr Ridley, economic and monetary union was 'a German racket designed to take over the whole of Europe' with the French 'behaving

like poodles to the Germans'. Interview given to *The Spectator* on 1 July 1990. Quotation according to *Newsweek*, 23 July 1990.

4. Memorandum prepared in the Bureau of German Affairs, 11 February 1950, in *Foreign Relations of the United States* (FRUS), 1950, Vol. IV, pp. 597–602.

5. Kennan Paper, 8 March 1949, in *FRUS* 1949, Vol. III, p. 87.

6. The Secretary of State to the Embassy in France, 19 October 1949, in *FRUS* 1949, Vol. IV, p. 471.

7. Kommission der Europäischen Gemeinschaft, *EG-Informationen* (DDR Extra), No. 12, March 1990.

8. 'Overcoming the Division', in *Europäische Zeitung*, December 1989, p. IV (official translation).

9. 'Thatcher vs. Europe', in *The Economist*, 3 November 1990.

10. Speech by Margaret Thatcher on Europe, in Bruges, 20 September 1988.

11. 'Changing Tracks with Mr Major', in *The Economist*, 8 December 1990.

12. Speech given by the Rt. Hon. Robin Leigh-Pemberton, Governor of the Bank of England, at the Deutsche Bank/ECU Banking Association Conference in Berlin, on 13 October 1990.

13. 'Going for it', in *The Economist*, 13 October 1990.

14. Resumé of the European Council, 25–6 June 1990, in *EG-Nachrichten*, p. 10, 29 June 1990.

15. For detailed evaluation of the possibilities, cf. Elfriede Regelsberger, 'Von der politischen Zusammenarbeit zur Vergemeinschaftung. Reformvorschläge für die EPZ', in *Integration* 4/90, pp. 179–99.

16. Message of President Mitterrand and Chancellor Kohl to the Acting President of the European Council, Charles Haughey, 18 April 1990, in *Europa-Archiv* (EA) 11/1990, Vol. 45, p. D283; Message of President Mitterrand and Chancellor Kohl to the President of the European Council, Giulio Andreotti, 6 December 1990, in *EA* 1/1991, Vol. 46, pp. D25–27.

17. Charles Krauthammer, 'How the war can change America', in *Time* (International), 28 January 1990.

18. Remarkably, 70 per cent are for European integration, and of those 13 per cent for total integration. Kommission der Europäischen Gemeinschaft, *Eurobarometer*, No. 33, June 1990, Vols. I and II, Brussels, 1990.

19. William Wallace, *The Transformation of Western Europe*. London, 1990.

MICHAEL WOLFFSOHN

Fear of Germany and Security for Europe

Fear of Germany and security for Europe – a double topic for endless discussion and debate. In an attempt to impose some limits, I shall concentrate on a socio-political approach supported by data from public opinion surveys, assessing the latter in their historical context. But first it is necessary to identify the institutional framework of security policy.

A. The Institutional and Empirical Approach

I. *Security Issues*

Existing Structures German reunification has long been the object of limitless speculation. Not least prominent among the anxiously posed questions have been these: 'Will Germany once again seek to set its own particular course? Will Germany abandon the Western alliance?'

Such fears have not been entirely without foundation – and they are certainly nothing new. In the late fifties, Karl. W. Deutsch and Lewis Edinger found that the preference of a substantial portion of the West German electorate was for neutrality in foreign relations under the military protection of the United States.[1] Apart from certain cyclical deviations, nearly all subsequent public opinion surveys have shown that a relatively stable 30 to 40 per cent of public opinion in West Germany has favoured in principle this alchemist's prescription for neutrality and security.[2]

Its supporters were not limited to the old–new rightist fringe, or to the Greens and leftist Social Democrats. Among CDU/CSU voters, about a third were also in favour of the principle of neutrality. Nevertheless, at least in West Germany, and, again, with the exception of cyclical deviations, both before and since reunification a broad consensus has prevailed with regard to the second-best solution: NATO membership. And that only the USA can be counted on for military support in an emergency was once again demonstrated by the Gulf War. Recent polls confirm that this consensus still obtains. In the autumn of 1990 67 per cent of the Germans surveyed were in favour of German membership in NATO. According to party preference, 85 per cent of the supporters of the CDU/CSU, 83 per cent of the Free Democrats, and 58 per cent of the Social Democrats, but only 33 per cent of the Greens were for NATO membership.[3]

Those belonging to the third of public opinion favouring neutrality can certainly be counted on to make use of every opportunity to press for their own agenda, but their chances for success remain minimal, as the overwhelming majority of the political élite does not share their position – the sole exceptions being the Greens, whose influence is confined to that of a junior coalition partner to the SPD in state governments, and the rapidly declining PDS, the successor organisation to the former East German Socialist Unity Party.

Considerably more West Germans than East Germans were convinced of the necessity of the NATO alliance. In September 1990 64 per cent of the West Germans, but only 31 per cent of the East Germans polled considered NATO 'necessary'.[4]

Neutralism would not only be tantamount to political and military suicide for Germany, it would also be economically foolish, as it would only rekindle a mistrust (but not fear!) of Germany that is structurally inherent and cannot be expected to disappear in the near future. The decision to purchase products from abroad is not determined by the quality of the goods alone. It also involves a political–psychological dimension. Goods 'Made in Germany' are popular not only for their quality, but also because the new (West) Germany has gained respect and popularity. The most recent case in point: in early 1991 BMW chairman von Kuenheim deplored the dramatic drop in BMW sales in the USA. The reasons, according to von Kuenheim, were not purely economic in nature.

The public discussion within Germany both before and since

reunification has once again demonstrated that the Germans would prefer to slip into the role of *Homos oeconomicus*. They will thus adjust their political course according to the prevailing trade winds. Thus: no cause to fear Germany!

Completely apart from this, the newly united Germany in its now 'definitive borders' in accordance with Article 1/1 of the 'Two-Plus-Four' treaty is firmly anchored within the NATO alliance. Article six of that treaty specifically provides for the right of a united Germany to belong to alliances, with all consequent rights and obligations. In other words: the Federal Republic of Germany was a member of NATO. In compliance with the provisions of Article 23 of the West German constitution, the GDR joined the Federal Republic, which remains in NATO. The united Germany thus also belongs to the alliance. And the United States remains a part of the European security system, simultaneously providing both guarantees and checks. In a period of uncertainty with regard to the future course of the CIS, this is of no small consequence for Germany, for Europe, for the USA and for the world at large. The former Soviet Union may have arrived at an economic dead end, but it remains a nuclear power – and as such its behaviour is less predictable today than was the case two years ago.

In Article 1/3 of the 'Two-Plus-Four' treaty, Germany declares that it has 'no territorial claims against other states and will not raise such claims in the future'. Well before reunification, the pledge that 'only peace will originate on German territory' belonged to the standard bromides of political speechmaking in Germany. Article two of the treaty raises this prescription to the sanctity of international law. What is more, Article two also provides that it is 'unconstitutional' and a punishable offense for Germany to 'disturb' the peaceful coexistence of the peoples, especially to make preparations for an offensive war. As the doctor and liberal German politician Rudolf Virchow said (and Lenin later repeated), 'Trust is good, controls are better.' Following this principle, the united Germany has renounced the 'production and possession of and the control over atomic, biological and chemical weapons' (Article 3/1) and has pledged to dramatically reduce the manpower of its armed forces to 370,000 (Article 3/2).

Futurology: NATO, WEU or Neutrality? Western Europeans in general, most especially the French, but also the Germans, want to strengthen the 'European pillar' of their security policy. Within the framework of the WEU they are striving for a closer and more intensive European 'identity' in foreign, security and defence policy. It can hardly be denied that France is thus pursuing late- or post-Gaullist ideals. And it is hardly surprising that Great Britain is resisting such tendencies, as are also the Netherlands, Portugal and Denmark. These countries fear that the NATO alliance may be thrown out of balance. The United States also remains sceptical. While the one side speaks of building a 'bridge between the EC and NATO' the other warns against 'hollowing out' the NATO alliance.

This is certainly a most interesting discussion. If we, however, consider the willingness of West Europeans and their governments (with the exception of Great Britain and, perhaps to a lesser extent, France) to follow up their words with actions, for example in the Gulf War, we find we are left with a largely theoretical tug-of-war. If military security is to be maintained and guaranteed, then any European security system without ties to the United States can only be highly insecure. This is a decision currently being faced not by the Germans alone, but by all members of the WEU.

B. The Historical and Socio-Political Approach*

II. Fight for Germany?

There is no reason to fear the armed forces of the united Germany. The goal of the integration of the German armed forces into a larger political-military framework was not and is not controversial. Nevertheless, in October 1977 a significant minority of public opinion abroad regarded the German military with suspicion. The sceptics were a majority of 51 per cent in Sweden, and numbered 41 per cent in Denmark, 40 per cent in Greece, 34 per cent in the Netherlands, 33 per cent in France, 28 per cent in Great Britain, 22 per cent in the USA and 21 per cent in Italy.

And the percentage of those who did not express reservations? They came to 51 per cent in the USA, 47 per cent in the Netherlands, 46 per cent in Great Britain, 30 per cent in Denmark and France, 24 per cent in Italy, 22 per cent in Sweden and 16 per cent in Greece.[5]

---

* Some parts of this section of the original lecture dealing with personalities have been omitted by the editors.

In early 1990 more than a third of the Dutch parliamentarians (36 per cent) would not discount the possibility that a united Germany might become 'militarily expansionist'.[6]

'Israelis, and not only Israelis, are worried about the possible rebirth of German military power.' Readers in Germany found this statement in their papers on 26 June 1990. In the same newspaper the same day they could also read: 'Armed forces not attractive for volunteers. Manpower replacement in 1990 seriously endangered. . . . The numbers for 1990 show the steepest drop of the last five years.' Is this the 'increasing nationalism' that critics believe to have been observed in both parts of Germany since late 1989?

Even before the German October Revolution, the willingness of Germans to serve in their armed forces was at an extraordinarily low level in international comparisons. In the context of the 'International Value Survey' in 1981–2 leading public opinion research institutes in various countries posed the following questions: 'We all hope that there will never be another war. But if it ever comes to a war, would you be prepared to fight for your country?' In the Federal Republic of Germany only 35 per cent responded that they were prepared to fight, but in Sweden it was 78 per cent, in the USA 69 per cent, in Great Britain 62 per cent, in the Netherlands 44 per cent and in France 42 per cent. Only in Italy (28 per cent) and Belgium (25 per cent) was less willingness to defend one's country registered.[7]

By the summer of 1989 the will to fight had declined even further among West Germans: only 15 per cent were willing to defend their country without reservation; another 36 per cent were prepared to do so under certain conditions.[8] At the same time, 77 per cent in the United States, 63 per cent in the Soviet Union, 49 per cent in Great Britain and 41 per cent in France said 'yes' without reservations.[9]

In almost all the former Allies of the Second World War, in the summer of 1989 as well as in earlier polls, the willingness to fight for one's country was consistently higher than in the nations that had been on the losing side. The one exception was Italy, where 34 per cent were prepared to 'fight for their country' in the summer of 1989. In Japan only 6 per cent were willing, and only 17 per cent in Austria. Japan and (West) Germany stood at the bottom of the list of 32 countries in which the survey was conducted[10] – an important finding.

Similarly, in November 1989 only 58 per cent of those polled in (West) Germany and a mere 55 per cent in Italy agreed to the 'necessity of a strong national defence force'. Only in Belgium (43 per cent) and in the Netherlands (48 per cent) were the percentages lower. Greece was the leader with 90 per cent, followed by Great Britain with 81 per cent and France with 72 per cent. The EC average was 65 per cent.[11]

There is no need to fear the Germans and their military. Indeed, there is every reason to fear *for* the German military, as a state without armed forces is subject to blackmail and thus virtually unable to conduct policy. Defence preparedness among the people of Germany is significantly lower than in other countries. One may applaud or regret this, but the fact is that talk of a resurrected German military power is groundless. The fact that the number of conscientious objectors to military service reached record levels during the Gulf War once again demonstrated the new-German aversion to the use of force in international relations. Need we fear these Germans?

How 'militaristic' is the political leadership of the new Germany? The title of the first democratically legitimate chief of the 'National People's Army' of the GDR, Pastor Eppelmann, was not 'Minister of Defence' but 'Minister of Disarmament and Defence'. Eppelmann had never served in the military, and, according to Martin Walser, was a 'practising pacifist'.

In July 1990 the government of West Germany decided to reduce the period of compulsory military service from 15 to 12 months, and to trim 3 per cent from the defence budget. The SPD opposition labelled the planning of the defence budget a 'numbers trick'. Perhaps it was. But that the government felt it necessary to employ such a 'trick' would only prove that, in the new Germany, in contrast to the old, more military means fewer votes. Militarism?

III. The German Hun as Softy

The German Reich aspired to rank among the Great Powers; during the reign of the Kaiser Germans spoke of a 'place in the sun'; the Weimar Republic was revisionist through and through; and Hitler wanted to rule the world. The drum-thumping, sabre-rattling aggressive and destructive foreign policy of a would-be superpower made Germany unpopular, to say the least. A foreign policy eschewing the use of force as an instrument of international relations has made the new German middle-size power welcome and popular in the world community. There is nothing to indicate that a united Germany intends to change anything about this approach.

The renunciation of violence has been so internalised by West Germany's society and polity that Bonn political scientist and historian Hans-Peter Schwarz quite accurately speaks of Germany's switching from a mode of *Machtversessenheit* to one of *Machtvergessenheit*, which can be roughly translated as switching from the aberration to the abjuration of power. It may be naïve to abjure the use of power, but 'after Auschwitz' it certainly gains sympathy. We are now witnessing the same process among the former East Germans. Their motives and convictions are obvious: the East German Revolution of 1989 was a gentle revolution. And it was successful – first and foremost *because* it was gentle.

The defensive posture of German foreign policy was, as we all know, not entirely voluntary. It was insisted on by the victorious Allies and written into Germany's constitution. The re-education of the Germans has now achieved its goal, but the former teacher, Uncle Sam, has not always been pleased with his model pupil. After 1945 the Germans were required to forswear the politics of force. Now they do so of their own free will. The result has led to frictions under Presidents Carter, Reagan and Bush.

Let us recall some of the irritations. First came the controversy concerning the proposed construction and deployment of the neutron bomb, beginning in 1977. Jimmy Carter was in favour; the West German public (and not just the 'peace movement') resisted. In 1979–80 Western oil supplies appeared endangered. Iran threatened to close off the Straits of Hormuz and thus the greater part of Middle Eastern oil exports. President Carter proposed the creation of an international fleet to secure the Persian Gulf and thus the flow of oil. West German navy vessels were to participate. A similar plan was proposed by President Reagan in 1987–8. The West German government was not even prepared to dispatch minesweepers in order to protect shipping in the Gulf.

'Germans to the Gulf?' was the question debated anxiously in Germany, and a resounding 'No, thank you!' was the answer given first by Chancellor Helmut Schmidt and later by Chancellor Helmut Kohl. In both cases the decisions of the government were supported by the opposition and by public opinion. The United States government and public were piqued: their view was that Germany's behaviour as an ally of the USA was anything but partner-like. Moreover, following the imposition of a US trade embargo on Iran,

West Germany profited from the consequences: West German trade with Iran grew by leaps and bounds.

For the West Germans it became even more evident: the abjuration of military power pays – quite literally – whereas the use of power is costly. In the summer of 1988 Washington pressured the Federal Republic to agree to participate in a proposed UN peacekeeping force that was to secure the fragile truce between Iran and Iraq. Bonn's reply was no different than before: the West German constitution prohibits the use of German armed forces outside the NATO region. In 1989 Bonn and Washington argued over the stationing of modernised short-range missiles in Germany. Bonn was opposed. For a time the German October Revolution appeared to end the controversy, as no one wanted to point new Western rockets at the new East Germany and the new Eastern Europe.

A short while later the crisis and war in the Persian Gulf once again illustrated lack of German–American synchronisation, this time in even sharper contours. Up until (and also after) the outbreak of hostilities, a large portion of the German public opposed the use of force, 'for historical reasons' it was argued. These Germans referred to the actual or perceived lessons of the years 1939 to 1945, the Second World War and the Holocaust. They did not (or did not want to) recognise that the Western powers, and the United States in particular, were also drawing upon the lessons of history. Their considerations, however, were guided not only by the history of the Second World War but also of the period immediately preceding that war: the years 1938–9, the era of appeasement, the Conference at Munich, the dismemberment and eradication of Czechoslovakia. Both sides, Germans and Americans, were thinking in terms of *Realpolitik* as well as in moral categories; but the actions, reactions, intentions and reflections of each side were centred on their own particular historical trauma.

Even before the gentle revolution of 1989 there was an element of the grotesque in the American irritations with Germany. That the one-time German Hun had turned into a softy was the result of Uncle Sam's own efforts. The re-education of Germany was necessary and right, and those who promoted it after 1945 were in no position to have their complaints about the results taken seriously. In the 1970s and 1980s the fruits of this re-education had a bitter aftertaste for the American teacher; but for the German pupil they were a sweet delight.

After 1945 the goal was to build a new Germany. And in fact, a

new, and most particularly a non-aggressive Germany was created.
Have the Germans learned their lessons too well? In the summer of
1989 this appeared to be the case. The same can be said of the
reactions of the German public and government to the Gulf crisis in
1990–1. The lessons of the past do not always prove an accurate
guide to mastering the present and the future.

IV.   Who is Afraid of a United Germany?

The World?   The division of Germany after the Second World War
had to do with more than the simple division of the world into an
eastern, Soviet-dominated and a Western, American-dominated
sphere of influence. The division of Germany was in accordance
with the will of all the victor nations. The Anglo-Saxon countries,
and certainly France, were, as Andreas Hillgruber observed, determined 'to prevent Germany from once again presenting a danger to
the peace of Europe and the world, and to carry out the struggle
against the national-socialist and "militaristic" Reich not only to its
military but also its political capitulation'.[12] For the Soviet Union
the advance of the Red Army into Central Europe was intended
permanently to remove the danger of a recurrence of the kind of
Soviet vulnerability that brought the country to the brink of collapse
in 1941.[13]

In contrast to what happened in 1918–19, the victorious Allied
Powers succeeded in 1945 in creating a buffer zone in Central
Europe between the two rival spheres of influence. This arrangement was similar to the European order prevailing between 1815
and 1866–71, that is between the Congress of Vienna and Bismarck's unification of Germany.[14] In terms of power politics this
could be interpreted as an attempt to restore a modified version of
an earlier, pre-Napoleonic constellation in Central Europe, in which
the Holy Roman Empire, with no significant political weight of its
own, served in an important role as a buffer between the Great
Powers in Western and Eastern Europe.[15]

In attempting to subjugate ever larger slices of Europe militarily,
Hitler sought to alter Germany's geographic position in the centre of
the continent. Politically, he was unable to change Germany's position. After conquests in all directions, Germany once again found
itself surrounded by alien and alienated states. Hitler had succeeded
in turning competitors and even friends into enemies of Germany.

The situation of a country caught in the middle is certainly not unique to Germany. Even nations located in geographical extremities can end up in the middle: Korea, for example. The Korean peninsula has always been in the middle between China and Japan. For various reasons, Korea has, in general, assumed a defensive posture, to which Germany's offensive reactions in the twentieth century present a sharp contrast. Hitler was not the sole reason for the desire after 1945 to get Central Europe, Germany, back under control, as it had been for centuries. In this context the role of Hitler is often overestimated.

The Postwar Order   Even a (true or presumed) 'cold warrior' such as President Eisenhower's Secretary of State, John Foster Dulles, stated as late as 1952 his preference for a sovietised over a neutral Germany. Dulles once told Willy Brandt that, despite all the outstanding differences between the USA and the USSR, there was one common interest: to prevent Germany from attaining a position in which it could, as a neutral, independent and armed power, act as a loose cannon between the front lines.[16]

With an almost brutal candour Henry Kissinger wrote of the presumed necessity of the division of Germany. Kissinger argued that the Soviet Union had forced a communist regime upon the eastern third of the country, that it was absurd for the community of nations to accept, even support, the imposition of a regime against the will of the people, particularly in Central Europe, the birthplace of nationalism. The same sort of 'imperialism', wrote Kissinger, would have led to angry protest and demonstrations in Asia or Africa, whereas it was commonly viewed as a sign of reasonableness to accept the status quo in Central Europe. Kissinger observed that the Western Allies had decided against assuming any significant risks for the sake of German reunification, in part also because the prospect of a reunified Germany stirred fears of a potential German hegemony among many Western Europeans and Americans.[17]

The most effective means to guard against unilateral moves on the part of Germany was Berlin – for all four Allied powers, as Kissinger noted elsewhere in his memoirs. The prime concern of the post-war order in Europe and most especially in Germany was stability, not justice.

Reunification: 'No, thank you'?   When Kissinger described Western reservations with regard to German reunification he was expressing the will and the opinion of the politicians. Where did international public opinion stand? And how did Germans perceive international public opinion?

In 1964 60 per cent of the French considered the division of Germany 'desirable'.[18] In 1979 36 per cent of those polled were still of the opinion that a reunited Germany represented a threat to the peace; 33 per cent did not respond; and only 31 per cent would have welcomed unification as a 'chance for peace'.[19]

Five years later, in 1984, 25 per cent continued to reject German unification and 32 per cent were undecided, but fewer than half of the French, namely 43 per cent, were in favour. However, 50 per cent of the interviewees under the age of thirty were in favour of unification, in contrast to only 29 per cent of those over the age of sixty.[20]

In a survey also conducted in early 1984 in the United States, slightly more than half of the respondents, 54 per cent, viewed German unification favourably. This was just 3 per cent more than in Great Britain, where 51 per cent said they were for reunification.[21]

In general the responses tended to be less than enthusiastic, but cannot be interpreted as rejectionist. The exception was Poland, where, in October 1987, 27 per cent were for and 47 per cent against the unification of Germany.

As is so often the case, the answers depended on how the question was put. 'Reunification by peaceful means' received high approval ratings: 87 per cent in Sweden in 1977, 72 per cent in the Netherlands, 66 per cent in Great Britain and Greece, 65 per cent in the USA, 64 per cent in Denmark, 58 per cent in France and 49 per cent in Italy.[22]

Even the results in the Netherlands and Italy should not really come as a surprise. Public opinion in the Netherlands with regard to Germany has long been more positive than is generally assumed. It is well known that in Italy the myth of the *resistenza* cloaks the fascist past.

The decisive conclusion: With regard to peaceful reunification, public opinion abroad has been surprisingly positive for a surprisingly long time.

How do the (West) Germans regard public opinion towards reunification in other countries? How did they answer the question posed by the Allensbach Institute: 'Do you believe that America (England/Italy/France) is in favour of German reunification or not?'

In 1967 only 39 per cent of the West Germans polled believed that Americans were for unification, and in 1969 it was only 37 per cent.[23]

The attitude of the French was believed to be even more sceptical. In 1967 only 20 per cent of the West Germans thought that the French were for reunification. By 1969 the proportion of optimists had risen to 28 per cent.

Despite a basic scepticism, there was a slightly more optimistic view of the British. In 1967 25 per cent believed that the English favoured unification, and 32 per cent in 1969.

Not without foundation was the growing doubt with regard to Italy. In 1967 only 22 per cent thought that the Italians were for German unification, and by 1969 only 20 per cent expressed this opinion.[24]

As Wolfgang Bergsdorf aptly summarised it: 'Germans felt abandoned by their allies with regard to reunification – and this despite actual attitudes.'[25]

No fear of Germany! Not even of a reunited Germany. That is the view of public opinion outside Germany. What is more, the (East) German revolution further reduced the already minimal residue of fear in most other countries. The actual image of the Germany of the Gentle Revolution, and not the old caricatures of foreign and domestic opinion-manipulators is what has influenced public opinion. The manipulators of opinion do not necessarily prove to be the moulders of opinion. There are, nevertheless, exceptions; and Poland is the most obvious.

First the international polls conducted by the Allensbach Institute. In September and October of 1989 citizens of eight countries were asked if they agreed with the statement: 'A united Germany would be better for world peace.' In Sweden 71 per cent agreed, in France 68 per cent, in Italy 66 per cent – a true surprise in view of other data – in Great Britain and the Netherlands 62 per cent – once again a friendly view on the part of the Dutch – in Spain 45 per cent, in Japan 38 per cent and in the USA 36 per cent.[26]

As always, one ought to take into account not only the individual poll at a particular point in time, but also the results over a period of time. The results of previous surveys taken in the USA, Great Britain and France are available. The long-term view reveals that support for reunification shrank in the United States. In 1984 54 per cent were in favour, in 1989 only 36 per cent.

In Great Britain and France the tendency went in the opposite direction. In 1984 51 per cent of the British were for a peaceful reunification of Germans; in the autumn of 1989 the proportion had risen to 62 per cent. In France the increase in favourable opinion was even more impressive: from 43 per cent in 1984 to 68 per cent in 1989.[27]

The German revolution in late 1989 not only demolished the Berlin Wall, it also significantly strengthened public opinion in other countries in favour of reunification. Between 12 October and 22 November 1989 the Spanish sceptics were transformed into glowing adherents of German unification, which was now favoured by 84 per cent. In Portugal and Greece 83 per cent were for unification, in Ireland 81 per cent, in France and Italy 80 per cent (a further sign of easing anxieties), in the Netherlands 76 per cent (which, by now, should no longer be a surprise), 71 per cent in Belgium and Great Britain, 63 per cent in Luxemburg and 59 per cent in Denmark. The overall average for the European Community was 78 per cent, which was exactly the same as the average for West Germany itself. This data was gathered by the 'Eurobarometer' of the European Commission.[28]

Thus, an almost grotesque situation had come about: in late 1989 public opinion in many countries was more 'German' than among the (West) Germans themselves!

By early 1990 the enthusiasm had dampened somewhat. The fashionable passion for Germany had passed. To have expected a lasting love affair would have been to place an exaggerated value on the role of states. But the sympathy seems to have remained. The average for the EC was 71 per cent in early 1990. Opinion in Spain remained the most positive with 81 per cent, Denmark and Luxemburg exchanged places as least enthusiastic, and the average in the Federal Republic was 77 per cent, somewhat above the EC average.[29]

The lingering doubts which had been registered in the USA up to October 1989 appear to have been blown away, albeit more so among average Americans on the street than among those with higher educations. In late November 1989 57 per cent of college graduates, but 72 per cent of Americans with only a high school education agreed with the statement that Germany ought to be reunited.[30] The trend continued in a positive direction. In January 1990 61 per cent of all Americans polled were for German unification; only 13 per cent were opposed.[31] As in the case of Spain, a mood of scepticism apparently changed to buoyant optimism. With regard to the possible dangers of German reunification Americans were now less worried than the British or the French.[32]

In March 1990 the University of Michigan Institute for Social

Research measured an even higher approval rate: exactly two-thirds of the US public (66 per cent) were for German unification.[33] The positive shift in public opinion would appear to have influenced the Bush Administration, which supported German unification at an early date and without reservation. In April 1990 President Bush stated that the time had come to forgive the mass murder of the Jews,[34] a view which goes a long way towards accommodating those who want to 'close the books' on the past – too far, in my opinion.

Do Eastern Europeans have a different view of German reunification from Western Europeans? In mid-January 1990 surveys were conducted in the Soviet Union, Hungary and Poland. Some 68 per cent of the Hungarians, 51 per cent of the Soviet citizens, but only 26 per cent of the Poles interviewed were in favour of reunification.[35] In Hungary 22 per cent, in the Soviet Union 30 per cent and in Poland 64 per cent were opposed.[36]

A poll also conducted in mid-January in Poland by the British MORI Institute also found a majority against reunification, but the margin between majority and minority was much closer: 44 per cent of the Poles questioned were against, 41 per cent in favour.[37]

The Polish broadcasting network OBOP polled the Polish public in October 1987, November 1989 and March 1990 with regard to the German question.[38] In the overall political context and especially in comparison with other data from Poland, these results are sensational indeed. In answer to the question whether the two German states should be united, 48 per cent were 'definitely' or 'more' in favour of unification in March 1990. In November 1989 the total was 47 per cent, and in October 1987 27 per cent.

In March 1990 39 per cent were 'definitely', or 'more' against unification. In November 1989 the total was 32 per cent and in October 1987 47 per cent. The increase in opposition between November 1989 and March 1990 was not insignificant; but nevertheless nearly half the Poles interviewed were in favour of a fusion of the two German states. Whereas the polarisation between those in favour and those opposed had increased somewhat since late 1989, a relative majority remained positively disposed towards German unification.

These results are all the more surprising, as the number of those who feared disadvantages for Poland as a result of German unity dropped from 59 per cent in October 1987 to 45 per cent in November 1989, but increased again dramatically to 67 per cent in March 1990. These anxieties appear to be deep-seated. Some 69 per cent agreed that a united Germany presented a 'danger to Poland's borders', and only 17 per cent disagreed.

Owing to their fear of Germany 47 per cent wanted to make the withdrawal of Soviet military forces from Poland dependent on developments in Germany. Only 23 per cent wanted to see the Red Army leave immediately.

Nevertheless, 67 per cent of the Poles polled desired 'closer co-operation' with the Federal Republic of Germany. At the same time, Poles wanted to keep the new GDR at arm's length: only 36 per cent favoured closer co-operation, which was most desired with the United States (95 per cent), Great Britain (89 per cent), Japan (88 per cent), France (88 per cent), Sweden (83 per cent) and Italy (83 per cent).

This desire on the part of the Poles for 'closer co-operation' with the Germans seems to be based more on a perception of necessity than on sympathy. On a 'temperature' scale between +50 and −50 the Poles placed both Germanies at the bottom of the negative zone, below Cuba, China, Israel and the Soviet Union. (The Polish 'temperature' with regard to the USA was 28, for Italy 23, France 22, Japan and Great Britain 21, Hungary 20, the USSR 8, Israel −2, China −5, Cuba −6, the Federal Republic of Germany −6 and the GDR −11.)

Almost a year after the massacre on the 'Square of Heavenly Peace', the People's Republic of China ranked above both German states, which enjoyed a peace that really was almost heavenly. Psychologically and historically deeply rooted aspects of the Polish national psyche are manifest here. The traditional recollection of a murderous Germany distorts the reality of a new and peaceful German entity. The perspective is understandable, but the view is nevertheless inaccurate – a classic example of how the lessons of the past can present a burden for policy in the present.

The results of the public opinion polls from Poland are highly contradictory, much more so than the surveys from any other country. Pollsters will have a hard time explaining the reasons, if they succeed at all. What is more, it is politically, and in the final analysis also methodologically, questionable whether the polls taken before the change in government (1987) can be compared with the results of 1989 and 1990.

In the case of other countries we have found that public opinion and the attitudes of politicians and 'opinion-makers' can diverge significantly. Perhaps public opinion in the new Poland is also not identical with the positions of the people's representatives. Are there any indications for this? There are indeed. For instance, the fact that thousands of Poles have come pouring into Germany. They come not just to buy Western goods or to sell their own wares. Great numbers are striving to remain in Germany and to become citizens. They do not make such decisions in order to tear their political and national souls asunder, nor are they only after the meat in German pots. They come because they know that Germany is a state worth living in. In and with this state one can live well and in peace. Even before the democratic revolution in their country, many Poles cast their own ballot on the German Question – on foot. Is this form of referendum less revealing than the mood reflected in the polls? Hardly. Public opinion polls register largely unbinding opinion. Voting with their feet, leaving their Polish homeland to emigrate to Germany ('of all places', one might add for the sake of historical argumentation) represents a decisive turning-point in their lives.

Like many Jews of the post-Holocaust generations, their Polish contemporaries seem attracted to the role of hereditary martyrdom. With respect to the Jewish side I feel competent to render personal judgement, but I do not possess sufficient knowledge of the Polish situation to do so. In a passage in his remarkable novel '*The Beautiful Mrs Seidenman*' the great Polish author Andrzej Szczypiorski offers a clear description and judgement of the phenomenon:

> The people [in Warsaw] who lived on top of the bones of Henryk Fichtelbaum [a Polish Jew murdered by the Germans in the Holocaust] rarely thought of him, and when they did so it was with an inordinate kind of vanity, as though they were the greatest martyrs under the sun. They were doubly wrong. First, because martyrdom is not a kind of nobility that one can inherit like a coat-of-arms or an estate. Those who lived on top of Henryk Fichtelbaum's bones were not martyrs at all. They were only clipping coupons from the martyrdom of others, which is always foolish and unworthy. Second, they did not notice that the world had moved on, and left the history of the war with Adolf Hitler far behind it.

Poland was not alone in feeling a certain uneasiness with regard to German unification. Not just other nations, but the Germans themselves kept them company. The West Germans were afraid for their Mark; the East Germans were afraid of the market, and others, too, shared economic fears. Even in France, where support for reunification was especially strong, in an April 1990 poll conducted by the IPSOS Institute 54 per cent agreed with the proposition that German unification could present problems for the French economy. At the same time they expressed unusual confidence in the pace towards European unity: 69 per cent agreed that the pace would be accelerated by the 'events in Eastern Europe' (including the GDR).[39] The rival SOFRES organisation arrived at an entirely different conclusion – albeit with a slightly different question. In November 1989, 40 per cent agreed that German unification would tend to make European political union 'more difficult' to achieve. In April 1990 the proportion had risen to 43 per cent.

Do the numbers reveal all? Or don't they tell us anything? They demonstrate that the French, like any other nation, are not prophets with a foreknowledge of the future. The data clearly document the fact that the French favoured German reunification. What that would bring, no one knew. Like the Germans, others were worrying about a future that no one could know. The past is known. Because it is past, and the years 1933–45 were a murderous past, a sense of grief is doubly appropriate. And since neither Germans nor non-Germans can see into the future, they have their worries and, yes, their fears. Not necessarily a fear of Germany, but a fear of what the future might bring.

To sum up   In May 1990 Alfred Grosser confessed: 'For twenty years I repeated a falsehood. Time and again I said that France was in favour of reunification, as long as it was not possible.' Rare indeed is the expert or professional conference participant who can approach Grosser's sovereign style.

After the exposure of their numerous, but human and thus forgivable errors, the 'experts' should have been found lying flat on their backs. At the least we might have expected some self-criticism or a measure of modesty. Quite the contrary! The international carousel of conferences careened at an even crazier pace. By telephone and fax the experts were rounded up and sent jetting off from one symposium to another. The day before, one expert knew as much as the other, namely nothing. And today they know just as much about tomorrow. In view of the earlier error-rate we may be permitted to remain sceptical. Public opinion in other countries towards German unification was, despite the available data, incorrectly estimated. Political discourse all too often equated published with public opinion – an elementary error, as we have seen.

Before, and even more so following, the German October Revolution, public opinion in nearly all other countries evidenced amazingly little antipathy towards reunification. Scepticism or rejection were much more frequently characteristic of published opinion and the pronouncements of politicians. Here the great exception was President Bush. Gradually, the political clouds seen hanging over Germany began to disperse, as politicians in other countries began to follow his example.

The Jews? 'We Jews cannot regard the unification of Germany without feeling an inner resistance. We will have to think over the consequences more than once,' Elie Wiesel told *Der Spiegel* in the final days of 1990.[40] Plural 'we'? All Jews? Meaning the real Jewish martyrs, *and* those who were not persecuted, *and* the latter-born as well? Is Elie Wiesel the elected representative and spokesman for all Jews? Is he in possession of the political, that is the democratic, legitimation to speak in the name of all Jews? Of course not!

Is his 'we' morally justified? Yes, if one remembers that he lived through the hell of Auschwitz. Nevertheless, past suffering does not guarantee that the martyrs of the past will always be able to measure up to the moral demands of the present and the future. Individually, this may be possible, perhaps in the case of Elie Wiesel. I cannot pass judgement in this regard, and do not wish to. But in the case of collectives there is no guarantee. Like every other collective, 'we' Jews have our black sheep. Their guilt, however, is not ours, even if the collective must assume the liability. In this we are like the Germans: the individual hero of the resistance is liable for his people, as well as those who passively acquiesced to, and most especially those who actively participated in the regime.

The history of the Jewish people perhaps contains more suffering than the history of any other people. But Jews are not better, and of course also not worse, than any other people. 'We' do not have a monopoly on morals. 'We', too, often enough refuse to open our eyes, ears and mouths. On the other hand, 'we' also have those who see, hear and protest. 'We', too, are human beings with all of the bright and dark sides of humanity. Let us therefore be more careful with this 'we'. Sometimes it is convenient and pleasant, sometimes not. Let us examine a few current examples of 'our' ability to play deaf, blind and mute. 'Our'?

Certainly numerous South African Jews were to be found among the civil rights advocates; but the representatives of the South African Jewish community did not denounce apartheid until 1985.[41]

'We too were silent' while the demonstrators were being beaten and shot in the Romanian city of Temesvar, as the Israeli historian

Moshe Zimmermann was moved to reproach his people and government.[42]

Until Ceausescu's end in December 1989, the chief rabbi of Romania was anything but sparing in submissive verbal gestures to the dictator. Equally abject, repugnant and, in the final analysis, immoral were the public pronouncements of Jewish representatives in the GDR. Nor do the internal protocols of the meetings of the council of the Jewish community in East Berlin provide morally uplifting reading material.

In June 1990 the rabbi of Prague, Daniel Meyer, publicly confessed to having been a paid agent of the Czechoslovakian secret police.[43] Soon afterwards, the general secretary of the Jewish community in Budapest, Gustav Zoltai, told the world that, 'Under communist rule all community leaders were in the same situation.'[44] Averted eyes, silence and conformity were not all. The representatives of 'our' community were also active participants. Quite rightly Zoltai recalled the Talmudic warning not to judge anyone if you have not been in his position. We ought to refrain from rendering judgement. We can and must attempt to understand the position of those who decided to participate. Who is able to resist a dictator? Only heros. And heros are the exception rather than the rule. But of course, even if they are one of 'us', those who chose to go along are in no case moral role models.

Can 'our' Jewish-Israeli policy of occupation be considered moral?

Do 'we' with 'our' Holocaust memorials demonstrate sufficient solidarity with other peoples, millions of whom were also murdered – the Armenians, for example? Where were the voices of American Jews when Senator Robert Dole proposed that a commemoration of the Armenian genocide take place in April 1990? Between 1915 and 1923 Turkey was responsible for the brutal murder of approximately 1.5 million Armenians. To this day, Turkey refuses to acknowledge this crime. In concert, President Bush, the governments of Israel and Turkey and a number of American–Jewish leaders prevented the realisation of the proposed day of commemoration. They all had their 'good reasons', which were politically understandable. Were these 'reasons' also moral? Did 'we' protest 'We' did not. I did.[45] Individual exculpation at best, but not collective.

To Sum Up   Even among 'us' Jews there are those who preach water and drink wine. So what? This only proves the obvious fact that 'we' Jews are simply human beings. No one is immune to human frailties. Once again: We, too, live in a glass house. Everyone does.

With a shock therapy of quotations one can prove everything and nothing. For every quote one can find a counter-quote. What has not been written and said on the subject of German reunification, including Jews, the Diaspora and Israeli? I shall thus dispense with a collection of Jewish quotations on the topic of German unity, especially as such a collection already exists.[46]

In the confusion of Diaspora–Jewish voices and moods a certain pattern can be recognised: official Jewish representatives and active members of Jewish organisations have in general adopted a more arms-length view of reunification than Jews who would, on the one hand, not dream of concealing their Jewishness, but on the other hand would not choose to run with the crowd just because it was Jewish.

It would be much too easy, and also cheap, to damn the actions of the Jewish community leaders. It is possible to understand their position even if one does not agree with it. As official representatives they must work within collectively established limits. Like any other collective, the Jewish communities want to survive as collectives. An organised minority, however, can only survive as a collective when it does not permit divergence and resists change. The 'case' of Spinoza provides a historical case in point. Baruch (Benedictus) de Spinoza (1632–77), the eminent Jewish philosopher, was banned from the Jewish community in Amsterdam because he was a dissident. Spinoza was a kind man a genial thinker, but as such he disquieted not so much the rabbis as the bulk of the community members. Of course, 'we' Jews were not the only ones faced with such problems.

'Only for idiots is the German the perpetual Nazi.' Such a sentence cannot be expected to issue from the mouth or pen of an official Jewish representative, but the French–Jewish philosopher André Glucksmann can afford to utter such a thought without further ado.[47] As an individualist, philosopher and Jew he enjoys a certain licence in a predominantly non-Jewish society. Free from organisational constraints – and thus in sovereign freedom – such prominent Jewish personalities as the political scientist and publicist Alfred Grosser, and musicians Yehudi Menuhin, Daniel Barendoim and Leonard Bernstein could respond with joy to the fall of the Berlin Wall. The last of these directed celebratory German concerts immediately after 9 November 1989. Significantly, Bernstein chose Beethoven's Ninth Symphony, based on the 'Ode to Joy' by the poet

Friedrich Schiller 'Seid umschlungen Millionen . . . Dieser Kuß der ganzen Welt.' The reference 'der ganzen Welt' is to the whole world. Not just Jews or Germans; the whole world.

These prominent Jewish individualists are responsible only for themselves, not for the collective of Diaspora–Jewish communities involved in the search for a lost identity, and thus understandably unwilling to allow themselves to be further irritated. Nevertheless there were also individual Diaspora-Jewish organisations which reacted positively to German unification. Among these were the Armonk Institute and a large portion of the American Jewish Committee.

The Jewish State, Israel, is also confronted with a deep identity crisis, and is thus in search of means for generating identity. Among the chief instruments of this, if not already the most important instrument of it, is the history Jewish suffering, especially the catastrophe of the Holocaust. If the catastrophe and thus Germany were required as a means of establishing identity, it followed that the division of Germany was to be regarded as a form of retribution for the genocide of the Jews. The fall of the Berlin Wall and German unification clouded this functional view. The gathering in the Diaspora in connection with the re-creation of the Jewish State, Israel, in 1948, served to contradict the traditional Christian view of the Jews as the perpetually banished people of God.

Holocaust and reunification form a double link between German and Jewish identities. Political mechanisms applied to the Jewish people led to the absurd charge of guilt for the murder of Christ. Guilt for the murder of Jews is the linchpin of the political mechanics applied to Germany. A comparison of the political mechanisms does not say anything about the validity of the charges or the character and extent of the purported or actual crimes. Neither is judgement rendered as to their comparability. The 'political mechanics' being identified and described here involve only the reaction of the outside world, which demonstrates reflexive rather than reflective attitudes. On the basis of political-historical reflexes an interpretation of history is derived which claims to explain the German situation: Germany's punishment for the murder of millions of Jews was its division.

But suddenly Germany is (re)united and thus its sentence commuted. Reunification leads Germany into a Jewish situation for a second time: as was the case with the re-founding of the Jewish State, it contradicts traditional historical views held by Germany's critics and opponents.

When a prevailing view of the world is turned upside down or reversed, a revolution in the literal sense of the word takes place, a turning around of relations. Revolutions cannot be intellectually digested in a matter of a few weeks or months. Established views of history must be rethought and then rewritten. It would thus be best to show a bit more understanding and patience with regard to some of the more extreme utterances of Israeli and Diaspora–Jewish opinion-makers and leaders. The ideologues and interpreters of the world suddenly find the carpet pulled out from under their feet. They are in search of a new standpoint, and will eventually arrive at one, as every challenge requires an answer. That the former victims and perpetrators unintentionally and unexpectedly find themselves in a similar situation is both difficult to comprehend and to deal with.

Public Opinion and Actual Behaviour – Israel   In Israel, too, the reaction of public opinion to the gentle October Revolution in Germany was considerably more relaxed than published opinion in the country. After initial panicked reactions, calm also prevailed among the politicians. In the final analysis a remarkable process had taken place: it was not the supposed leadership, the opinion-makers and the politicians doing the governing, but the purportedly governed who brought about the change in course.

Rather than acting, the politicians reacted. They reacted to public opinion, but also to the actions of their political opponents. In mid-March 1990 Minister of State Schäfer of the (West) German Ministry of Foreign Affairs met with Arab diplomats in Bonn. 'May reunification succeed – for the benefit of peace and of the German people' declared the doyen of the Arab diplomatic corps, Qatar ambassador al-Khal. And he added that the Palestinians also long finally to be able to exercise their right of self-determination. The next morning's newspapers reported that the Minister of State, known for his critical approach to Israel and for his pro-Arab sympathies, had thanked the Arab countries for their positive approach to the process of German unity during the previous months.

Schäfer's well-chosen words of thanks were a signal that could not be overlooked. Translated from diplomatic into everyday language, the message was: you understand us: the Israelis criticise us. Then Schäfer got down to the nitty-gritty. The changes in Germany and Eastern Europe would not make Bonn lose sight of the problems in the Middle East, he said. A dialogue between the Israelis and the Palestinians must commence.[48] 'We have always maintained that the Israeli settlements in the occupied territories were illegal.' Schäfer referred to various declarations of the EC, and called for Israel to refrain from all measures that would burden the peace process. At the same time (in this context!) he appealed to Prime Minister Shamir to keep the door open for an understanding and a compromise with the Palestinians.

Schäfer and the Arab ambassadors certainly cannot be counted among Israel's close political partners in Bonn. But what if other, more favourably disposed German politicians should decide to distance themselves from Israel? Preventive measures were in order. For Shamir, historical reproaches were one thing, the realities of politics another, more important matter. This, too, was in the tradition of Israeli relations with Germany. Ben-Gurion was really the only Prime Minister of Israel who did not attempt to separate the one from the other. Shamir's ambassador in Bonn, Benjamin Navon, demonstrated considerably more understanding for Germany's enthusiasm for unification, and thus certainly contributed to the deepening of friendships.

As late as November 1989 Prime Minister Shamir conjured up the German devil in an appearance on US television. Shamir raised the spectre of a unified Germany once again attempting to murder millions of Jews.[49] In April 1990 the tone was completely different: 'The Jewish people have memories, doubts and questions. It is therefore difficult to say that we are enthused by the thought of German unification. Nevertheless, we understand that the time for German unity has come.'[50]

A few days before, the almost sensational results of a poll conducted in March 1990 had been published. Two-thirds of the Israelis interviewed said they had nothing against German unification; 26 per cent were actually in favour, 41 per cent undecided, and only 33 per cent were opposed.[51] What was even more significant for the long term from both the political and social vantage-points was that younger Israelis expressed fewer reservations with regard to unification. For geographical as well as political–psychological reasons, Israelis of oriental (North-African or West-Asian) background were more at ease, with only 24 per cent opposed, whereas 42 per cent of the Israelis from European backgrounds said they were against reunification.

By the beginning of the 1990s the majority of Israelis had

achieved a certain generational and geographical distance from the events of the Holocaust. Professor Moshe Zimmermann agreed. Critics argued that it was methodologically incorrect to count the 41 per cent of those who did not express a clear opinion as being in favour. Zimmermann countered that what really counted was not the addition proponents but the numbers of the opponents of German unification, and added a decisive argument: contrary to the claims of politicians and the media, the reaction of the majority of Israelis to the events in Germany was neither automatic nor energetically against reunification. If the public had indeed behaved as they were generally purported to feel, then the results would have been clearly and emphatically against German unity.[52] In other words: the expected reflex-reaction to the stimulus 'Germany' did not take place.

In May 1990 Zimmermann had another poll conducted. In March the question had been 'Are you for or against the unification of the two Germanies?' In May the question was 'Should Israel support or oppose the unification of Germany?' This time, the interviewee was being asked to decide in the role of representative of the State of Israel, and thus to conform more to general expectations. One might well have expected a less favourable response. Wrong! The opposition to reunification actually declined, from 33 per cent to 21 per cent.[53] (Some 27 per cent favoured support, and 41 per cent expressed no opinion.)

Courageously continuing to explode myths with sober numbers, Moshe Zimmermann posed further a question in May 1990, 'Does the unification of Germany, in your opinion, pose a danger for Jews?': 49 per cent said no, a considerable 34 per cent said yes, and 17 per cent did not know.

Only 21 per cent were against reunification, but 34 per cent recognised a danger for Jews. Is there a contradiction here? Not necessarily. Zimmermann's convincing explanation is that Israelis have learned to distinguish between dangers to Israel and to the Jewish Diaspora. As an Israeli one can support German reunification from the standpoint of the State of Israel. The Jews living in other countries are, in the eyes of the Israelis, more likely to be endangered.[54]

To what conclusions do these data lead? We may assume that the great majority of Israelis, about two-thirds, view relations with Germany as a normal matter, despite all the political background noise. Public opinion in Israel has evidently turned a cold shower on the expectations of ideologues, politicians and opinion-makers. 'Yes, I consider relations with Germany as normal' was a statement agreed with by 63 per cent of the Israelis surveyed in May 1990.[55]

It is therefore no surprise that in May 1990 only 10 per cent of the Israelis polled agreed with the statement: 'All the Germans living today bear guilt for the Holocaust.'[56] There was no significant change in comparison with a survey conducted in 1982, in which 9 per cent agreed with the same statement.

'Yes, there is another Germany' (different from the old, National-Socialist Germany responsible for the Holocaust) was agreed to by 64 per cent of the Jewish Israelis polled in May 1990.[57] In June 1981, shortly after Prime Minister Menachem Begin had made strong anti-German statements with regard to collective guilt, only 41 per cent of the Israelis agreed that there was a 'new Germany'; but by March 1982 the number was the same as in May 1990, namely 64 per cent.[58]

Is there a difference between the *behaviour* of Israelis and their *attitudes* towards Germany? No. Despite their weak currency, the Israeli press reports that 'streams' of Israeli tourists are pouring into the (former) GDR.[59]

A realistic picture of Germany has been formed and now dominates the Israeli's image of Germany. This is a remarkable, if rarely noticed, fact. Israelis are not afraid of Germany. One need not possess the gift of political prophecy to predict that few indeed will dare to spread this news and thus narrow the gulf between Germans and Israelis. Like Don Quixote, these few, armed with hard data, will challenge the windmill of published opinion – and lose. The ideologues are still running the mill, and that which cannot be must not be.

No, it must not be. In February 1990 the readers of the *Süddeutsche Zeitung* were informed by an Israeli historian: 'It is of no help to repeatedly point out that there is a guiltless "new Germany" . . . Israelis from all parts of the spectrum are sceptical of the Federal Republic's claim to represent the "new Germany". Despite close diplomatic relations and numerous close ties, the new Germany still also stands for the "old Germany". Despite the countless pronouncements of politicians, Jewish reactions depend not on current political calculations but on feelings derived from past experiences.[60]

Perhaps our historian might have found one public opinion survey or another more helpful with regard to the reliability of her presenta-

tion than the appeal to emotions. Feelings can be positive or negative, but they are not necessarily conducive to reliable scholarship.
Some emotions or observations are only occasionally representative
of the overall society. But what ideologue will willingly surrender the
tools of the trade? The arguments of the historian can be better
applied to the Jewish Diaspora than to Israel.

The Jewish Diaspora   The attitudes of the Jewish Diaspora towards
Germany are, in fact, ambivalent. In contrast to the Israelis, Jews
living outside the Jewish State display mixed feelings about the
newly united Germany. A majority of American Jews are not at ease
with the reunited Germany. In March 1990 42 per cent considered
this development 'very alarming', an additional 32 per cent found it
'alarming' and only 24 per cent did not consider German unity
alarming.[61] This was the complete reverse of the results in Israel. Why?

It is difficult to arrive at a definitive explanation. One suspicion is
that, despite the identity problems, the Israeli–Jewish feeling of
community is more solid than that prevailing among Diaspora Jews.
It can be said that the Diaspora has lost both of the legs upon which
it had stood for centuries: the Jewish religion and the more than
three thousand years of Jewish history. As a result of secularisation
the majority of Jews have lost contact with the religious tradition,
and Jewish history has been largely foreshortened to the twelve most
horrible years of a history rich in horrors: the Holocaust. In place of
historical traditions, a sort of prosthesis has been offered: Israel. But
this prosthesis could never really fit, since the Jewish State, from the
beginning, regarded itself as the antithesis to the Diaspora. Its hope
and demand was that the Diaspora should disappear as a consequence of immigration to Israel. This has not happened, as Diaspora Jews would rather send money to Israel than migrate themselves. But the Diaspora has not developed sufficient traditions of its
own.

Within the last decade, the prosthesis 'Israel' has become rather
uncomfortable. The policy of the Jewish State towards the Palestinians has made it increasingly difficult for Diaspora Jews to identify
with Israel completely and without qualification. What remains is
the Holocaust, and thus Germany – not the real, but the old,
murderous Germany – as a means of generating identity.

Henryk Broder has offered a different, both remarkable and
thought-provoking explanation for the attitude of American Jews
towards Germany. The criticism of Germany serves to mask a bad

conscience for not having done enough for the German and European Jews during the Holocaust.[62] According to the military motto that offence is the best form of defence, the historical–psychological tactic was to redirect self-criticism into criticism of Germany. The explanation of the mechanics is convincing; but on the other hand the majority of Jews in the United States today were born after the Holocaust, and bear no guilt for the failures of their parents and grandparents, although they must bear the consequences. In this role their reactions ought to be less agitated than that of the generations bearing the guilt. But Broder is right nevertheless: with a bad conscience it is much easier to criticise others, too.

The immigration of Soviet Jews presents an entirely different picture. Their behaviour towards Germany stands in stark contrast to that of American Jews. Rather than attempting to avoid any contact, the exodus of Russian Jews has chosen Germany as one of its prime goals. Of the approximately 6,000 members of the Jewish community in West Berlin about half are originally from the Soviet Union. The flow of Russian-Jewish immigration to Germany, only a dribble in the 1970s, widened to a stream in the 1980s. In West Berlin the Jewish community was able to wrest residency and work permits from a reluctant city administration. Not that the (West) Berlin Senate had turned anti-Semitic. Its desire was merely to avoid worsening the already crowded and tense situation for the inundation of foreign residents in the city. Good will was and is shown, but could one grant privileges to Jews that were being denied to Turks? In view of the difficulties, a cautious approach was necessary. Without this well-intended and circumspect approach the number of Jewish immigrants in Germany would probably have been much higher.

The final days of the GDR also witnessed an immigration of Soviet Jews, beginning in May 1990. By the beginning of June 160, by the beginning of July about 500 had arrived.[63] They left the Soviet Union because they were forced to flee from the anti-Semitic violence in their homeland. They came to Germany because they did not want to go to Israel. Germany, the 'land of the murderers', became for them a place of refuge. An irony of history? Why irony? Nothing in history is as permanent as change, and that applies to German history as well.

Notes

1. Karl W. Deutsch and Lewis J. Edinger, *Germany Rejoins the Powers*, 2nd edn, New York, 1973, p. 22 (1st edn Stanford, 1959).
2. Cf. Michael Wolffsohn, *West Germany's Foreign Policy in the Era of Brandt and Schmidt. An Introduction*, Frankfurt am Main, 1986, p. 12, with empirical data.
3. Hans-Joachim Veen, 'Die Westbindungen der Deutschen in einer Phase der Neuorientierung', in *Europa Archiv*, No. 2, 1991, p. 40.
4. Ibid.
5. Emnid, *Das Deutschlandbild aus der Sicht der Bevölkerung in 8 ausgewählten Ländern*, Bielefeld, December 1977, p.48.
6. Jan Hoedeman, *Elsevier*, April 7, 1990, p. 37.
7. Elisabeth Noelle-Neumann and Renate Köcher, *Die verletzte Nation*, Stuttgart, 1987, p. 61.
8. Gallup International, Summer 1989, unpublished manuscript, p. 15, kindly provided by Norman Webb of Gallup International.
9. Ibid. This poll contained data from 32 states and countries.
10. Ibid.
11. *Eurobarometer, Public Opinion in the European Community*, No. 32, December 1989, Vol. I: Report, p. A40. For example, in January 1987, considerably more Germans (57 per cent) and Italians (62 per cent) were in favour of cuts in defence spending than was the case in France (35 per cent) and Great Britain (27 per cent). Data from the *Index to International Public Opinion 1986–87*, Westport, Connecticut, 1988, p. 610.
12. Andreas Hillgruber, *Die Gescheiterte Großmacht. Eine Skizze des Deutschen Reiches 1871–1945*, (4th edn), Düsseldorf, 1984, p. 106 f.
13. Ibid., p. 107.
14. In 1918–19 the 'Soviet Union factor' precluded the establishment of such an order (cf. Hillgruber, ibid. p. 60).
15. For quote and further details see ibid., p. 9.
16. Quoted by Ernst Nolte, *Deutschland und der Kalte Krieg*, Munich–Zurich, 1974, p. 688, note 29. Nolte quotes from an interview with Willy Brandt conducted by Gordon A. Craig on 13 August 1964, to be found in the John Foster Dulles Oral History Project. For Dulles's position with regard to a soviet or neutralised Germany, see also Nolte, ibid. p. 295, in which Nolte quotes from Louis L. Gerson, *John Foster Dulles*, New York, 1967, p. 308.
17. Henry A. Kissinger, *Memoiren 1968–1973* (German edn), Munich, 1979, p. 441. See also pp. 442, 566.
18. *Gallup France*, Vol. I, p. 454. In 1955 31 per cent were for the division, ibid., p. 185.
19. Louis Harris France poll for *L'Express*, 17–23 March 1979.
20. IFOP for Allensbach and *Stern*, in *Stern*, 26 April 1984, p. 72.

21. Louis Harris in USA and Research Services in Great Britain for *Stern*, in *Stern* 26 April 1984, p. 72.

22. EMNID, *Das Deutschlandbild aus der Sicht der Bevölkerung in 8 ausgewählten Ländern*, Bielefeld, October, 1977, p. 45.

23. Elisabeth Noelle and Erich Peter Neumann (eds), *Jahrbuch der öffentlichen Meinung 1968–1973*, Allensbach and Bonn, 1974, p. 507.

24. *Jahrbuch 1968–1973*, p. 507.

25. Wolfgang Bergsdorf, 'Wer will die Deutsche Einheit? Wie sich die Meinungen im In- und Ausland entwickelten', in *Die politische Meinung*, No. 248, Jan.–Febr. 1990, p. 18.

26. Institut für Demoskopie Allensbach, *Das Deutschlandbild im Ausland*, November 1989, p. 29.

27. Ibid., p. 31.

28. *Eurobarometer*, No. 32, Dec. 1989, Vol I, p. 33.

29. *Eurobarometer*, qouted in *Frankfurter Allgemeine Zeitung*, 1 June 1990. The Gallup Institute discovered a much less favourable attitude towards Germany in Denmark in January, 1990: only 26 per cent supported reunification, and 56 per cent were opposed: Niels Norlund, *Berlingske Tidende Magazin*, 1 February 1990.

30. *New York Times*/CBS poll, in *New York Times*, 1 December 1989.

31. George Skelt, *Los Angeles Times*, 26 January 1990 and *The Economist* (London), 27 January 1990, p. 29.

32. Ibid. The survey included questions about a possible 'German domination in Europe' or a German economy growing 'too strong'.

33. Gibowski / Semetko, *Öffentliche Meinung*, p. 1 and 6.

34. *Frankfurter Allgemeine Zeitung*, 17 April 1990.

35. Poll by CSA Institute Eric Du Pin for *Libération* (Paris), 19 February 1990.

36. Poll by CSA Institute Eric Du Pin for *Libération* (Paris), 19 February 1990.

37. MORI poll for *Los Angeles Times*, 26 January 1990 and *The Economist*, 27 January 1990.

38. OBOP, Report No. 10/552, March 1990. Text and translation kindly provided by Mr Silbergerg of the German embassy in Warsaw.

39. Ipsos Institute poll for *Les Echos* (Paris), Françoise Crouigneau in *Les Echos*, 2 May 1990.

40. Interview with Elie Wiesel in *Spiegel*, No. 1, 1990, p. 105.

41. Joaw Karni, *Haaretz*, 11 May 1990.

42. Mosche Zimmermann, *Haaretz*, 8 January 1990.

43. Jehuda Lahav, *Haaretz*, 12 June 1990.

44. A. Rabinovich, *Jerusalem Post*, 30 June 1990.

45. Michael Wolffsohn, 'Der armenische Holocaust: politisch verharmlost', in *Frankfurter Allgemeine Zeitung*, 28 October 1990.

46. See also Michael Wolffsohn, 'Die Reaktionen Israels und der diaspora-

jüdischen Welt auf den 9. November 1989', in G. Trautmann (ed.): *Die häßlichen Deutschen?*, Darmstadt, 1990.

47. Interview with André Glucksmann, in *Passages* (Paris), No. 23, December 1989, pp. 21 f.

48. (Bernd) Co(nrad), *Die Welt*, 14 March 1990. dpa (Deutsche Presseagentur) reports concerning this meeting in *Süddeutsche Zeitung*, 14 March 1990.

49. Printed in *Deutschland-Berichte*, March 1990, pp. 8 f.

50. A. Eldar, *Haaretz*, 5 April 1990.

51. PORI poll, March 1990, for Moshe Zimmermann, *Haaretz*, 26 March and 19 April 1990.

52. Cf. the controversy in the Israeli newspaper *Haaretz*, 19 April 1990.

53. PORI poll, May 1990, for Moshe Zimmermann, who kindly made the data available to the author.

54. Moshe Zimmermann, *Haaretz*, 25 May 1990.

55. Cf. PORI poll conducted for Moshe Zimmermann, 15 May 1990.

56. Ibid.

57. Ibid.

58. Polls conducted by PORI Institute. For additional details, see Michael Wolffsohn, *Deutsch–Israelische Beziehungen. Umfragen und Interpretationen. Umfragen 1952–1983*, Munich, Bayerische Landeszentrale für politische Bildung, 1986.

59. Cf. Zohar Blumenkranz, *Haaretz*, 9 July 1990.

60. Shulamit Volkov, director of the Institute for German History of the University of Tel Aviv, in *Süddeutsche Zeitung*, 8 February 1990.

61. Hart–Teeter poll for *The Wall Street Journal* and NBC, *The Wall Street Journal*, 16 March 1990.

62. ARD (German television) *Pressclub*, 13 May 1990.

63. Cf. *Haaretz*, 23 May 1990; Voice of Israel, Anita Kugler, in *Tageszeitung* (taz), 6 June 1990; Irene Runge, in: *Sonntag* (East Berlin) No. 24, 1990; *Berliner Morgenpost*, 10 June 1990; Daniel Dagan, *Haaretz*, 13 July 1990.

PETER GRAF KIELMANSEGG

Germany – A Future with Two Pasts

I.

The latest edition of a well-known dictionary of the English language which was published in 1987, two years before the sudden collapse of the German Democratic Republic, informs its users about the meaning of the word Germany as follows: 'Germany – a former country in the centre of Europe'. The statement was probably meant as definitively as it sounds. But our dictionary can claim, as could everybody else, that the turn European history has taken in the years 1989–90 is one of the great political miracles of this century: what has happened is still unbelievable.

What would a correct definition of Germany be in 1991, a few months after the reappearance of the 'former country'? Is it already and again 'a country in the centre of Europe'? The most precise description possible at present might well be 'Germany – a future country in the centre of Europe'. By this I mean: unification has only just begun. It is a process, not a single act – a process that will take years. Two states can be unified by a legal act, two societies cannot. And two separate societies do exist in Germany.

The reintegration of these two societies is now on the agenda. All the political rhetoric of the last forty years notwithstanding, this reintegration will in effect be an effort to rebuild a nation that has lost much of its coherence in the period of division. There is no guarantee of success. And the chance to steer, to control the process may well be smaller than the term 'rebuild' suggests.

What I intend to do is to look somewhat more closely at the

starting-point of this process. To be precise: I am interested in the impact the Eastern past might have on the common future. The extent to which the new Federal Republic of Germany will really be a new republic obviously depends on the strength and the direction of this impact. It is not my intention to discuss in detail the acute transition crisis, with its specific problems, that we are facing right now.

But before taking this road I would like to exclude two historical analogies that might come to one's mind as misleading. The first, although perhaps far-fetched, is 1871: the first unification of German states in a single German national state. It is obvious that there are all sorts of dissimilarities between 1871 and 1990. Let me mention three of them, which are of particular relevance to my argument. In 1871 national unity was achieved, although by war, as the fulfilment of a long-cherished dream. It was a ripe fruit, so to speak. Nationalism also played a part as a powerful integrating and assimilating force. And the Germany that had to be integrated, the pre-1870 Germany, had been split up into more than two dozen states, but not into several distinct and antagonistic societies.

The situation of 1990 was and is different in all these respects. This time the Germans were taken completely by surprise. Most of them had no longer thought of unification as a real possibility. Secondly: the Germans now faced each other as two separate, fundamentally different societies. Some of these differences will have to be discussed in greater detail later. Thirdly: the rebuilding of the nation will have to be done without the impulse of a strong patriotism. The striking absence of national enthusiasm in the whole process of unification, except perhaps for a few short moments, may have been one of the conditions that made the reunification of Germany acceptable to the rest of Europe. But it certainly does not make the task of reintegrating the two German societies easier.

The other historical analogy is of course the post-1945 period, the so-called economic and, we should not forget, democratic miracle in West Germany. Should not East Germany forty years later be able to repeat this performance under what seem to be more favourable conditions? Indeed, the conditions are in some important respects more favourable for East Germany than they were forty years ago for West Germany. But not in all. The common effort in the late forties and early fifties of a poor people that had barely survived an extreme catastrophe, supported by international development, was something very different from the effort, supported by major redistribution within the country, of the less fortunate half of that people to catch up with the more fortunate half that is now required. More important than anything else is perhaps the fact that the political climate is different. There is no patience, there probably can be no patience, because there are those enormous disparities between the two halves of the country. In the post-war years most people were grateful for their bare survival, for the gradual recovery from war, destruction, defeat. The prevailing experience of the East Germans since 3 October 1990 has been, and will be for some time to come, that the transition period is much harder and will last longer than they had expected. Moreover, the devastating effects of four decades of a socialist totalitarian dictatorship are in some respect much more serious than the legacy of Hitler's Germany, with which post-war Germany had to start, simply because the socialist system of the GDR lasted so much longer.

So there is some room for doubt whether the post-war history of West Germany really proves that East Germany, as we all hope, can move in a very short time from where it is now to where West Germany has arrived after forty years of democracy and a market economy. It will be altogether a new story.

II.

To discuss the process of rebuilding the nation and of reintegrating the two societies, to study the impact of the East German legacy on the emerging new Federal Republic, it is helpful to distinguish between different levels or aspects of integration. Let me mention three of them.

Most obviously, there is the institutional suprastructure of society. Reintegration at this level is, although an enormous challenge in a more technical sense, relatively easy to accomplish, because the institutional suprastructure is basically a legal structure. You can alter it and replace it by taking political decisions. For this reason I shall largely neglect it.

The second aspect of the process of integration of the two societies that has to be considered is the adaptation or even transformation of the social structures underlying the institutional suprastructure. The social structure is a much more resistant element of reality. Reintegration at this level in a free society is a process that may be influenced, but certainly cannot be controlled, by politics. Whereas almost nothing of the East German institutional set-up will remain, the social structure that has been shaped by forty years of communist rule will not be totally transformed or submerged in the process of reintegration. It will, to a certain extent, become an element of the common future, which of course means that Germany will have to live with certain structural cleavages. But the impact – this is at least my assumption – of the East German past on German society as a whole in structural terms will remain quite limited. A few remarks to illustrate what kind of cleavages might result from the deeper and more lasting effects of those forty years will therefore be sufficient.

The third, and in my view the most interesting, dimension is that of 'mentality' or attitudes. It is, indeed, the great unknown factor in the process of social reintegration I am talking about. It may well be the decisive one. I shall therefore concentrate upon this factor.

But let us begin with the two other dimensions of the process of integration I have mentioned. On the institutional level integration is in fact the wrong word. Not only the political institutions but the whole set of institutions in almost all spheres of life, from public health to higher education, from social security to labour relations, not to mention the economy, and the whole legal system has been or is being transferred from West to East. From a legal point of view this is the logical consequence of the fact that unification took place as by means of the accession of the German Democratic Republic to the Federal Republic. Whether this total imposition of institutions was politically wise in every respect, is another question. Perhaps it was unavoidable. Apparently there was no time to sort out carefully those elements of the institutional suprastructure that might have qualified for survival, and to develop the necessary legal flexibility for giving them a chance. On the other hand, the fact that no single element of the institutional structure did separately survive the collapse of the political core is perhaps what one should expect in the case of a totalitarian system.

On the whole, the transfer of institutions, despite myriads of problems in the transition period, is likely to be a successful operation. But there may be repercussions on the institutions being transferred which are not yet foreseeable. The party system is an interesting case in point. The first all-German parliamentary elections of December 1990 seem to be proof of an almost unbelievably successful transplantation of the party system from West to East. The election results in East and West Germany are almost identical, if one adds the PDS-vote to the SPD-vote in East Germany.[1] But the figures are misleading. Whereas in West Germany almost two-thirds of the electorate have developed relatively stable party loyalties, in East Germany at present it is only one out of five voters.[2] No party has an identifiable social base yet. In other words: the party system is still in a highly fluid state. The final distribution of the East German vote – and this means, 25 per cent of the German electorate now being East Germans, the structure of the party system of the new Federal Republic – is still an open question.

As to social structure, all I want to do is to give three examples which illustrate that East German society is indeed structurally different, and is likely, at least to a certain extent, to remain different for the foreseeable future as part of a greater German society. As a first example, take religion: in the old Federal Republic both major Christian churches comprised almost one half of the population – 43 per cent of the West Germans being Catholics and 42 per cent Protestants. Of the remaining 15 per cent the great majority had no affiliation to any Christian denomination, most of them living in the urban centres of the old Federal Republic. In East Germany Christianity has become the religion of a minority: 60 per cent of the East Germans have no affiliation to a Christian (or to any other) church, 34 per cent are Protestants, and 6 per cent Catholics – East Germany having of course historically always been a predominantly Protestant rather than Catholic region. The figures are even more dramatic, when we look at the youngest generation. Of 15-year-old East Germans 86 per cent do not belong to a Christian church. The corresponding figure for West Germany is 16 per cent.

Two obvious consequences of this are: first, that the established balance between the Catholic and the Protestant churches will be – if only slightly – affected; and second, that there will be a strong minority of Germans, one out of four, heavily concentrated in one region, who have nothing to do with the Christian churches.

The effects these shifts will have are difficult to predict. But it is hard to believe that they will have no effect at all. One might argue that the figures for West Germany are misleading: that only a minority of church-tax payers are active members of their respective churches. That is certainly true. But is the difference between no affiliation whatsoever to a Christian church – the situation of the majority of East Germans – and at least a legal affiliation being preserved – the case with the overwhelming majority of West Germans – really culturally irrelevant? The Protestant churches in West and East Germany certainly do have conflicting views of their role in society and *vis-à-vis* the state derived from that difference. And if it is culturally relevant, it will have its impact not only on the churches themselves but also on political discourse in general. It might also be the case that voting Christian Democrat in East Germany will have less to do with being an active churchgoer than it has in West Germany, which means that the party system could be directly affected.

My second example is female employment. In the former GDR the proportion of women who worked was 81 per cent in the relevant age-group, the percentage of men being only insignificantly higher. In the former Federal Republic the percentage was 55 per cent, almost 30 percentage points below the figure for men. It is obvious that these figures indicate much more than just a different composition of the labour-force. They indicate that family life, the system of public child-care, the educational system, the relations between the sexes must be different – and indeed they are. High unemployment in the transitional period will presumably hit women more than men. But there is little doubt that East Germans have accepted high female employment, including the employment of mothers with young children, not just as an economic necessity: it has become a way of life. And they will certainly try, with slight modifications, to maintain their way of life.

My third example is agriculture. Land was socialised in the former GDR in the fifties. Agriculture was organised in huge, highly specialised farms under collective ownership. The once-independent farmers became workers in a kind of agricultural industry, whereas West Germany stuck to the tradition of independent farming as a family enterprise. As a result, villages in the East and villages in the West have almost nothing in common but the name. Their economies and their social fabrics are totally different.

Apparently most of the Eastern agricultural workers hesitate to return to independent farming with its risks of entrepreneurship. Which means that whereas industry, trade, and craft will be reorganised in accordance with Western patterns rather quickly, the future of agriculture is quite open.

III.

In turning to what is my main point, to the third factor, the third dimension of the process of reintegration of the two German societies, i.e. the matter of the divergent 'mentalities' and how they might or might not merge, the first question has to be: what do we know about the mentality of East Germans? Is there something like a distinct East German mentality? Pollsters have been quite busy in 1990; they have collected interesting material, and have already discovered short-term trends. But as all the data we have are from the last twelve months the empirical base is quite narrow – the first snapshots, so to speak. It may well be that many of the answers that were given to the pollsters were related to and conditioned by the extraordinary events of an extraordinary period of history, and do not yet reveal stable attitudes. In any case, we have to bear in mind that the knowledge we have so far about the impact the totalitarian past has had on how East Germans see the world, on their value systems, on their way of thinking, is not very substantial and solid. What we do know is that forty years are a long time.

This is how Helmut Klages, a West German sociologist and leading contributor to the 'materialism–postmaterialism debate' in West Germany, reads the data of the recent surveys.[3] East Germans are not terribly different from West Germans. They are somewhat less religious, a bit more conservative, somewhat more materialistic; personal relations are more important for them. The East Germans he discovered in the public opinion poll data of 1990 reminded him very much of the West Germans of the fifties and early sixties – i.e. the West Germans before the great value-shift that transformed Western industrial societies, West German society among them, from the late sixties onwards.

This picture is, with certain variations, confirmed by other reports, based on other sets of data. Ursula Feist[4] ascribes a 'lead in modernity' to the West Germans as compared to the East Germans. Using Inglehart's categories, she tells us that the 'silent revolution', the shift from materialistic to postmaterialistic values, has made much more progress in West than in East Germany, which is hardly a surprise, if we accept Inglehart's premises. This implies that the cleavage between the two groups is more visible and more distinct in West Germany. Others have found hints that the gap between the generations is less deep in East Germany, at least within families, although in general the same pattern of relations between age and attitude seems to prevail in both parts of Germany. This corresponds to the impression that the family is still a more relevant social unit for East than for West Germany, probably because it has been important as a retreat and as source of support in facing the intricacies of daily life in the former GDR.

All these findings seem to confirm the idea that Communist rule has somehow frozen the societies of Eastern Europe, that it has blocked certain modernising evolutions for decades, rather than directing them towards its own goals.

This may be an element of what is the whole truth – but it is certainly not the whole truth. It is unreasonable to assume that the post-communist-totalitarian societies of Eastern Europe are just Western societies lagging behind. The experiences of four decades must have left their mark, even if such experiences do not immediately show up in the opinion polls. The political culture, in particular, of these societies, of which East Germany as a part of a divided country and nation was obviously a very special case, must have some very specific traits. From what East Germans themselves have said and written about themselves since the breakdown of the communist dictatorship such traits can be easily deduced. I shall briefly describe two of them.

East Germans have always felt that they were citizens of a second-class country, and second-class Germans in particular. In that respect their experience has been quite different from that of all the other East Europeans. East Europeans could distinguish between country and regime, East Germans could not. There was no focus for loyalty, for identification but the regime. East Germans, if they didn't accept their regime, had nothing to fall back upon – except perhaps an abstract idea of socialism for some intellectuals. At the same time this regime could never stand the test of comparison with the other Germany. Some kind of latent political inferiority complex was bound to result from these conditions. That they are now citizens of a democracy and of a united Germany is largely their own achievement. But the circumstances of the process of unification have certainly not helped East Germans to overcome that complex.

As citizens they feel no longer at home in their own country, which has never been, in a political sense, *their* country. And they certainly do not yet feel at home in the larger Federal Republic. Perplexity is the natural result of this condition, perplexity even in regard to democracy. Their attitudes toward democracy are shaped by two factors:[5] a total lack of experience with democracy as an institutional system – East Germany after all has had to live through almost sixty years of dictatorship; and the experience of a peaceful revolt that was successful against a crumbling dictatorship. With this background distrust of institutions and an emphasis on protest, on spontaneity in general as the core of democratic participation is natural. You would hardly expect in East Germany that solid trust in the institutions of the Federal Republic, which a majority of West Germans, after forty years of a successful experiment, consistently demonstrate in public opinion polls. Nor would you expect a balanced view of the essentials of democracy and of the citizen's role in the democratic process.

In the long run it may well be that their unique experience with totalitarian dictatorship will enable the East Germans to make a significant contribution to a democratic political culture in Germany. But presumably as a first step some kind of transitional political culture will develop in East Germany, shaped by the legacy of the past on the one hand and the shock of rapid change on the other, which will be a 'culture', if I may so put it, of perplexity and confusion, without stable attitudes, but with an extreme sensitivity to the ups and downs of events. This will be a factor of instability and incalculability, with which democracy in Germany will have to live for some time.

My second remark concerns the East Germans' view of the world. For the West Germans the integration of their part of the country into the community of Western peoples – West European and beyond – has been perhaps *the* most fundamental political experience of the post-war period. And it has been a *personal* experience for almost everybody. East Germans haven't had this or a comparable experience. They have lived in isolation – enforced isolation towards the West, and voluntary isolation, so to speak, towards the East. Russia was nothing but the intensely disliked hegemonic power for them. And as to the neighbouring East European countries, both sides kept their distance, perpetuating rather than transcending the bad traditions of German–Slavonic relations.

That this isolation has had consequences for general attitudes towards foreign policy is, I think, beyond doubt. During the Gulf War, public opinion polls showed remarkably different reactions among East and West Germans.[6] Whereas in West Germany majorities were consistently in favour of using force against the aggression as a last resort, the East Germans were as consistent in saying 'No' to force. Whereas a slight majority of West Germans thought that Germany would have to come to the aid of Turkey if the country were attacked, a majority of East Germans gave the opposite answer. Whereas a majority of West Germans said that the lesson their own history had taught the world was not to yield to an aggressive dictator, for a majority of East Germans the lesson was that peace was more important that anything else.

The idea that there is no justification for the use of force in international relations under any circumstances has, of course, much support in West Germany as well. Both German political cultures seem to have difficulties in accepting the ideas not only of legitimate force, but even of legitimate power. This may be a post-totalitarian phenomenon. But forty years of membership in alliances and federations of free nations have helped West Germans to realise that their own peculiar historical experience is not the only relevant experience in international relations. They have learned something about the implications of partnership between nations and states. A certain familiarity with these implications, a certain willingness to accept them has, as we hope, become an element of West German political culture. East Germans did not have this chance in the past.

IV.

What is going to happen? What kind of democracy will the new Federal Republic develop? Just a continuation of the old one? In terms of institutions this is indeed likely to be the case. It will be, with some modifications, the same constitution, the familiar parliamentary system, it will be federalism – a structure of crucial importance for the transitional period, because it gave the East Germans from the very beginning political institutions of their own – it will be the constitutional court, and presumably even the same party system. As we have seen, the same holds true for almost the entire institutional set-up of the old Federal Republic.

But will these institutions function in the same way they have functioned in the past? What about the prerequisites of their functioning that cannot be simply transferred? More precisely, what kind of common political culture will emerge from the two pasts? From what I have said about East Germany, it is obvious that what is taking place is not a merger of two different but inherently stable political cultures. East German attitudes towards politics, as I have described them, are necessarily unstable. They are being reshaped by the turmoils of the transition period. Two factors are of particular importance for the outcome of this process: let me term these factors moral regeneration and economic regeneration. Whether we like it or not, the economic regeneration of East Germany will be crucial for the new Federal Republic, as the economic regeneration of West Germany in the fifties was crucial for the old Federal Republic. But before turning to the political implications of the economic development, a few words about the process of 'moral regeneration' are also necessary.

The moral and legal problem of handling the legacy of a totalitarian dictactorship, i.e. a dictatorship that forces almost everybody into some sort of corrupting collaboration, is of course a familiar problem in Germany. The dimensions and intensity of the problem may have been different after 1945, but not its structure. After 1945 both Germanies, West and East, failed in different ways. Neither's answer was adequate. It is still undecided, what the answer will be this time; far more so, whether it will prove adequate.

Again the problem is to draw the line between three categories of people. There are thousands, who by the normal standards of civilised countries under the rule of law have committed crimes. The legal problems of prosecuting such crimes, which were authorised by the system and were an integral part of the practice of government, are formidable. But the first question is, whether there is the political will to solve these problems. At present, no clear line of action is discernible.

In the second category there are hundreds of thousands, who have actively served the system, have taken advantage of this service, have frequently misused their share of power, and have done wrong to other people without committing crimes. There is widespread agreement that these people are no longer qualified for public service. Evaluations have been started, for instance for judges and university professors. But it turns out that the practical problems of sifting the chaff from the wheat are immense.

The third category: millions of people, who have at least taken part in the rituals of loyalty to a fundamentally immoral system, and must now ask themselves what this has done to their personal integrity – the ruling party alone had 2.3 million members, and it is not a question of party membership alone. For this third group the problem of coming to terms with the past is a question of individual sincerity and the willingness to learn. It can't be anything else.

There are two aspects of these problems that are clearly new. One question results from the former division of the country. What should the respective roles of East and West Germans be in the process of working off the past? Western interference is unavoidable – I have mentioned, to give but one example, the necessity of evaluating former judges and professors. This can't be done without Western assistance. But Western interference is also likely to produce the wrong results. The second question is related to the remarkable fact that the ideology on which the system was built pleads not guilty, and that quite a few intellectuals accept this plea. Will not the somewhat vague idea that the intention was good and only the execution went wrong, serve as a strategy of avoiding the need to face the truth about the past?

How we handle the problems of what I have labelled 'moral regeneration' is important. But to repeat it once more: the decisive factor in the process of reintegration of the two German societies is the economy. I do not wish to discuss the enormous problems of the transition period. They are by now obvious. And it is also obvious that wishful thinking has seriously underestimated them. All I want to do before discussing the political consequences of economic success and failure is to recall a few data and facts to show where the process of transforming the bureaucratic state economy of the former GDR into a market economy had to start.

The GNP of the former GDR is estimated to have been less than 10 per cent of the GNP of the former Federal Republic. This means that the productivity of labour in the East was only about 50 per cent of what it is in West Germany. So was income. When the GDR ceased to exist, the average income there was only about 45 per cent of the average West German income. And the average old age pension in the East was even lower, at 35 per cent. Latent unemployment was very high. The machinery in most plants was hopelessly obsolete. And the state of the environment was so disastrous that even those who had expected the worst were shocked.

Whether East Germans knew this or not, when they voted for unification they expected the market economy to bring about a miracle. And perhaps they were promised a miracle. They are now discovering that the market economy is not a mechanism which produces wealth automatically. Which means: they are now facing the ugly side of the market economy. They feel threatened, as they have lost the one security they had – job security, so long as they met certain political conditions.

How will East Germans react to this new experience of insecurity? Four decades of socialism have taught them to wait for orders, for things to happen, rather than to take the initiative. Klages has described this attitude as – to use a French word – *attentisme*. *Attentisme* is not the disposition of mind the market economy requires. The market is after all a system of chances that have to be actively sought and exploited. Most people agree that *attentisme* can and will be overcome. East Germany is not Russia. But this is only one of the

factors that are crucial for the experiment of transforming a rotten
bureaucratic state economy into a market economy within a democratic political framework – that is to say, under enormous time-
pressure.

Two scenarios therefore have to be taken into consideration.

Scenario 1. The Germans succeed in getting a self-sustainable
market economy started in the East, one that provides sufficient jobs
and improves the standard of living visibly, within a rather short
period of time. Three or four years are here for obvious political
reasons a critical period, during which substantial and visible progress has to be made.

In this scenario we could expect the feeling of being different
gradually to fade away. It would be there for a long time to come,
but it would not be the organising principle, the dominant stimulus
of democratic politics in East Germany. Alliances and cleavages
would cross the former borderline between West and East, and
would not be conformed to it. Patterns of political thinking and
political behaviour which have developed in West Germany would
become dominant in the whole of Germany, not only because West
Germans outnumber East Germans by 4 to 1, but also because those
patterns would spread among East Germans. But in the East the
fifties and early sixties and the late sixties, seventies, eighties would
not be, as they were in West Germany, consecutive, but contempor-
aneous periods of development. For the majority the overwhelmingly important question would be how to raise one's standard of
living. Minorities, on the other hand, would commit themselves to
what social scientists have termed 'postmaterialistic values':
– for participatory democracy, an ideal that implies serious criticism of the established representative democracy of the Basic
  Law;
– for the environment; and
– for equal rights for women
to give but a few examples.

These are familiar themes. But they would be put forward with
special Eastern accents. On abortion, for instance, East Germans
think somewhat more progressively than West Germans. There may
also be more concern about the state of the environment, simply
because the situation is so much move serious. People know that at
least in the southern parts of East Germany pollution is an immediate threat to their health. But just as the 'Eastern accent' in some
cases would mean a somewhat more radical approach to politics, it

could also mean a more conservative approach in others. Socialism will remain a negative word. And the experiences they have had under socialist rule will continue to have an impact not only on the population in general, but also on where East German Social Democrats and Greens stand within their respective parties. But in some respects they will also remain *more* 'socialist' than the West Germans; in their ideas about the responsibilities of the state, for instance.

As to foreign policy, it will take East Germany some time to become familiar with the confederation and alliance of free nations they now belong to; to develop a certain loyalty towards such a framework. After all, the only experience they have had for four decades is that of being subjected to the interest of a hegemonic power. The EC will be more readily accepted than NATO. Pacifist sentiments will become stronger in Germany. And the Protestant Churches in the East will support these sentiments with much less reluctance than the Protestant Churches of the West have shown in the past.

Scenario 2. All this, let me remind you, is part of scenario 1. What about scenario 2, the consequences of economic failure? In this case, East Germany would develop a new, separate, post-GDR political identity that had its roots in disappointment and bitterness. East Germans would probably remember that unification was their decision – the East German parliamentary elections of March 1990 were in fact a plebiscite for unification, whereas West Germans have never been asked and could not be asked, because the Basic Law granted East Germany the right of accession. In October 1990, when the two Germanies were reunited, East German support for unification was as high as 86 per cent (80 per cent among West Germans).[7] But they would feel that they had been betrayed, betrayed by Western politicians who hadn't kept their promises, and not by their own hopes and illusions. They would feel, that having paid the price for the German defeat in the Second World War – to quote an East German woman 'We have lost the war every day again, for forty years' – they are the losers again. And the imposition of Western institutions by Western experts would be viewed as a kind of domestic colonialism.

Politics in East Germany would then be organised around this separate identity. The cleavage between East and West would be a major determinant of politics in Germany. East–West migration would of course become a permanent phenomenon, and, in a vicious spiral, this in itself might render the East–West problem definitively insoluble.

What this would mean for democracy in Germany, for the development of its party system in particular, and what kind of split political culture would result from all this, nobody can predict precisely. Would Germany then resemble Italy, with an East German *Mezzogiorno*? Two societies, two mentalities that do not understand each other, two economies under one institutional roof – in effect two realities in one country? This is perhaps a somewhat fantastic perspective. But a worst-case scenario (and the case would be much worse for Germany than it is for Italy) may help us to realise that the challenge for the old Federal Republic, which had become used to being successful, is extraordinary. We did not have a terribly good start. We cannot afford to go on underestimating the challenge.

Notes

1. The election results:

	West	East
CDU/CSU/ (CDU/DSU in East Germany)	44.2 %	42.8 %
FDP	10.6 %	12.9 %
SPD (+ PDS in East Germany)	35.9 %	24.3 % + 11.1 %
Greens	4.7 %	6.0 %

Figures for West Germany without West Berlin.

Source: Wolfgang G. Gibowski and Max Kaase, 'Auf dem Weg zum politischen Alltag. Eine Analyse der ersten gesamtdeutschen Bundestagswahl vom 2. Dezember 1990', in *Aus Politik und Zeitgeschichte*, B 11–12 / 91.

2. Ursula Feist, 'Zur politischen Akkulturation der vereinten Deutschen', in *Aus Politik und Zeitgeschichte*, B 11–12 / 91.
3. *Frankfurter Allgemeine Zeitung*, 16.2.1991.
4. See note 2. See also Willi Herbert and Rudolf Wildenmann, 'Deutsche Identität. Die subjektive Verfassung der Deutschen vor der Vereinigung', and Petra Bauer, 'Freiheit und Demokratie in der Wahrnehmung

der Bürger in der Bundesrepublik und der ehemaligen DDR', in Rudolf Wildenmann (ed.), *Nation und Demokratie*, Baden-Baden, 1991.
5. See note 4.
6. Unpublished Allensbach-data.
7. Werner Kaltefleiter, 'Die Struktur der deutschen Wählerschaft nach der Vereinigung', in *Zeitschrift für Politik*, 38 (1991), S. 21.

Chronology

March 1989:	Elections to the Congress of People's Deputies in the Soviet Union.
2 May 1989:	The Hungarians begin to remove the frontier fence at the frontier to Austria.
7 May 1989:	Communal elections in the German Democratic Republic rigged in the traditional way: 98.85 per cent of the votes go to the candidates of the National Front. Protests and ·demonstrations against the election fraud.
8 June 1989:	The People's Chamber of the GDR unaminously declares its understanding for the measures of the party leadership in China to restore order with armed force.
End of July 1989:	Refugees from the GDR begin to crowd the embassies of the Federal Republic in Budapest, Prague and Warsaw and its 'Permanent Representation' in East Berlin.
19 August 1989:	661 refugees from the GDR make use of a Pan-Europa Festival at the Hungarian–Austrian border to escape to Austria.
25 August 1989:	The Hungarian Prime Minister Nemeth and Foreign Minister Horn meet Chancellor Kohl in Bonn to discuss the refugee problem.
11 September 1989:	Hungary opens its border to Austria for refugees from the GDR. Up to the end of the month more than 25,000 leave the GDR via Hungary.
6 October 1989:	Fortieth anniversary of the foundation of the GDR.
7 October 1989:	Gorbachev urges Honecker in East Berlin to follow the example of *Pérestroika*. Brutal suppression of demonstrations against the SED regime in many East German Cities.
9 October 1989:	Contrary to expectations, a large demonstration in Leipzig is not dissolved by the security forces. The regime no longer dares to use force against demonstrators.
18 October 1989:	Erich Honecker has to resign as General Secretary

196

of the SED and member of the Politbureau. His successor is Egon Krenz.

9 November 1989:
The GDR opens its frontier to the Federal Republic and to West Berlin.

13 November 1989:
Hans Modrow (SED) becomes Chairman of the Council of Ministers.

28 November 1989:
Chancellor Kohl announces a 10-Point programme with the final aim of achieving unification.

7 December 1989:
The Round Table talks begin in East Berlin.

8 December 1989:
The Party Congress of the SED elects Gregor Gysi as Party Chairman. The Party is renamed SED–PDS ('Party of Democratic Socialism').

19 December 1989:
Chancellor Kohl visits Dresden. He is welcomed by more than 100,000 citizens demanding unification.

20 December 1989:
President Mitterand begins his state visit to the GDR.

15 January 1990:
Chairman of the Council of Ministers Hans Modrow for the first time takes part in the 'Round Table' discussions. A demonstration against the Stasi (state security service) ends with the demonstrators storming the Stasi headquarters in East Berlin.

28 January 1990:
Hans Modrow proposes a 'Government of national responsibility', including members of the opposition groups represented at the Round Table.

30 January 1990:
Modrow in Moscow. Gorbachev refuses to support Modrow's endeavours to stabilise the GDR as an independent state.

5 February 1990:
A 'government of national responsibility', including the SED, the former *bloc* parties, and the oppositional groups, is constituted.

7 February 1990:
The government of the Federal Republic of Germany proposes a currency union with the GDR.

13 February 1990:
Kohl and Modrow agree upon a commission of experts to prepare a currency union and economic union.

At Ottawa, the Four Powers and the two German states agree to begin talks about the international aspects of German unification.

18 March 1990:
Free elections to the People's Chamber. The 'Alliance for Germany' (CDU 163 seats, DSU 25, DA 4 seats) gains an unexpected victory.

12 April 1990:	Lother de Maizière (CDU) is elected as Chairman of the Council of Ministers by the People's Chamber.
7 May 1990:	Local elections in the GDR. The strongest party is the CDU (34 per cent), followed by the SPD (21 per cent) and the PDS (14.5 per cent).
1 July 1990:	The Deutsche Mark is introduced in the GDR.
16 July 1990:	Chancellor Kohl meets President Gorbachev in Kislovodsk. Gorbachev agrees to the united Germany's membership of NATO.
12 September 1990:	The 'Two-plus-Four-Talks' end with the Moscow agreement.
3 October 1990:	The GDR, dissolved into five states, accedes to the Federal Republic of Germany.

Basic Literature

Hermann Weber, *DDR: Grundriß der Geschichte* 1945–1990, Hanover, 1991

Karl Dietrich Bracher, Theodor Eschenburg, Joachim C. Fest and Eberhard Jäckel (eds), *Geschichte der Bundesrepublik Deutschland*, Vols 1–5, Stuttgart, 1983–7

Werner Weidenfeld and Hartmut Zimmermann (eds), *Deutschland Handbuch: Eine doppelte Bilanz 1949–1989*, Munich, 1989

Werner Weidenfeld (ed.), *Die Identität der Deutschen*, Munich, 1983

Karl Kaiser, *Deutschlands Vereinigung. Die internationalen Aspekte*, Bergisch-Gladbach, 1991

Timothy Garton Ash, *The uses of adversity. Essays on the fate of Central Europe*, New York, 1989

Gerhard Wettig, *Changes in Soviet Policy Towards the West*, London–San Francisco 1991, especially: 'The Soviet Union and the Political Transformation in Eastern Europe', p. 123

Europa Archiv, Zeitschrift für internationale Politik, Bonn, Vol. 12/1989, Vol. 13/1990, Vol. 14/1991.

Deutschland Archiv, Zeitschrift für das vereinigte Deutschland, Cologne, Vol. 22/1998, Vol. 23/1990, Vol. 24/1991.

Index

Adenauer, 2, 34ff., 47, 50, 88
Afghanistan, 6
Alleinvertretungsanspruch, 39
Alliance 90 (Bündnis 90), 22, 104
Allianz für Deutschland, 21, 83, 93
Alsace-Lorraine, 101
Article 23 of the Basic Law, 29, 81
Atlantic Alliance, 37, 47
Austria, 154
Austrian solution, 38

Bahr, Egon, 5, 40
balance of power, 136, 138ff., 143
Barendoim, Daniel, 169
Barzel, Rainer, 43–4
Basic Law (see Grundgesetz)
Basic Treaty (see Grundlagenvertrag)
Begin, Menachem, 174
Belgium, 154, 155, 162
Ben-Gurion, David, 172
Berlin, 30, 41, 44
    Crises, 38
    East, 46, 80
    West, 3
    Wall, 2, 10, 16, 39, 46, 56, 60
Bernstein, Leonard, 169
Bismarck, 101
bloc parties, 17, 21, 58, 77, 82ff.
Böhme, Ibrahim, 81
Bonn convention, 95
boundaries, 33, 40, 48ff.
Brandt, Willy, 3, 39ff., 47ff., 93, 159
    Ostpolitik, 4ff., 43
Brezhnev Doctrine, 7, 90
Broder, Henryk, 175
brother countries, 56, 66
Bündnis 90, 22
Bürgerbewegungen, 73, 81ff.
Bulgaria, 40
Bundesbank, 29, 95, 114ff., 133
Bundesrat, 97, 130
Bundestag, 97
    Committee for German unity, 98
Bundesverfassungsgericht, 42, 44, 49,
    103, 120
Bundeswehr, 30

Burgfrieden, 38
Bush, George, 93, 95, 163

Cambodia, 41
'chancellor democracy', 88
Carstens, Karl, 44
Carter, Jimmy, 156
Central Europe, 158
CDU (East), 17, 74ff., 82
CDU (West), 20ff., 38ff., 93, 104, 194
Ceaucescu, 8
citizens' movements (see
    Bürgerbewegungen)
civic action groups, 12
civil rights groups, 22ff., 64
change through rapprochement, 5
China, 35, 164
China syndrome, 62
Christian Democrats (see CDU)
Christian Democratic–Liberal
    Coalition, 5
churches, 14, 18, 76, 184
    Protestant, 49, 57, 64ff.
CIS, 137, 152
Coalition (Christian Democratic–
    Liberal), 5
communists, 67, 81, 89
Conference at Munich, 157
Conference on Security and Co-
    operation in Europe, 44ff., 79
Congress of People's Deputies, 7, 13
conscientious objectors, 155
constitution, 29
Constitutional Court (see
    Bundesverfassungsgericht)
counter-élite, 67
coup d'état, 68
CPSU, 7, 12
CSU, 42, 83, 104
Cuba, 164
Czechoslovakia, 3, 41ff., 56ff., 73, 80

Delors, Jacques, 139, 147
de Maizière, Lothar, 22, 28ff., 80, 82,
    94, 98ff., 113
democracy, 73, 79, 182

200

Democracy Now, 22, 58, 74ff.
Democratic Awakening, 21, 74ff., 83, 93
demonstrations, 15ff., 21ff., 58ff., 62, 79
Denmark, 153, 160, 162
détente, 2, 34, 39, 79
Deutsche Mark (DM), 26, 137
Deutsch, Karl W., 150
Deutschlandvertrag, 37
Dresden, 75
DSU, 83, 93
Dulles, John Foster, 159

East Berlin (*see* Berlin, East)
Eastern Europe, 68, 79, 86, 143, 148, 187
Eastern treaties, 3
East Germany, 79
  economy, 26
East-West conflict, 101
EC (*see* European Community), 25, 39, 46ff., 94, 155, 162, 172, 193
economic and monetary union (Germany), 27, 95
economic growth, 24
Economic, Monetary and Social Union (Germany), 88, 114, 125, 133
  state treaty, 28ff., 96
economic summit in Houston, 99
Edinger, Lewis, 150
elections, 183
  to the Volkskammer (18 March 1990), 20, 81ff., 88
  campaign (for 18 March 1990), 21, 28
  GDR local elections (6 May 1990), 29
  Bundestag (2 Dec 1990), 105
élite, 67
EMU (*see* European Community),
European Central Bank, 144
European Community (EC), 25, 39, 46ff., 94, 155, 162, 172, 193
  EC summit in Dublin, 99
  European Agreements, 140
  Monetary Union (EMU), 108, 133, 140ff., 143, 147
  Political Union, 140ff., 144, 146
  Single Market, 143
European Defence Community (EVG), 36
European economic integration, 36, 39
European Economic Space, 140
European Free Trade Association (EFTA), 140ff.
exodus, 10, 14, 24ff., 57ff., 62

FDP, 3, 41ff.
federalism, 189
Federal Republic of Germany, 28, 56, 164
  peace note (March 1966), 40
  Basic Treaty, 42
  financial matters, 92
  military, 154, 157
Feist, Ursula, 186
fortieth anniversary celebrations, 15
Four plus Two talks, 28
Four Powers, 30ff.
France, 25, 28, 31, 138ff., 145ff., 153ff., 160ff.
Franco-German relationship, 137, 148
Free Democrats (*see* FDP)
French Revolution, 68

GDR (*see* German Democratic Republic)
GEMSU (*see* Economic, Monetary and Social Union (Germany))
Genscher, Hans-Dietrich, 28, 31, 45, 92ff.
Germany, 30
  division, 4, 160
  economy, 137
  German-German Treaty, 4
  partition, 1
  reunification, 2, 25
  single German citizenship, 43ff.
  territorial claims, 152
  German Problem, 138, 143
German Democratic Republic (GDR), 3ff., 9ff., 17ff., 24, 28ff., 38ff., 43, 72ff., 164
  declaration: accession to the Basic Law, 29
  unemployment, 185
  agriculture, 185
German National Bank (*see* Bundesbank)
German-German Economic Commission, 92
German-German entrepreneurial conference, 92
German Social Union, 21
German Unity Fund (Fonds Deutsche Einheit), 131
glasnost, 7ff., 12, 61
Glorious Revolution, 67

Glucksmann, André, 169
Gorbachev, 1, 6ff., 12ff., 20, 27ff., 30,
    61, 81, 90ff., 99
Gorbachev–Kohl, 4
government of 'national responsibility',
    20ff.
Grand Coalition, 40ff.
Great Britain, 25, 28, 31, 138ff., 153ff.,
    160ff.
Greece, 147, 153, 155, 160, 162
Greens, 48, 104, 194
Grewe, Wilhelm, 38
Grosser, Alfred, 166, 169
Grundgesetz, 2, 81, 86, 120, 192
Grundlagenvertrag, 4, 42
Gulf crises, 157ff.

Hallstein Doctrine, 38ff., 43
Helsinki Conference, 57, 64
Hitler, 182
Holocaust, 157, 170, 174
Holy Roman Empire, 158
Honecker, Erich, 8, 12, 14ff., 56, 61, 90
Hungary, 1ff., 9ff., 13ff., 24, 40, 56ff.,
    73, 80, 163ff.
Hurd, Douglas, 25
Husak, 8
Inglehart, 186
Inquiry Commission, 63
Initiative for Peace and Human Rights,
    57
integration, 2
investment, 11
Iraq, 41
Israel, 41, 154, 164, 170ff.
Italy, 153ff., 160ff.

Japan, 154, 161, 164
Jaruszelski, 6
Jaeger, Wolfgang, 88, 106
Jews, 163, 165, 167ff.
    American Jewish Committee, 170
    American Jews, 175
    Soviet Jews, 176

Kaiser, Jakob, 51
Kiesinger, Kurt Georg, 40
Kissinger, Henry, 159
Klages, Helmut, 186
Kohl, Helmut, 4, 9, 25, 27ff., 30, 45,
    49, 82, 86, 88, 90ff., 102, 105, 112ff.,
    140ff., 145
    ten-point programme, 25ff., 46, 90,
    140

Korea, 159
Krause, Günther, 98
Krenz, Egon, 15ff., 25, 58, 61, 64, 90

Lafontaine, Oskar, 48, 82, 115
Lehnrevolution, 68
Leipzig, 15, 17, 26, 58, 62, 65
Liberals, 21ff., 27
Ligachev, 9
Luxemburg, 162
local elections, 13

magnetism theory, 36
market economy, 24, 182
Major, John, 142, 144, 148
Masur, Kurt, 15
materialism-postmaterialism, 186
Matthäus-Maier, Ingrid, 27
Mende, Erich, 42
Menuhin, Yehudi, 169
Mertes, Alois, 45
Meyer, Daniel, 168
Mielke, Erich, 63ff.
Ministry of State Security, 63
Mitterand, François, 25, 31, 99, 138,
    141, 145
Modrow, Hans, 12, 17ff., 23, 27, 57,
    63, 67, 80ff., 91ff., 112
Möllemann, Jürgen, 121
monetary union, 26ff.
Monday Demonstration, 65
Moscow, 28, 30ff.
    Moscow agreement of 12 September,
    31

Nationalism, 181
NATO, 25, 30, 36, 39, 46, 49, 99,
    151ff., 193
Nemeth, Niklas, 9
Netherlands, 153ff., 160ff.
networks (*see* Seilschaften)
Neues Ökonomisches System (New
    Economic System), 111
neutrality, 36ff., 151, 152
New Economic System (*see* Neues
    Ökonomisches System)
New Forum, 14ff., 19, 22, 58, 74ff.
new groups and parties, 19ff., 74ff.
Nikolai, Kirche, 58
Nomenklatura, 10, 12, 15, 17ff., 23
non-aggression agreement, 40ff.
Non-violence, 23
NPD, 42

Oder–Neisse frontier, 4, 30, 42ff., 46, 49, 96, 101
Office for National Security, 63
opposition groups, 57ff., 64ff., 73ff., 83
Ostpolitik, 35ff., 47
Ottawa, 28

party system, 81, 183
PDS (Party of Democratic Socialism), 17ff., 62, 74ff., 82, 104, 183
peace movement, 12
peace note (March 1966), 40
Peking, 13
People's Army, 31
People's Chamber (*see* Volkskamme)
People's Police, 63
People's Revolution, 66
perestroika, 6ff., 12, 55, 61, 64
Pfleiderer, Karl-Georg, 51
Pöhl, Karl Otto, 27
Poland, 1ff., 30, 40ff., 56ff., 73, 160ff.
Solidarity, 7ff.
policy of strength, 36
Politbureau, 12ff., 23
political culture, 187
Portugal, 147, 153, 162
Poszgay, Imre, 9
Prague, 14, 40
Prayers for Peace, 58
Protestant Church, 57, 64ff.

Quadripartite Agreement on Berlin, 42

Reagan, Ronald, 156
re-education, 156
refugees, 9ff., 14, 49, 56, 79
reunification, 2ff., 21ff., 26ff., 81, 159
rehabilitation, 61
revolution, 22, 66ff., 72
Ridley, Nicholas, 137
Rohwedder, Detlev, 122
Romania, 40
Roth, Wolfgang, 27
Round Table, 18ff., 62, 66, 74ff., 81
Discussion, 18
Russia, 145, 137
Russian Revolution, 68

Sachverständigenrat zur Begutachtung der gesamtwirtschaftlichen Entwicklung, 122ff.
Schäfer, 171
Schäuble, Wolfgang, 98
Scheel, Walter, 42

Schiller, Karl, 127
Schmidt, Helmut, 126, 156
Schumacher, Kurt, 36
Schuman Plan, 139, 144
SDP, 74ff.
SED (Sozialistische Einheitspartei), 8, 12ff., 46, 59ff., 75, 91, 111
SED-PDS, 17ff., 62, 74ff., 82, 104, 183
Seilschaften (networks), 67, 73
Sethe, Paul, 51
Shamir, Jitzhak, 172
Shevardnadze, 28, 30ff., 105
short-range missiles, 157
Social Democrats (*see* SPD)
Social Market Economy, 108, 114, 133
socialism, 57, 187
socialist economies, 11
Socialist Unity Party (SED), 8
Solidarity, 7ff.
Soviet Union, 1ff., 24ff., 28, 31ff., 35ff., 66, 72, 86, 154, 163ff., 188
Note of March 1952, 36
Spain, 161ff.
SPD, 3, 20ff., 37ff., 74ff., 93, 183, 194
SPD–FDP Coalition, 47
SDP/SPD, 74ff.
South Yemen, 41
Staatsraison, 101, 106
standard of living, 11
State Security Service (Stasi), 12ff., 19, 21, 60, 62ff., 67, 80
Sudan, 41
Sweden, 153ff., 160ff.
Syria, 41
Szczypiorski, Andrzej, 165

ten-point programme (*see* Kohl)
Thatcher, Margaret, 138, 141ff., 148
Tietmeyer, Hans, 114
totalitarian dictatorship, 182
totalitarianism, 89
trade missions, 40
Treuhandanstalt, 120ff.
Two plus Four talks, 30ff., 88, 92, 95, 99
treaty, 152

unification, 25
treaty, 28ff., 88, 97ff.
United Kingdom, 28, 31
United States, 2, 25, 28, 31, 92, 138ff., 145ff., 150, 153ff., 156, 160ff.

Volkskammer, 29, 77, 80, 88
    election campaign, 93

wages, 11
Walters, Vernon, 90
Warsaw, 14
Warsaw Pact, 8ff., 30, 41
West Berlin (*see* Berlin), 3
West Germany (*see* Federal Republic of

Germany), 3
WEU, 152ff.
Wiesel, Elie, 167

Yugoslavia, 40

Zhivkov, 8
Zimmermann, Moshe, 173
Zoltai, Gustav, 168